Reinhold Niebuhr's Works

a bibliography

Reinhold Niebuhr's Works

a bibliography

D. B. ROBERTSON

G.K.HALL&CO.

70 LINCOLN STREET, BOSTON, MASS.

Copyright © 1979 by D. B. Robertson

Library of Congress Cataloging in Publication Data

Robertson, D. B.
  Reinhold Niebuhr's works.

  Includes index.
  1. Niebuhr, Reinhold, 1892-1971 — Bibliography.
Z8628.R6 1979   [BX4827.N5]   016.23   79-4037
ISBN 0-8161-8237-X

This publication is printed on permanent/durable acid-free paper
MANUFACTURED IN THE UNITED STATES OF AMERICA

Contents

Preface

Reinhold Niebuhr may have written publishable material earlier, but by 1911, when he was in his nineteenth year, he published an article in The Keryx, student publication at Eden Theological Seminary. He continued to write for publication into the year he died— 1971. From the time of his twenties he became known as a churchman, a notable preacher, ecumenical leader, political activist, and later as a teacher of theology students at Union Theological Seminary in New York. He became known as a writer whose works were and are read by persons interested in public affairs, by politicians, as well as by students of religion and ethics.

Dr. Niebuhr used to say that he began writing in order to piece out his small salary as pastor of Bethel Church in Detroit. The two articles in The Atlantic Monthly support this statement. His publishing record, however, shows that he was publishing before the appearance of these paid articles and that the greatest number of his articles were published in journals that were not paying affairs.

Niebuhr developed a facility for writing articles of varying length; he could write on impulse or request an article of one or two pages or more substantial pieces. He could always come out with a prescribed number of words and pages, and he rarely rewrote anything, including major portions of his books. This meant, among other things, that there would be considerable repetition. Dr. Niebuhr sometimes remarked that every preacher has only one sermon, and he works it over and over in different combinations. John Bennett once noted that Reinhold Niebuhr always wrote each article as if he had never thought of anything like it before. For all of the repetition, this habit gave his work a freshness and made it consistently interesting. The same "Biblical truths" were recovered and appreciated over and over again as history moved on and as the faces of national and international life altered their aspects.

Persons who knew Niebuhr or who have read his works know that he always recognized the ephemeral nature of running comments on historical events. Perhaps this is one of the reasons why so many of Dr. Niebuhr's titles through the years, including the title of his first book, were presented in the form of questions. This applies especially to the captions of many articles and book reviews. The listing of the vast number of published articles and the indexing of the titles may appear to overwhelm in importance his many books. This, of course, is not the case. The importance of these shorter writings, however, is suggested by the pioneer work on them by Ronald H. Stone in his Reinhold Niebuhr: Prophet to Politicians and elsewhere.

It is only fair to the spirit of Reinhold Niebuhr to mention the fact that any reader can observe: he often lent his name to a new journal or magazine by contributing an article during the first year of publication. Just as important was his generous willingness to write "forewords" and "introductions" for ever so many writers and editors of books.

Over a span of sixty years Niebuhr wrote articles for particular journals for a time and then moved on to others, in some cases because the journal ceased publication. In a few instances he wrote occasionally and sometimes regularly for journals throughout h s writing career, or as long as the journal lasted. Examples of the latter are The Nation, The Christian Century, The New Republic, The World Tomorrow (folded in 1935), Radical Religion, Christianity and Society, Christianity and Crisis (which he launched in February of 1941). No doubt The Christian Century is a special case. Niebuhr began publication in this journal in November of 1922. He published his last article here in 1969. In that forty-seven year period he had written more articles for The Christian Century than anyone else—— 112 signed articles [The Christian Century, June 16, 1971, p. 735]. The New Republic published articles between October 24, 1928, till past the middle of 1967. Many book reviews appeared in The New York Herald Tribune Books beginning in September of 1929. A constant companion for Niebuhr, beginning in the 1940's and going into 1970, was The New Leader. Most of Niebuhr's articles in this journal appeared after 1950, and there was a constant flow in particular years in that period. All of these were journals appearing regularly in any listing of Niebuhr publications. If one tries to number all the others, it will be discovered that there were over one hundred publications carrying his articles through the years.

Most of Niebuhr's shorter writings in any given time period were presented to a single journal or only a few. There was a short period, though, during which he did a syndicated column——for Religious News Service. From June 1946 to December 1948 he wrote a regular column for RNS. When the column ceased, The Lutheran and The Messenger made arrangements for a biweekly column that continued into Dr. Niebuhr's last years. Following is a list of clients receiving the column when RNS made its widest distribution: The Jacksonville Journal, The Boston Globe, Pontiac Daily Press, St. Louis Globe-Democrat, The Abertan, Michigan Christian Advocate, The Christian Evangelist, Friedensbote, The Lutheran, Presbyterian Life, The Presbyterian Outlook, The Religious Herald, The Southern Churchman, and The Messenger.

Preface

One item in the Niebuhr works I have not been able properly to identify as to date and place of publication. There was an interview by John Gunther entitled "Are We Strong Enough to Live Without God?" The interview can definitely be dated before Dr. Niebuhr's first illness in 1952; beyond that, all efforts at identification have been unsuccessful. Another article I have not seen at all. Dr. Niebuhr recalled on at least two occasions that he published an article in Charm--when the editor asked him to lunch and expressed a wish to widen the interests of his readers. As Dr. Niebuhr recalled, the article was on race relations.

Other Niebuhr sources should be noted: The Library of Congress, Manuscripts Division, has Dr. Niebuhr's private papers. The collection has been supplemented by Mrs. Ursula Niebuhr and others. The Department of Oral History at Columbia University has material supplied by Dr. Niebuhr. Researchers into the early Niebuhr will need to explore the holdings of the Eden Theological Seminary Archives. The New York Public Library holds a collection of Union For Democratic Action materials. The following movies have been made: Huston Smith made two movies, showing Dr. Niebuhr discussing with Smith the subjects of "Morality" and "Progress." These films are available at the Audio-Visual Services, National Educational Television, at The University of Indiana, Bloomington, Indiana. Another 40-minute movie called simply "Reinie" has been available at Peter M. Robech & Company, Inc., 230 Park Avenue, New York, N. Y., 10017. A sermon by Dr. Niebuhr on a cassette tape has been available at Union Theological Seminary, Broadway at 120th Street, New York, N. Y., 10027. Title: "Advent in a Nuclear Age." Other tapes are being prepared for distribution by the Reigner Library, Union Theological Seminary, 3401 Brook Road, Richmond, Virginia, 23227.

The writings about Niebuhr are extensive. Surely not all articles are listed here; many short pieces have been omitted. The major attempt has been to find and list writings about Dr. Niebuhr that represent the widest possible range of interpretations and approaches to the study of his life and thought.

It will be noted that there are occasional brief annotations, mostly of Niebuhr articles. This was done where the title gave little clue to the content of the article.

The Index undertaken here, it should be clearly understood, is limited in this way: it is an index of terms and ideas evident in Niebuhr titles and in the writings about Niebuhr. The content of the articles is indexed only as it is revealed in the titles or in the limited number of annotations. No indexing of books is included.

A number of partial listings of Reinhold Niebuhr's works have been made. In 1942 Professor Asher Hinds of Princeton University set his students to searching for Niebuhr writings, and he produced an extended mimeographed list that was not widely distributed. In 1954

Preface

Berea College Press published my first listing of Niebuhr works--spanning the period from 1916 to 1953. A selected bibliography was prepared for the Kegley-Bretall volume: Reinhold Niebuhr: His Religious, Social and Political Thought (New York: The Macmillan Co., 1956). In 1971 Ronald H. Stone and Joann M. Stone listed most of the Niebuhr writings between 1953 and 1971. This useful work was published in the Union Seminary Quarterly Review, 27, no. 1 (Fall 1971), 10-29.

The present work builds on, adds to, and in many places corrects, all previous listings. The earlier work of others is gratefully acknowledged in the preparation of this bibliography.

A particular note of thanks is due to Mr. William Chrystal, formerly Archivist of Eden Theological Seminary. His work was notably important in searching out the very earliest writings. One result of his work has been a collection of early Niebuhr writings, Young Reinhold Niebuhr: 1911-1930, published by Eden Publishing House in 1977. Two others were helpful in that we exchanged bibliographical materials over a period of time--Dietz Lange and J. Dell Johnson.

D. B. Robertson

Journal Abbreviations

Abbreviations of journals in which Niebuhr articles appeared--listed
in the order of their appearance in the bibliography.

EH	The Evangelical Herald
NR	The New Republic
WT	The World Tomorrow
N	The Nation
CCY	The Christian Century
NYHT	The New York Herald Tribune Books
RR	Radical Religion
CS	Christianity and Society
CC	Christianity and Crisis
NL	The New Leader
M	The Messenger
L	The Lutheran
EC	Episcopal Churchnews

Books by Reinhold Niebuhr

Does Civilization Need Religion? A Study of the Social Resources and
    Limitations of Religion in Modern Life. New York: The Macmillan
    Company, 1927.

    I.   The State of Religion in Modern Society
   II.   Nature and Civilization as Foes of Personality
  III.   The Social Resources of Religion
   IV.   The Social Conservatism of Modern Religion
    V.   Religion and Life: Conflict and Compromise
   VI.   Social Complexity and Ethical Impotence
  VII.   Transcending and Transforming the World
 VIII.   A Philosophical Basis for an Ethical Religion
   IX.   Conclusion

Leaves From the Notebook of a Tamed Cynic. New York: Willett, Clark
    and Company, 1929.

The Contribution of Religion to Social Work. New York: Columbia
    University Press, 1932. Reprinted by AMS Press, Inc., 1971.

       Introduction by Porter R. Lee
    I.   Religion in the History of Social Work
   II.   The Limitations of a Religiously Inspired Philanthropy
  III.   Religion as a Source of Mental and Social Health
   IV.   Religion as a Cause of Personal and Social Maladjustment
    V.   Religion as a Resource for the Social Worker

Moral Man and Immoral Society, A Study in Ethics and Politics. New
    York: Charles Scribner's Sons, 1932.

    I.   Man and Society: The Art of Living Together
   II.   The Rational Resources of the Individual for Social Living
  III.   The Religious Resources of the Individual for Social Living
   IV.   The Morality of Nations
    V.   The Ethical Attitudes of Privileged Classes
   VI.   The Ethical Attitudes of the Proletarian Class
  VII.   Justice Through Revolution
 VIII.   Justice Through Political Force
   IX.   The Preservation of Moral Values in Politics
    X.   The Conflict Between Individual and Social Morality

Books by Reinhold Niebuhr

<u>Reflections on the End of an Era</u>. New York: Charles Scribner's Sons, 1934.

- I. The Life and Death of Civilizations
- II. Prophecy and Doom
- III. The Wise Men and the Mighty Men
- IV. The Significance of Fascism
- V. The Brief Glory of the Business Man
- VI. The Social Struggle in America
- VII. The Virtues of a Bourgeois Civilization
- VIII. The Individual and Individualism
- IX. Christian and Bourgeois Individualism
- X. Mythology and History
- XI. The Executors of Judgment
- XII. Neither Votes Nor Bullets
- XIII. The Peril of Barbarism in the Spirit of Vengeance
- XIV. The Conflict Between Christianity and Communism
- XV. The Political Realism of Christian Orthodoxy
- XVI. A Radical Political Theory
- XVII. The Balance of Power in Politics
- XVIII. The Liberal Spirit in Morals
- XIX. Radicalism and Religious Disinterestedness
- XX. The Assurance of Grace

<u>An Interpretation of Christian Ethics</u>. New York: Harper and Brothers, 1935.

- I. An Independent Christian Ethic
- II. The Ethic of Jesus
- III. The Christian Conception of Sin
- IV. The Relevance of an Impossible Ethical Ideal
- V. The Law of Love in Politics and Economics (Criticism of Christian Orthodoxy)
- VI. The Law of Love in Politics and Economics (Criticism of Christian Liberalism)
- VII. Love as a Possibility for the Individual
- VIII. Love as Forgiveness

<u>Beyond Tragedy, Essays on the Christian Interpretation of History</u>. New York: Charles Scribner's Sons, 1937.

- I. As Deceivers, Yet True
- II. The Tower of Babel
- III. The Ark and the Temple
- IV. Four Hundred to One
- V. The Test of True Prophecy
- VI. The Ultimate Trust
- VII. Childhood and Maturity
- VIII. Christianity and Tragedy
- IX. The Suffering Servant and the Son of Man
- X. Transvaluation of Values
- XI. The Things That are and the Things That are Not
- XII. Zeal Without Knowledge

XIII. Two Parables About Judgment
 XIV. The Kingdom Not of This World
  XV. The Fulfillment of Life

<u>Christianity and Power Politics</u>. New York: Charles Scribner's Sons,
     1940.

   I. Why the Christian Church is Not Pacifist
  II. The War and American Churches
 III. Germany and the Western World
  IV. Democracy and Foreign Policy
   V. Idealists as Cynics
  VI. Peace and the Liberal Illusion
 VII. Greek Tragedy and Modern Politics
VIII. Ideology and Pretense
  IX. Synthetic Barbarism
   X. The False Answers to Our Unsolved Problems
  XI. Modern Utopians
 XII. Hitler and Buchman
XIII. An End to Illusions
 XIV. Optimism, Pessimism and Religious Faith--I
  XV. Optimism, Pessimism and Religious Faith--II
 XVI. The Christian Church in a Secular Age

<u>The Nature and Destiny of Man</u>, Volume I. New York: Charles Scribner's
     Sons, 1941.

   I. Man as a Problem to Himself
        <u>The Classical View of Man</u>
        <u>The Christian View of Man</u>
        <u>The Modern View of Man</u>
  II. The Problem of Vitality and Form in Human Nature
        <u>The Rationalistic View of Human Nature</u>
        <u>The Romantic Protest Against Rationalism</u>
        <u>The Errors of Romanticism</u>
        <u>Romantic Elements in Marxism</u>
        <u>The Social Bias of Conflicting Theories</u>
 III. Individuality in Modern Culture
        <u>The Christian Sense of Individuality</u>
        <u>The Idea of Individuality in the Renaissance</u>
        <u>Bourgeois Civilization and Individuality</u>
        <u>The Destruction of Individuality in Naturalism</u>
        <u>The Loss of Self in Idealism</u>
        <u>The Loss of Self in Romanticism</u>
  IV. The Easy Conscience of Modern Man
        <u>The Effort to Derive Evil From Specific Historical Sources</u>
        <u>Nature as a Source of Virtue</u>
        <u>The Optimism of Idealism</u>
   V. The Relevance of the Christian View of Man
        <u>Individual and General Revelation</u>
        <u>Creation and Revelation</u>
        <u>Historical and Special Revelation</u>

3

Books by Reinhold Niebuhr

2. The Individual and History
3. The Unity of History

The Children of Light and the Children of Darkness, A Vindication of Democracy and a Critique of its Traditional Defense. New York: Charles Scribner's Sons, 1944.

    I. The Children of Light and the Children of Darkness
   II. The Individual and the Community
 III. The Community and Property
 IV. Democratic Toleration and the Groups of the Community
   V. The World Community

Discerning the Signs of the Times, Sermons for Today and Tomorrow. New York: Charles Scribner's Sons, 1946.

    I. Discerning the Signs of the Times
   II. Anger and Forgiveness
 III. The Age Between the Ages
 IV. The Nemesis of Nations
   V. The City Which Hath Foundations
 VI. Today, Tomorrow and the Eternal
 VII. Humor and Faith
VIII. The Power and Weakness of God
 IX. Mystery and Meaning
   X. The Peace of God

Faith and History, A Comparison of Christian and Modern Views of History. New York: Charles Scribner's Sons, 1949.

    I. The Current Refutation of the Idea of Redemption Through Progress
   II. The History of the Modern Conception of History
 III. Time as the Stage of History
 IV. Similarities and Differences between Classical and Modern Ideas of Meaning in History
   V. The Extravagant Estimates of Freedom in the Progressive View of History
 VI. The Identification of Freedom and Virtue in Modern Views of History
 VII. The Biblical View: The Sovereignty of God and Universal History
VIII. The Biblical View: Moral Meaning and Moral Obscurities of History
 IX. The Foolishness of the Cross and the Sense of History
   X. The Validation of the Christian View of Life and History
 XI. Beyond Law and Relativity
 XII. False Absolutes in Christian Interpretations of History
XIII. Fulfillments in History and the Fulfillment of History
 XIV. The Church and the End of History

Books by Reinhold Niebuhr

The Irony of American History. New York: Charles Scribner's Sons, 1952.

I. The Ironic Element in the American Situation
II. The Innocent Nation in an Innocent World
III. Happiness, Prosperity and Virtue
IV. The Master of Destiny
V. The Triumph of Experience Over Dogma
VI. The International Class Struggle
VII. The American Future
VIII. The Significance of Irony

Christian Realism and Political Problems. New York: Charles Scribner's Sons, 1953.

I. Faith and the Empirical Method in Modern Realism
II. The Illusion of World Government
III. Why is Communism so Evil?
IV. The Anomaly of European Socialism
V. The Foreign Policy of American Conservatism and Liberalism
VI. Ideology and the Scientific Method
VII. Democracy, Secularism, and Christianity
VIII. The Christian Witness in the Social and National Order
IX. Augustine's Political Realism
X. Love and Law in Protestantism and Catholicism
XI. Coherence, Incoherence, and Christian Faith

The Self and the Dramas of History. New York: Charles Scribner's Sons, 1955.

PART I
1. The Uniqueness of the Human Self
2. The Internal Dialogue of the Self
3. The Dialogue Between the Will and Conscience of the Self
4. The Ladder of the Self's Ambitions, Desires and Qualms of Conscience
5. The Self in Space and Time
6. The Self and its Body
7. The Dialogue Between the Self and Others
8. The Self and Its Communities
9. The Self as Creator and Creature in Historical Drama
10. The Self and the Dramas of History
11. The Problem of Historical Knowledge
12. The Self and Its Search for Ultimate Meaning
PART II
13. The Hebraic and the Hellenistic Approaches to the Problem of Selfhood and History
14. Faith and Dogma in the New Covenant Community
15. Dogma and Ontology in the Christian Consensus
16. The Self and its Dramas: Reason and Nature in the Disintegration of the Medieval Synthesis

17. Understanding Nature and Misunderstanding Human Nature
18. The Climax of an Empirical Culture: Its Blindness to Some Obvious "Facts"

PART III

19. The Resources of the Christian Faith in a Dynamic Civilization and an Expanding Society
20. Organism and Artifact in Democratic Government
21. Property, Social Hierarchy and the Problem of Justice
22. The Integration of the World Community
23. Individual and Collective Destinies in the Contemporary Situation

Pious and Secular America. Charles Scribner's Sons, 1958. Published in England as The Godly and the Ungodly. London: Faber and Faber, 1958.

I. Pious and Secular America
II. Frustration in Mid-Century
III. Higher Education in America
IV. Russia and America: A Study in Historical Contingency
V. Liberty and Equality
VI. Justice to the American Negro From State, Community and Church
VII. The Relations of Christians and Jews in Western Civilization
VIII. The Impulse for Perfection and the Impulse for Community
IX. Mystery and Meaning

The Structure of Nations and Empires, A Study of the Recurring Patterns and Problems of the Political Order in Relation to the Unique Problems of the Nuclear Age. New York: Charles Scribner's Sons, 1959.

I. Introduction
II. The Two Imperial Nations of Today
III. Community and Dominion in Nation and Empire
IV. Democracy and Authority
V. The Anatomy of Empire
VI. The Encounter Between Christianity and Empire
VII. The Lessons From the Three Empires
VIII. The Uniqueness of Western Christendom
IX. The Historical Basis for National Autonomy
X. The World of Autonomous Nations
XI. The Vague Universalism of Liberal Democracy
XII. The Character of National Imperialism
XIII. The Utopian Basis of Soviet Power
XIV. Communist Universalism and Imperialism
XV. Empires, Nations, and Collective Security in a Global Situation
XVI. The Cold War and the Nuclear Dilemma
XVII. The Creative and Destructive Possibilities of Human Freedom

Books by Reinhold Niebuhr

A Nation So Conceived, Reflections on the History of America From its
Early Visions to Its Present Power. (with Alan Heimert). New
York: Charles Scribner's Sons, 1963.

  I.   American Character: Endowment and Destiny
  II. The Quest for National Identity and Unity in a Growing Nation
 III. From an Agrarian to an Industrial Economy
  IV. The American Sense of Mission: From our Original Dreams to
       Global Responsibilities and Frustrations

Man's Nature and His Communities, Essays on the Dynamics and Enigmas
of Man's Personal and Social Existence. New York: Charles
Scribner's Sons, 1965.

  I.   Introduction: Changing Perspectives
  II. Man's Nature and His Communities
 III. Man's Tribalism as One Source of His Inhumanity
  IV. Man's Selfhood in Its Self-seeking and Self-giving

The Democratic Experience, Past and Prospects. (with Paul E. Sigmund).
New York: Frederick A. Praeger, 1969.

  I. The Democratic Experience in Western History
       1. Democracy and Communism: Two Utopian Ideologies
       2. The Hazards of Racial, Linguistic, and Religious
           Pluralism
       3. The Impact of Industrialization
       4. The Arrested and Reclaimed Democracies of Western
           Europe
       5. The Lessons of the Democratic Experience in Western
           History
  II. The Prospects for Democracy in the Developing Areas
       6. Africa: Tribalism, the One-Party State, and the Rise
           of the Military
       7. The Middle East: Authoritarian Modernizers and
           Islamic Traditionalism
       8. Latin America: Democracy Imposed on Feudalism
       9. Asia: The Success and Failure of Democracy
      10. The Prospects for Democracy: A Review of the
           Literature

Collections of Reinhold Niebuhr's Shorter Writings and Sermons

III. Why is Communism So Evil?
IV. The Anatomy of American Nationalism
V. The United Nations and the Free World
VI. The Illusion of World Government
VII. The Limits of Cultural Co-operation
VIII. The Limits of Military Power
IX. What We Can Learn From Sputnik

Essays in Applied Christianity, The Church and the New World. Edited
  by D. B. Robertson. New York: Meridian Books, 1959.

   Introduction by D. B. Robertson
I. The Weakness of Common Worship in American Protestantism
       A Christmas Service in Retrospect
       Sects and Churches
       Sunday Morning Debate
       Worship and the Social Conscience
       A Problem of Evangelical Christianity
       The Religious Pluralism of America
       The Weakness of Common Worship in American Protestantism
       Religiosity and the Christian Faith
II. Can the Church Give a "Moral Lead"?
       The Weakness of the Modern Church
       Moralists and Politics
       Church and State in America
       Which Question Comes First for the Church?
       Can the Church Give a "Moral Lead"?
       The Church and Equal Rights for Women
       Utilitarian Christianity and the World Crisis
       Social Christianity
       The Protestant Clergy and U. S. Politics
       Prayer and Politics
       Communism and the Clergy
       Literalism, Individualism, and Billy Graham
       The Security and Hazard of the Christian Ministry
III. Barthianism and the Kingdom
       Barth--Apostle of the Absolute
       Barthianism and the Kingdom
       Barthianism and Political Reaction
       Marx, Barth, and Israel's Prophets
       Karl Barth and Democracy
       Karl Barth on Politics
       We are Men and Not God
       An Answer to Karl Barth
       Why is Barth Silent on Hungary?
       Barth on Hungary: An Exchange
IV. The Catholic Heresy
       Arrogance in the Name of Christ
       Pius XI and His Successor
       The Catholic Heresy
       The Pope's Christmas Message
       Three Elements in Papal Leadership

13

24.   Berlin Notes (1924)
25.   Is Europe on the Way to Peace? (1924)
26.   Our Educational Program (1924)
27.   Tyrant Servants (1926)
28.   Winning the World (1926)
29.   An Aristocracy of Spiritual and Moral Life (1928)
30.   Youth and Religion (1928)
31.   Christianizing International Relations (1928)
32.   The Traditions of the Fathers and the Virtues of the
      Children (1929)
33.   Religion and Poetry (1930)
34.   Christianity at the Dawn of a New Era (1931)
35.   Christian Education and Society (1931)

Other Writings by Reinhold Niebuhr

1911

"The Attitude of the Church Toward Present Moral Evils." The Keryx,
1, no. 1 (February), 6-8.
Niebuhr was a charter staff member of this student publication
of Eden Theological Seminary. He was editor during the academic
year 1912-1913. This article is reprinted in Young Reinhold
Niebuhr.

"Ein Tag in Eden." The Keryx, 1, no. 2 (April), 3-6.

1913

"Die Gemeinde-Diakonie." Der Evangelische Diakonissen-Herold, 8,
no. 1 (October), 6-7.
This is a report of work done in St. John's Church in Lincoln,
Illinois, during the summer before he went to Yale. He had
"filled in" as pastor after his father died.

"Religion: Revival and Education." The Keryx, 3, no. 3 (June), 7-10.
Reprinted in Young Reinhold Niebuhr.

1914

"The Validity and Certainty of Religious Knowledge." B.D. thesis,
Yale University, 38 pp.
In Container no. 17, Reinhold Niebuhr Papers, Library of
Congress.

"Yale-Eden." The Keryx, 4, no. 5 (December), 1-4.
Reprinted in Young Reinhold Niebuhr.

1915

"The Contribution of Christianity to the Doctrine of Immortality."
M.A. thesis, Yale University, 40 pp.
Copy at Yale University Library.

1915

"Eine deutschen Predigt vom 75. Jubilee der deutschen Evangelischen
   Synode Nord Amerikas" (October), 13 pp.
      Manuscript anniversary sermon preached at Bethel Church,
   Detroit, Michigan, October 15, 1915. Copy at Eden Theological
   Seminary Archives. A translation is included in Young Reinhold
   Niebuhr.

"An English Sermon, preached on the occasion of the 75th anniversary
   of the German Evangelical Synod of North America at Bethel Church,
   Detroit, Michigan."
      Copy at Eden Theological Seminary Archives.

1916

"The Bible in the Sunday School." The Evangelical Teacher, 1, no. 11
   (November), 667-669.

"Failure of German-Americanism." The Atlantic Monthly, 118, no. 1
   (July), 13-18.

"The Nation's Crime Against the Individual." The Atlantic Monthly,
   118, no. 5 (November), 609-614.

"Paul and Christ's Most Formidable Foes." The Evangelical Teacher,
   1, no. 7 (July), 358-360.

"Paul the Champion of a Universal Faith." The Evangelical Teacher,
   1, no. 9 (September), 514-516.

"The Scylla and Charybdis of Teaching." The Evangelical Teacher, 1,
   no. 5 (May), 224-226.
      Reprinted in Young Reinhold Niebuhr.

"Sunday School or Church?" The Evangelical Teacher, 1, no. 10
   (October), 586-588.

1917

"Avoiding Abstractions." The Evangelical Teacher, 2, no. 2
   (February), 88-89.

"The Captivity and Restoration." The Evangelical Teacher, 2, no. 11
   (November), 750-751.

"The Future of Our Seminaries." The Keryx, 7, no. 1 (February), 5-8.
      Reprinted in Young Reinhold Niebuhr.

"How Large is Your Reserve Fund?" The Evangelical Teacher, 2, no. 3
   (March), 157-158.

"The Individuals in the Class." The Evangelical Teacher, 2, no. 6
   (June), 386-387.

"Isaiah the Prophet." The Evangelical Teacher, 2, no. 7 (July), 449-450.

"A Modern Sunday School." The Evangelical Teacher, 2, no. 10 (October), 678-679.
     Reprinted in Young Reinhold Niebuhr.

"Our Task." St. Louis: Eden Theological Seminary. n.d. [probably 1917].
     This pamphlet was prepared by Niebuhr to explain the work of the War Welfare Commission of the Evangelical Synod of North America. He served as the Commission's Executive Secretary. Copy at Eden Seminary Archives..

"The Spiritual Gospel." The Evangelical Teacher, 2, no. 1 (January), 16-18.
     From January 1917 until February 1918 Niebuhr served as Associate Editor of this denominational journal.

"Telling Children About Life After Death." The Evangelical Teacher, 2, no. 4 (April), 224-226.

"Telling Stories." The Evangelical Teacher, 2, no. 8 (August), 526-527.

"Written Work in the Sunday School." The Evangelical Teacher, 2, no. 9 (September), 603-604.

1918

"Love of Country." EH, 17, no. 16 (April 18), 2.

"A Message from Reinhold Niebuhr." The Keryx, 8, no. 4 (October), 2-5.
     Reprinted in Young Reinhold Niebuhr.

"Our Evangelical Boys in Military Camps." Evangelical Tidings, 4, no. 9 (March 3), 5.

"The Present Task of the Sunday School." The Evangelical Teacher, 3, no. 7 (July), 462-465.
     Reprinted in Young Reinhold Niebuhr.

"The Single Lesson Theme." The Evangelical Teacher, 3, no. 4 (April), 238-240.

1919

"Educational Principles in Church Schools." Sunday School Work in the Evangelical Synod of North America 1916-1919: Official Report of the Second National Convention of Evangelical Sunday Schools.

1919

St. Louis: Board of Sunday Schools, Evangelical Synod of North
America, pp. 104-106.

"Rebuttal on 'Where Shall We Go?'" Magazin für Evangelische
Theologie und Kirche, 47, no. 4 (July), 270-271.
    A response to F. W. Henninger, "Why Go At All?," in the same
journal, 47, no. 3 (March), 194-201. Reprinted in Young Reinhold
Niebuhr.

"The Twilight of Liberalism." NR, 19, no. 241 (June 14), 218.

1920

"The Church and the Industrial Crisis." The Biblical World, 54,
no. 6 (November), 588-592.

"The Evangelical Forward Movement From the Standpoint of a Liberal."
EH, 19, no. 26 (June 24), 5, 8.

"The Keryx and Our Educational Institutions." The Keryx, 10, no. 1
(February), 3-5.
    Reprinted in Young Reinhold Niebuhr.

"Religion's Limitations." WT, 3, no. 3 (March), 77-79.

1921

"Christian America." EH, 20, no. 32 (August 11), 5.
    The subcaption here is "A Review of Events and an Appraisal of
Tendencies in the Church Life of America." Niebuhr wrote a column with this title, "Christian America," until the middle of
1923. It was a series of short pieces about what was going on
in the various denominations. Except for the fact that the
writing was limited to the activities of churches, there is some
similarity to his later short pieces in "Ex Cathedra" and "editorial notes" in Christianity and Crisis and Christianity and
Society.

"Christian America." EH, 20, no. 36 (September 8), 5-6.

"Christian America." EH, 20, no. 40 (October 6), 6.

"Christian America." EH, 20, no. 45 (November 10), 5-6.

"Christian America." EH, 20, no. 51 (December 22), 6, 8.

"The Federal Council at Boston." EH, 20, no. 1 (January 6), 4, 6-7.

"Heroes and Hero Worship." N, 112, no. 2903 (February 23), 293-294.

"Making the Nation Christian." [Lesson for June 5.] The Evangelical
Home, 1, no. 2 (April), 115-119.

"Making the World Christian." [Lesson for June 12.] The Evangelical
Home, 1, no. 2 (April), 119-124.

"Shall a Minister Have an Education?" Magazin für Evangelische
Theologie und Kirche, 49, no. 3 (May), 208-211.
Reprinted in Young Reinhold Niebuhr.

1922

"The Chinese Church." EH, 21, no. 32 (August 10), 5.

"Christian America." EH, 21, no. 3 (January 10), 6.

"Christian America." EH, 21, no. 22 (June 1), 5-6.

"Christian America." EH, 21, no. 25 (June 22), 6-8.

"Christian America." EH, 21, no. 30 (July 27), 5.

"Christian America." EH, 21, no. 37 (September 14), 6.

"Christian America." EH, 21, no. 43 (October 26), 6.

"Christian America." EH, 21, no. 51 (December 21), 6.

"The Church and the Middle Class." CCY, 39, no. 49 (December 7),
1513-1515.

"Letter." NR, 29, no. 377 (February 22), 372.
In reply to an editorial, "War and Christian Ethics." NR, 29,
no. 371 (January 11), 166-169.

1923

"America and Europe." EH, 22, no. 44 (November 1), 695-696.
Reprinted in Young Reinhold Niebuhr.

"Christian America." EH, 22, no. 3 (January 18), 45-46.

"Christian America." EH, 22, no. 7 (February 15), 104-105.

"Christian America." EH, 22, no. 9 (March 1), 136-137.

"Christian America." EH, 22, no. 10 (March 8), 202.

"Christian America." EH, 22, no. 15 (March 29), 202.

"Christian America." EH, 22, no. 15 (April 12), 232-233.

"Christian America." EH, 22, no. 18 (May 3), 281-282.

"Christian America." EH, 22, no. 21 (May 24), 326.

"Christian America." EH, 22, no. 26 (June 28), 409.

1923

"The Despair of Europe." EH, 22, no. 38 (September 20), 601–602.
    Reprinted in Young Reinhold Niebuhr.

"Deutschlands verzweiflungsvolle Lage." Der Friedensbote, 74, no. 40
    (October 7), 635.
        English version in the September 13 issue of EH.

"Eine Fahrt durch das Ruhrgebiet." Der Friedensbote, 74, no. 35
    (September 2), 551–552.
        English version in August 9 issue of EH.

"Germany in Despair." EH, 22, no. 37 (September 13), 584–585.
    Reprinted in Young Reinhold Niebuhr.

"The Paradox of Institutions." WT, 6, no. 8 (August), 231–232.

"Protestantism in Germany." CCY, 40, no. 40 (October 4), 1258–1260.

"A Trip Through the Ruhr." EH, 22, no. 32 (August 9), 501–502.
    Reprinted in Young Reinhold Niebuhr.

"Wanted: A Christian Morality." CCY, 40, no. 7 (February 15),
    201–203.

"Youth Movement in Germany." CCY, 40, no. 44 (November 1),
    1396–1397.
        A version of the same article appears in the October 11 issue
    of EH. Reprinted in Young Reinhold Niebuhr.

1924

"Aus Berlin: Eindrücke eines Amerikaners in der deutschen Hauptstadt."
    Der Friedensbote, 75, no. 37 (September 14), 587.
        Appears in exact translation as "Berlin Notes: Impressions of
    an American in the German Capital." EH, 23, no. 38 (September 18),
    616–617. Reprinted in Young Reinhold Niebuhr.

"Christianity and Contemporary Politics." CCY, 41, no. 16 (April 17),
    498–501.

"The Dawn in Europe." EH, 23, no. 32 (August 7), 518–519.
    Reprinted in Young Reinhold Niebuhr.

"European Reform and American Reform—How They Differ." CCY, 41,
    no. 35 (August 28), 1108–1110.

"The German Clan." CCY, 41, no. 42 (October 16), 1330–1331.

"Is Europe on the Way to Peace?" EH, 23, no. 39 (September 25), 631.
        Published in German in the October 5 issue of Der Friedensbote.
    Reprinted in Young Reinhold Niebuhr.

"Is Protestantism Self-Deceived?" CCY, 41, no. 52 (December 25),
    1661–1662.

1926

"On Academic Vagabondage." The Keryx, 14, no. 1 (February), 1–4.
    Reprinted in Young Reinhold Niebuhr.

"Our Educational Program," in Report of the Fifth National Convention
    of the Evangelical Brotherhood, September 14–17, 1924, East St.
    Louis, Illinois. St. Louis: The Evangelical Brotherhood,
    pp. 84–87.
    Reprinted in Young Reinhold Niebuhr.

"What are the Churches Advertising?" CCY, 41, no. 48 (November 27),
    1532–1533.

1925

"Can Christianity Survive?" The Atlantic Monthly, 135, no. 1
    (January), 84–88.

"Can Schweitzer Save us From Russell?" CCY, 42, no. 36 (September 3),
    1093–1095.

"Capitalism––Protestant Offspring." CCY, 42, no. 19 (May 7),
    600–601.

"Foreword," to The Will of God: Can it, Shall It Be Done on Earth
    as it is in Heaven? By J. H. Norstmann. St. Louis: Eden Pub-
    lishing House, p. 3.

"Germany and Modern Civilization." The Atlantic Monthly, 135, no. 6
    (June), 843–848.

"Religious Values." CCY, 42, no. 43 (October 22), 1308–1309.
    Review of E. S. Brightman's Religious Values.

"Shall We Proclaim the Truth or Search for It?" CCY, 42, no. 10
    (March 12), 344–346.

"What Bethel Church Stands For." Bethel Brother (March), n.p.

1926

"Another Outline––And a Good One." CCY, 43, no. 47 (November 25),
    1458.
    Review of Lynn Thorndike's A Short History of Civilization.

"Bertrand Russell as a Family Man." CCY, 43, no. 32 (August 12),
    1016–1017.
    Review of Bertrand Russell's Education and the Good Life.

"Christ's View of the Kingdom." CCY, 43, no. 26 (July 29), 843.
    Review of Manson's Christ's View of the Kingdom of God.

"Does Religion Quiet or Disquiet?" WT, 9, no. 6 (November), 220–221.

1926

"The Foolishness of Preaching," in Best Sermons of 1926. Edited by
Joseph F. Newton. New York: Harcourt, Brace and Co., pp. 179-187.

"Henry Ford and Industrial Autocracy." CCY, 43, no. 44 (November 4),
1354-1355.
   This article is unsigned, but it is Dr. Niebuhr's. The reaction to the article was considerable and led to further articles
on Ford with Niebuhr's name on them.

"How Civilization Defeated Christianity." CCY, 43, no. 28 (July 15),
895-896.
   Review article of R. H. Tawney's Religion and the Rise of
Capitalism.

"How Philanthropic is Henry Ford?" CCY, 43, no. 49 (December 9),
1516-1517.
   Reprinted in Love and Justice.

"Impotent Liberalism." CCY, 43, no. 6 (February 11), 167-168.
   Unsigned but undoubtedly Niebuhr's.

"Is Western Civilization Dying?" CCY, 43, no. 20 (May 20), 651-652.

"Mr. Howie Talks it Over with Mr. Niebuhr." CCY, 43, no. 30
(July 29), 946-947.
   An exchange with a Mr. James M. Howie of Buffalo, New York, in
which Mr. Howie attacks Niebuhr's strictures on the Protestant
Ethic (particularly Niebuhr's article in The Atlantic Monthly of
June 1926). Niebuhr answers Howie here.

"Our Secularized Civilization." CCY, 43, no. 16 (April 22), 508-510.

"Puritanism and Prosperity." The Atlantic Monthly, 137, no. 6
(June), 721-725.

"Reverend Dr. Silke." CCY, 43, no. 10 (March 11), 316-318.

"Science and the Modern World." CCY, 43, no. 14 (April 8), 448-449.
   A review article of A. N. Whitehead's Science and the Modern
World.

"The Threat of the R.O.T.C." WT, 9, no. 5 (October), 154-156.

"Tyrant Servants," in Preachers and Preaching in Detroit. Edited by
Ralph M. Pierce. Detroit: Fleming H. Revell Co., pp. 149-159.
   Reprinted in Young Reinhold Niebhur.

"The Vice of Intolerance." EH, 25, no. 34 (August 26), 533.

"Winning the World," in Report of the Sixth National Convention of
the Evangelical Brotherhood, August 22-25, 1926, Buffalo, New
York. St. Louis: The Evangelical Brotherhood, pp. 120-123.
   Reprinted in Young Reinhold Niebuhr.

<u>1927</u>

"Allegorizing the Miracles." CCY, 44, no. 41 (October 13), 1203.
Review of L. C. Douglas's <u>Those Disturbing Miracles</u>.

"Beauty as a Substitute for Righteousness." CCY, 44, no. 39
(September 29), 1133-1134.

"Business is Business--Plus." CCY, 44, no. 1 (January 6), 15-16.
Review of Jerome Davis's <u>Business and the Church</u>.

"A Critique of Pacifism." <u>The Atlantic Monthly</u>, 139, no. 5
(May), 637-641.
Reprinted in <u>Love and Justice</u>.

"Ford's Five-Day Week Shrinks." CCY, 44, no. 23 (June 9), 713-714.
Reprinted in <u>Love and Justice</u>.

"A Gentleman, a Bishop, and a Christian." CCY, 44, no. 18 (May 5),
560-561.
Review of Bishop William Lawrence's <u>Memories of a Happy Life</u>.

"Governor Smith's Reply." CCY, 44, no. 21 (May 26), 661-662.
A letter to the Editor. Niebuhr argued against the idea that
Smith should take a stand against his church and declare unquali-
fied loyalty to the secular state.

"How Adventurous is Dr. Fosdick?" CCY, 44, no. 1 (January 6), 17-18.
A review article on Fosdick's <u>Adventurous Religion</u>.

"Missions and World Peace." WT, 10, no. 4 (April), 170-171.
In a series called "Building Tomorrow's World."

"The Practical Unbelief of Modern Civilization," in <u>Religion on the
Campus</u>. Edited by F. P. Miller. New York: Association Press,
pp. 11-21.

"A Religion Worth Fighting For." <u>The Survey</u>, 58, no. 9 (August 1),
444-446, 480.

"The State of Our Religion," in <u>A Survey of Our Student Life and of
the Present Religious Situation as it Affects American Students</u>.
By Reinhold Niebuhr, Bruce Curry, and G. A. Studdert-Kennedy.
Milwaukee: The National Student Conference, pp. 25-37.

"To Whom Shall We Go?" CCY, 44, no. 10 (March 10), 299-301.

"Why I am Not a Christian." CCY, 44, no. 50 (December 15), 1482-1483.
Also included in H. E. Luccock's <u>The First Fine Careless
Rapture</u>.

1928

"An Aristocracy of Spiritual and Moral Life," in <u>Adventures With Christ: Tenth National Report of the Evangelical League, August 7-12, 1928, Milwaukee, Wisconsin</u>. St. Louis: The Evangelical League, pp. 167-173.
    Reprinted in <u>Young Reinhold Niebuhr</u>.

"An Artist's Civilization." WT, 11, no. 12 (December), 521.
    Review of Clive Bell's <u>Civilization</u>.

"Barth--Apostle of the Absolute." CCY, 45, no. 50 (December 13), 1523-1524.
    Reprinted in <u>Essays in Applied Christianity</u>.

"The Best-Loved Saint." CCY, 45, no. 18 (May 3), 572.
    Review of Luigi Salvatorelli's <u>Life of St. Francis of Assisi</u>.

"Christianity and the Good Life." CCY, 45, no. 14 (April 5), 442.
    Review of A. D. Lindsay's <u>Christianity and the Present Moral Unrest</u>.

"Christianizing International Relations," in <u>Report of the Seventh National Convention of the Evangelical Brotherhood, September 16-19, 1928, Indianapolis, Indiana</u>. St. Louis: Evangelical Brotherhood, pp. 121-126.
    Reprinted in <u>Young Reinhold Niebuhr</u>.

"The Confessions of a Tired Radical." CCY, 45, no. 35 (August 30), 1046-1047.
    Reprinted in <u>Love and Justice</u>.

"For Preachers and Teachers." CCY, 45, no. 4 (February 2), 147-148.
    Review of Hugh Martin's <u>Christian Social Reformers of the Nineteenth Century</u>, together with B. Carrier's <u>The Kingdom of Love</u> and J. R. P. Schlater's <u>The Public Worship of God</u>.

"Idealism and Religion." CCY, 45, no. 35 (September 13), 1106.
    Review of E. E. Thomas's <u>The Ethical Basis of Reality</u>.

"Letter of Resignation." Niebuhr's resignation from Bethel Evangelical Church, Detroit. Back-of Church Bulletin for April 22.

"Life and the Soldier." WT, 11, no. 10 (October), 423.
    Review of A. Hopkinson's <u>Religio Militis</u>.

"Morality and the Supernatural." CCY, 45, no. 36 (September 6), 1076.
    Review of H. H. Scullard's <u>The Ethics of the Gospel and the Ethics of Nature</u>.

"Oriental vs. Occidental Strategy of Life." WT, 11, no. 1 (January), 21-23.

"Pacifism and the Use of Force." WT, 11, no. 5 (May), 218-220.
    Reprinted in <u>Love and Justice</u>.

"The Philosophy of Sharing," in <u>Students and the Future of Christian Missions</u>. Edited by Gordon Poteat. New York: The Student Volunteer Movement, pp. 145-154.

"The Present Germany." CCY, 45, no. 29 (July 5), 857.
  Review of G. H. Danton's <u>Germany Ten Years After</u>.

"Protestantism and Prohibition." NR, 56, no. 725 (October 24), 265-267.

"Religious Imagination and the Scientific Method," in <u>Proceedings of the National Conference on Social Work</u>. Chicago: The University of Chicago Press, pp. 51-57.

"The Reward of Righteousness." CCY, 45, no. 45 (November 8), 1364.
  Review of E. H. Hughes's <u>Christianity and Success</u>.

"Shoddy." WT, 11, no. 7 (July), 310.
  Review of Dan Brummit's <u>Shoddy</u>.

"Socialism Simplified." CCY, 45, no. 31 (August 2), 925-953.
  Review of Bernard Shaw's <u>The Intelligent Woman's Guide to Socialism and Capitalism</u>.

"Truth From the Trenches." CCY, 45, no. 23 (June 7), 731.
  Review of Fritz von Unruh's <u>Way of Sacrifice</u>.

"What the War Did to my Mind." CCY, 45, no. 39 (September 27), 1161-1163.

"Why We Need a New Economic Order." WT, 11, no. 10 (October), 395-396.

"The Winged Horse." WT, 11, no. 9 (September), 375.
  Review of Auslander and Hill's <u>The Winged Horse</u>.

"Would Jesus Be a Churchman Today?" WT, 11, no. 12 (December), 492-494.

"Youth and Religion," in <u>Adventures With Christ: Tenth National Convention Report of the Evangelical League, August 7-12, 1928, Milwaukee, Wisconsin</u>. St. Louis: The Evangelical League, pp. 180-185.

<u>1929</u>

"Americanization of the Soul." WT, 12, no. 11 (November), 473-476.
  Review of R. M. Freienfel's <u>Mysteries of the Soul</u>.

"Christian Pacifism." WT, 12, no. 5 (May), 234-235.
  Review of Leyton Richards's <u>The Christian Alternative to War</u>.

"Christianity and Redemption," in <u>Whither Christianity</u>? Edited by L. H. Hough. New York: Harper & Brothers, pp. 110-112.

Other Writings by Reinhold Niebuhr

1929

"Concerning Anepsiarchal." WT, 12, no. 4 (April), 184-185.
Review of J. H. Denison's Emotion as the Basis of Civilization.

"A Consistent Pessimist." CCY, 46, no. 18 (May 1), 586-587.
Review of Joseph W. Krutch's The Modern Temper.

"End of the Forsyte Saga." WT, 12, no. 2 (February), 90-91.
Review of John Galsworthy's The Swan Song.

"Harmonizing our Personal Relations With Our Social Ideals," in
J. H. Holmes. The Community Pulpit Series, No. 8, 1928-1929,
p. 11.

"Hebraism and Hellenism," in J. H. Holmes. The Community Pulpit
Series, No. 9, 1928-1929, p. 11.

"It Was a Sermon on Love." CCY, 46, no. 50 (December 11), 1540-1542.

"Jesus as Symbol." NYHT (September 22), p. 16.

"Jesus, Son of Man." WT, 12, no. 4 (April), 185.
Review of Kahlil Gibran's Jesus, the Son of Man.

"John Dewey." WT, 12, no. 11 (November), 472-473.

"The Minister as an Expert," in Effective Preaching. Boston: Boston
University School of Theology, Conference on Preaching, pp. 81-92.

"The Perils of American-European Relationships," in J. H. Holmes.
The Community Pulpit Series, No. 11, 1928-1929, p. 11.

"Political Action and Social Change." WT, 12, no. 12 (December),
491-493.

"A Prophet Come to Judgment." WT, 12, no. 7 (July), 313-314.
Review of Walter Lippmann's A Preface to Morals.

"Religion and Moral Experience," in "What Religion Means to Me." By
Reinhold Niebuhr, H. E. Fosdick, A. B. Curry, E. F. Tittle et al.
New York: Doubleday, Doran & Company, Inc.
    A shorter, and apparently earlier, version of this article
appears in an undated pamphlet entitled "Dynamic Religion, A
Personal Experience," published by Eddy and Page in the Personal
Problems Series, Number 11.

"A Religion to Save the World." NYHT (March 17), p. 25.
Review of Harry F. Ward's Our Economic Morality.

"Science vs. Morality." WT, 12, no. 3 (March), 136.
Review of W. K. Wallace's Scientific World View.

"Senator Norris and His Clerical Critic." WT, 12, no. 4 (April), 170.

"The Terrible Beauty of the Cross." CCY, 46, no. 12 (March 21),
386-388.

"The Unethical Character of Modern Civilization," in J. H. Holmes. The Community Pulpit Series, no. 10, 1928-1929, p. 10.

"The Unhappy Intellectuals." The Atlantic Monthly, 143, no. 6 (June), 790-794.

"The Use of Force," in Pacifism in the Modern World. Edited by Devere Allen. New York: Doubleday, Doran & Company.

"We Are Being Driven." CCY, 46, no. 18 (May 1), 578-579.

"Wealth for All." WT, 12, no. 10 (October), 423.
      Review of Javits and Wood's Make Everybody Rich.

"The West in Oriental Eyes." WT, 12, no. 1 (January), 44.
      Review of K. K. Kannan's The West.

"Would Jesus be a Modernist Today?" WT, 12, no. 3 (March), 122-124.

1930

"At Oberammergau." CCY, 47, no. 33 (August 13), 983-984.
      Editorial Correspondence.

"Awkward Imperialists." The Atlantic Monthly, 145, no. 5 (May), 670-675.

"Christian Faith in the Modern World," introduction to Ventures in Belief. Edited by H. P. Van Dusen. New York: Charles Scribner's Sons, pp. 5-22.
      Also published as "The Difficulty of Religion in the Modern World." The Christian, 6, no. 50 (October 30), 797-798.

"Church Currents in Germany." CCY, 47, no. 32 (August 6), 959-960.
      Editorial Correspondence.

"Church in Russia." CCY, 47, no. 38 (September 24), 1144-1146.
      Editorial Correspondence.

"England and the English." WT, 13, no. 8 (August), 347.
      Review of Wilhelm Dibelius's England.

"Europe's Religious Pessimism." CCY, 47, no. 34 (August 27), 1031-1033.

"The Genesis of the Social Gospel." WT, 13, no. 1 (January), 41.
      Review of C. C. McCown's The Genesis of the Social Gospel.

"The German Crisis." N, 131, no. 3404 (October 1), 358, 360.

"Germany Wrestles With Her Debts." CCY, 47, no. 31 (July 30), 935-936.
      Editorial Correspondence.

"Glimpses of the Southland." CCY, 47, no. 29 (July 16), 893-895.

Other Writings by Reinhold Niebuhr

1930

"Green Pastures." WT, 13, no. 6 (June), 280.
   Review of Marc Connelly's The Green Pastures.

"If You Were President--How Would You Proclaim Thanksgiving Day?"
   CCY, 47, no. 48 (November 26), 1452.

"Is Stewardship Ethical?" CCY, 47, no. 18 (April 30), 555-557.
   Reprinted in Love and Justice.

"Land of Extremes." CCY, 47, no. 42 (October 15), 1241-1243.
   On Russia.

"Mechanical Men in a Mechanical Age." WT, 13, no. 12 (December),
   492-495.
   Reprinted from Union Seminary Alumni Bulletin.

"Mr. McCabe Holds Forth." WT, 13, no. 4 (April), 185-186.
   Review of Joseph McCabe's The Story of Religious Controversy.

"Mr. Mencken as Theologian." WT, 13, no. 10 (October), 428.
   Review of H. L. Mencken's Treatise on the Gods.

"A Modern Theist." WT, 13, no. 8 (August), 346-347.

"Political Action and Social Change," in A New Economic Order.
   Edited by Kirby Page. New York: Harcourt, Brace & Company,
   pp. 301-312.
   Same title to be found in WT (December 1929).

"The Preaching of Repentance." CCY, 47, no. 25 (June 18), 779-781.

"The Quest of the Ages." WT, 13, no. 6 (June), 280.
   Review of Eustace Haydon's The Quest of the Ages.

"Religion and Poetry." Theological Magazine of the Evangelical Synod
   of North America, 58, no. 4 (July), 241-245.
   Reprinted in Young Reinhold Niebuhr.

"Renewing Religious Liberty." CCY, 47, no. 18 (July 9), 868-869.
   Review of A. E. Day's Revitalizing Religion.

"Russia Makes the Machine its God." CCY, 47, no. 36 (September 10),
   1080-1081.

"Russian Efficiency." CCY, 47, no. 40 (October 1), 1178-1180.

"Russia's Tractor Revolution." CCY, 47, no. 37 (September 17),
   1111-1112.

"The Speculation Mania." WT, 13, no. 1 (January), 25-27.

"The Spirit of Life," in Addresses and Proceedings. The National
   Education Association of the United States. New York: NEA,
   pp. 610-618.

"The Spiritual Life of Modern Man." Alumni Bulletin of the Union
   Theological Seminary, 5, no. 5 (June-July), 153-160.

"The Traditions of the Fathers and the Virtues of the Children."
Light Bearer, 4, no. 2 (February), 17–21.
Reprinted in Young Reinhold Niebuhr.

"Would You be Happy?" WT, 13, no. 11 (November), 473.
Review of Bertrand Russell's The Conquest of Happiness.

1931

"An American Approach to the Christian Message," in A Traffic in
Knowledge. Edited by W. A. Visser't Hooft. London: Student
Christian Movement Press, pp. 54–85.
An International Symposium on the Christian Message.

"Anti-Authoritarian." WT, 14, no. 10 (October), 330.
Review of Louis Lefevre's Liberty and Restraint.

"Barthianism and the Kingdom." CCY, 48, no. 28 (July 15), 924–925.
Comment on an article with this title by E. G. Homrighausen.
Reprinted in Essays in Applied Christianity.

"Christian Education and Society." Light Bearer, 5, no. 9
(September), 16–19, 40.
Reprinted in Young Reinhold Niebuhr.

"Christianity at the Dawn of a New Era." Light Bearer, 5, no. 8
(August), 9–12.
Reprinted in Young Reinhold Niebuhr.

"Christianity's Social Teaching." WT, 14, no. 12 (December), 409.
Review of Ernst Troeltsch's The Social Teaching of the Christian Churches.

"The Common Root of Joy and Pain," in What Can Students Believe?
(Sermons by Fosdick, Tittle, Coffin, Buttrick, Sperry, Niebuhr
et al.) Edited by E. M. McKee. New York: R. R. Smith,
pp. 129–138.

"Confusion of Tongues." WT, 14, no. 9 (September), 298–299.
Review of Living Philosophies, A Series of Intimate Credos
by Albert Einstein et al.

"Crisis in British Socialism." CCY, 48, no. 39 (September 30),
1202–1204.

"The Crisis of Society." The Congregationalist and Herald of Gospel
Liberty, 116, no. 35 (August 27), 1157–1159.
Also published in The Christian, 7, no. 43 (September 5),
682–684.

"Dissenters, Not Puritans." WT, 14, no. 3 (March), 90.
Review of T. C. Hall's The Religious Background of American
Culture.

Other Writings by Reinhold Niebuhr

1931

"Economic Perils to World Peace." WT, 14, no. 5 (May), 154-156.

"Education and Social Change." WT, 14, no. 12 (December), 407.
    Review of Harold Rugg's Culture and Education in America.

"Foreword," to He Stirreth Up the People. By Herman J. Hahn.
    Buffalo: Salem Evangelical Brotherhood, p. 8.

"The 'Gloomy' Dean." WT, 14, no. 7 (July), 234.
    Review of W. R. Inge's Christian Ethics and Modern Problems.

"Heterodox Orthodoxy." WT, 14, no. 2 (February), 59.
    Review of J. C. Ransom's God Without Thunder.

"Introduction," to "Toward a New Economic Society." A Program for
    Students by a Commission of the Student Christian Association
    Movement. Chairman, F. A. Henderson. New York: Eddy and Page.

"Labor's Story in England." WT, 14, no. 10 (October), 331.
    Review of Godfrey Elton's England Arise!

"Let Liberal Churches Stop Fooling Themselves!" CCY, 48, no. 12
    (March 25), 402-404.

"The Life of Lenin." WT, 14, no. 8 (August), 265-266.
    Review of F. Ossendowski's Lenin, God of the Godless, along
    with Vernadsky's Lenin, Red Dictator.

"Making Peace With Russia." WT, 14, no. 11 (November), 354-355.

"Not So Loud, Gentlemen!" WT, 14, no. 7 (July), 232.
    Review of Behold America, A Symposium, edited by S. D.
    Schmalhausen.

"The Present-Day Interpretation of the Christian Faith." Four
    lectures at the National Student-Faculty Conference on Religion
    and Education. New York: Association Press.
        Lectures: 1) "Religion and Modern Culture," 2) "The Christian
    Religion in Modern Civilization," 3) "Historic Protestantism and
    Student Religion," 4) "The Ethical Resources of the Christian
    Religion."

"Property and the Ethical Life." WT, 14, no. 1 (January), 19-21.

"Radicalism and Religion." WT, 14, no. 10 (October), 324-327.

"Religion in a Power Age." WT, 14, no. 5 (May), 165.
    Review of Paul Hutchinson's World Revolution and Religion.

"The Religion of Communism." The Atlantic Monthly, 147, no. 4
    (April), 462-470.

"A Social Survey of England and France." WT, 14, no. 9 (September),
    300.
        Review of C. W. Pipkin's Social Politics and Modern
    Democracies.

"Socialism and Christianity." CCY, 48, no. 33 (August 19), 1038-1040.
Editorial.

"The Weakness of the Modern Church." The Christian Herald, 10, no. 5
(May), 42-43.
Reprinted in Essays in Applied Christianity.

"What Causes Unemployment?" WT, 14, no. 11 (November), 372.
Review of V. A. Demant's This Unemployment.

"What Chance Has Gandhi?" CCY, 48, no. 41 (October 14), 1274-1276.

"What Price Efficiency?" WT, 14, no. 8 (August), 267.
Review of Gina Lombroso's The Tragedies of Progress.

"What the Future Holds in Store For Us." WT, 14, no. 6 (June), 203.
Review of Eugen Diesel's Germany and the Germans.

"When Virtues are Vices." CCY, 48, no. 3 (January 21), 114-115.

1932

"Catastrophe or Social Control, The Alternatives for America."
Harpers, 165, no. 6 (June), 114-118.

"A Communist Manifesto." WT, 15, no. 15 (October 26), 404-405.
Review of William Z. Foster's Toward Soviet America.

"Economic Forces in Modern Society." WT, 15, no. 3 (March), 89-90.
Review of Economic Behavior by W. E. Atkins et al.

"Epic of Russia." WT, 15, no. 6 (June), 187-188.
Review of Hans von Eckardt's Russia.

"Eternity and our Time." WT, 15, no. 23 (December 21), 596.
Review of Paul Tillich's The Religious Situation.

"The Ethic of Jesus and the Social Problem." Religion in Life, 1,
no. 2 (Spring), 198-208.
Reprinted in Contemporary Thinking About Jesus, edited by
T. S. Kepler. Also in Love and Justice.

"Events and the Man." WT, 15, no. 7 (July), 210.
Review of Leon Trotsky's The History of the Russian Revolution.

"Germany--Prophecy of Western Civilization." CCY, 49, no. 9
(March 2), 287-289.

"Germany's Darkest Hour." CCY, 49, no. 9 (March 2), 291-292.
Review of George Shuster's The Germans.

"Idealists and the Social Struggle." WT, 15, no. 15 (October 26),
395-397.
From the Introduction to Moral Man and Immoral Society.

1932

"Is Peace or Justice the Goal?" WT, 15, no. 10 (September 21), 275–276.

"Letter." N, 135, no. 3502 (August 17), 147.
 Urges voters to back Norman Thomas for President.

"Letter." NR, 72, no. 924 (August 17), 22.
 Invites readers to join The Committee of Five Thousand for Thomas for President.

"Moralists and Politics." CCY, 49, no. 27 (July 6), 857–859.

"More Pro and Con on Russia." WT, 15, no. 16 (November 2), 428.
 Review of Joseph Freeman's The Soviet Worker, along with I. D. Levine's Red Smoke.

"More Thunder Than Dawn." WT, 15, no. 5 (May), 151–152.
 Review of Glenn Frank's Thunder and Dawn, along with C. A. Beard's America Faces the Future.

"Must We Do Nothing?" CCY, 49, no. 13 (March 30), 415–417.
 A critique of an article by H. Richard Niebuhr entitled "The Grace of Doing Nothing."

"Optimism is Cowardice." WT, 15, no. 4 (April), 121.
 Review of Oswald Spengler's Man and Technics.

"Perils of American Power." The Atlantic Monthly, 149 (January), 90–96.

"Rebels and Renegades." WT, 15, no. 13 (October 12), 357.
 Review of Max Nomad's Rebels and Renegades.

"Religion and Class War in Kentucky." CCY, 49, no. 20 (May 18), 637–639.
 Reprinted in Love and Justice.

"Religion and 19th Century Man." CCY, 49, no. 22 (June 1), 708.
 Review of Rufus Jones's A Preface to Christian Faith in a New Age.

"The Revolt of the Masses." WT, 15, no. 18 (November 16), 477–478.
 Review of Jose Ortega y Gasset's The Revolt of the Masses.

"Socialism and Christianity." CCY, 49, no. 11 (March 16), 355.
 Review of G. C. Binyon's The Christian Socialist Movement in England.

"The Stakes in the Election." (A Letter.) CCY, 49, no. 45 (November 9), 1379–1381.

"Still on Probation." WT, 15, no. 20 (November 30), 525–526.
 Review of Sherwood Anderson's Beyond Desire.

"Waldo Frank in Russia." WT, 15, no. 9 (September 14), 261–262.

1933

"Ablest Interpreter of Marx." WT, 16, no. 20 (August), 476.
  Review of Sidney Hook's Towards the Understanding of Karl Marx.

"After Capitalism--What?" WT, 16, no. 9 (March 1), 203-205.

"A Christian Philosophy of Compromise." CCY, 50, no. 23 (June 7),
  746-748.
  Discussion continued in issues of July 26 and August 9.

"Christianity Today." NYHT (September 17), p. 18.
  Review of Contemporary Religious Thinking, edited by R. W.
  Searle and Frederick Bowers, along with Paul Hutchinson's The
  Ordeal of Western Religion.

"A Christmas Service in Retrospect." CCY, 50, no. 1 (January 4),
  13-14.
  Reprinted in Essays in Applied Christianity.

"Democracy in Crisis." WT, 16, no. 17 (May), 404.
  Review of Harold Laski's Democracy in Crisis.

"An Editorial Conversation." (with C. C. Morrison.) CCY, 50,
  no. 30 (July 26), 950-951.
  Conversation continued in issue of August 9, pp. 1006-1008.

"The Eleventh Commandment." WT, 16, no. 15 (April 12), 357.
  Review of Francis Neilson's The Eleventh Commandment.

"The Germans: Unhappy Philosophers in Politics." The American
  Scholar, 2, no. 4 (October), 409-419.

"Germany Must be Told." CCY, 50, no. 32 (August 9), 1014-1015.

"The Germany of Hitler." WT, 16, no. 25 (October 26), 598-599.
  Review of Adolph Hitler's My Battle, along with The Brown Book
  of the Hitler Terror, by the World Committee for the Victims of
  German Fascism, and Germany, Twilight or New Dawn? (anonymous).

"Germany: Two Views." WT, 16, no. 14 (April 5), 330.
  Review of E. A. Mowrer's Germany Puts the Clock Back, along
  with O. G. Villard's The Green Phoenix.

"Hitlerism--A Devil's Brew." WT, 16, no. 16 (April 19), 369-370.

"Illusions--Petty and Majestic." WT, 16, no. 1 (January 4), 20.
  Review of E. D. Martin's Civilizing Ourselves.

"In a Gentler Mood." WT, 16, no. 3 (January 18), 69.
  Review of Bertrand Russell's Education and the Modern World.

"Letter." CCY, 50, 11 (March 15), 363-364.
  A reply to George A. Coe's attack on Moral Man and Immoral
  Society.

1933

"The Liquor Traffic." WT, 16, no. 27 (November 25), 646.
 Review of Fosdick and Scott's Toward Liquor Control.

"Making Radicalism Effective." WT, 16, no. 29 (December 21), 682–684.

"Marxism and Religion." WT, 16, no. 11 (March 15), 253–255.

"Naive Individualism." WT, 16, no. 13 (March 29), 310.

"A New Strategy for Socialists." WT, 16, no. 21 (August 31), 490–492.

"Notes from a Berlin Diary." CCY, 50, no. 27 (July 5), 872–873.
 Editorial Correspondence.

"Notes from a London Diary." CCY, 50, 28 and 29 (July 12 and 19),
 903–904, 927–928.
 Editorial Correspondence.

"The Opposition in Germany." NR, 75, no. 969 (June 28), 169–171.

"Optimism and Utopianism." WT, 16, no. 8 (February 22), 179–180.
 A rejoinder to some of the reviews of Moral Man and Immoral
 Society.

"Protestantism, Capitalism and Communism," in Religion Today, A
 Challenging Enigma. Edited by Arthur L. Swift, Jr. New York:
 McGraw-Hill Book Company, pp. 138–154.

"A Rarely Successful Biography." NYHT (October 29), p. 4.
 Review of Abram Lipsky's Martin Luther.

"Religion and the New Germany." CCY, 50, no. 26 (June 28), 843–845.

"A Reorientation of Radicalism." WT, 16, no. 19 (July), 443–444.

"The Saga of Industry." WT, 16, no. 2 (January 11), 44–45.

"Streeter in Strange Fields." CCY, 50, no. 9 (March 1), 290–291.
 Review of B. H. Streeter's The Buddha and the Christ.

"Trotsky's Classic." WT, 16, no. 5 (February 1), 116–117.
 Review of Leon Trotsky's The History of the Russian Revolution,
 volumes II and III.

"Why German Socialism Crashed." CCY, 50, no. 14 (April 5), 451–453.

1934

"Barthianism and Political Reaction." CCY, 51, no. 23 (June 6),
 757–759.
 Reprinted in Essays in Applied Christianity.

"A Bourgeois Takes a Stand." N, 139, no. 3615 (October 17), 455–456.
 Review of Ludwig Lewisohn's The Permanent Horizon.

Other Writings by Reinhold Niebuhr

"The Church and Political Action." CCY, 51, no. 31 (August 1), 992-994.

"Churches in Germany." The American Scholar, 3, no. 3 (Summer), 344-351.

"Class War and Class Hatred." WT, 17, no. 1 (January 4), 21.
    Review of Nicholas Berdyaev's Christianity and Class War.

"Comment on An Appeal to the Socialist Party by 47 Members." WT, 17, no. 8 (April 12), 185-186.

"Comment on 'The Christian Cult of Violence.'" Religion in Life, 3, no. 3 (Summer), 439-441.
    Comments on an article by Jerome Davis.

"Ethics and the Family." NYHT (January 21), p. 15.
    Review of G. E. Newsom's The New Morality.

"Ex Cathedra." WT, 17, no. 1 (January 4), 2.
    Notes on Dr. Nicholas Murray Butler's "Christmas Message."
    Niebuhr raises questions about Butler's point that "the man of
    courage must be a man of faith"; the German court verdict con-
    victing Van der Lubbe of arson in the Reichstag fire; and the
    recent report of the Lavenburg Foundation on housing, concluding
    that "Housing for the poor is impossible on the basis of private
    enterprise, even when it is financed by the government."
    [In its last year of publication, 1934, The World Tomorrow pub-
    lished a column called "Ex Cathedra." The last two columns of the
    year were identified as Reinhold Niebuhr's. All the earlier ones
    were signed "Pronuncio." From internal evidence it would seem
    certain that Dr. Niebuhr wrote all of the pieces. The content,
    style and format are similar to his later "Brief Comments" and
    "Editorial Notes" in Christianity and Crisis and Christianity and
    Society. A paragraph in the May 10th issue ties Niebuhr to this
    series of columns--a reference to his 1926-1927 articles "debunk-
    ing" Henry Ford: "I see that Henry Ford is not yet completely
    debunked. One preacher writes: 'The service motive can be pre-
    dominant in capitalism, as exemplified by Henry Ford.' I thought
    I had debunked Mr. Ford so that every preacher in America under-
    stood. Wearily I must take up my pen once more." The series and
    a summary of the contents follows.]

"Ex Cathedra." WT, 17, no. 2 (January 18), 26.
    A note on the controversy in the Fellowship of Reconciliation
    about "just how much violence will be necessary and permissible
    in the day of crisis." The question is academic because there
    is no organized radical movement present that may have to face
    it; the old system has not yet broken down sufficiently to permit
    questions of alternative systems. Roosevelt's "measures" will
    prolong the days of the old system. It is important to build a

1934

radical political force, and the discussion carried forward about the nature of human society and collective behavior, whether transition from capitalism to socialism, can be made within parliamentary democratic tradition, political strategy and social conflict.

"Ex Cathedra." WT, 17, no. 4 (February 15), 74.
    Notes on the "signs of hope" "amidst the general gloom of a sad world." The signs called to the writer's attention seem to be a "fair symbol of the political confusion in which our nation lives."

"Ex Cathedra." WT, 17, no. 5 (March 1), 98.
    Notes about the resistance of Socialists in Vienna to Nazi disarmament of the workers. The gesture was too little and too late but rightly made. The tragedy is increased by the fact that rival factions of workers and peasants fight each other as well as the Nazis; the death of King Albert "has again filled the newspapers with assurances about the 'democracy' of Kings." It will be good to have it all over so that we don't have to "read about democratic kings for a while."

"Ex Cathedra." WT, 17, no. 6 (March 15), 122.
    Notes about the response of sixty college presidents who think "that democratic habits are so deeply ingrained that neither communism nor fascism is a peril to our democratic institutions." Niebuhr is skeptical about this judgment if a real crisis should come. Notes that the recent reports on high salaries of executives of industry is a sign that "The old law still holds. Privilege always flows in the direction of power, whatever the social consequences." Considers the publication by the German Minister of Agriculture, Herr Darre, of a book on the significance of the pig for Nordic and Semitic culture which offers "conclusive proof of the complete incompatibility of Nordic and Semitic culture"; the revelation of monopolistic tendencies of the NRA; Secretary Wallace's statement about the problem facing American agriculture as "the most statesmanlike utterance that has come from the present administration"; and Roosevelt's first year in office. The optimism he has imparted to the nation has given him great prestige, but whatever prosperity there is is due mostly to government spending. "Let us see what happens when Roosevelt is forced to balance his budget."

"Ex Cathedra." WT, 17, no. 7 (March 29), 146.
    Notes on Mussolini's moves in the Danube Basin posing certain dilemmas for Nazi Germany; on Otto Bauer's analysis of the mistakes of the Austrian Socialist Party, showing the same weakness and mismanagement as the German Party and suffering the same fate, in spite of the last minute courage of the workers; on Walter Duranty's report of a Moscow decree penalizing workers falling

1934

short of their quotas; on Col. Lindberg's long suspected reactionary tendencies being fully revealed; on military budgets in
the U. S., Britain and France spelling the death of disarmament.
Notes that "the power of our industrial bourbons is far from
being broken, but the Roosevelt Administration deserves credit"
for some curbs on the mighty empires, and now Andrew Mellon is
to be tried for tax evasion.

"Ex Cathedra." WT, 17, no. 8 (April 12), 170.
    Notes John D. Rockefeller, Jr.'s "optimism," in contrast to
that of "the poor devils" who have lost their jobs; the apparent
slackening of tension in the Orient, although Russian power will
press Japan toward war; "poor old Samuel Insull's vain flight
from the majesty of American law"; opposition of the German Church
to Nazism in contrast to the incomprehensible capitulation of the
universities; the pretension of Chancellor Dollfuss that the new
Austrian Constitution derives from "God Almighty." The Cuban
government is revealed to be more and more reactionary. General
Motors profit for 1933 as compared with 1932 shows the New Deal
places no limits on profits.

"Ex Cathedra." WT, 17, no. 9 (April 26), 194.
    Notes that the Senate's stance is more radical than that of
the House, as seen in a new tax bill that is opposed by the House;
that the taxi union of New York City has dismissed their Communist
leaders, who were responsible for the loss of a recent strike;
that the political events in Cuba point to a coming crisis that
suggests a Communist revolution: "Communism has a better chance
of staging a real revolution than in any other part of the world."
Considers the student anti-war demonstrations and the National
Student League, "which seemed as anxious to commit the students
to a defense of the Soviet Union as to a consistent anti-war
attitude"; the "gorgeous" first diplomatic reception held by the
Russian Ambassador; and the imposition by Congress of a three per-
cent excise tax on Philippine cocoanut oil soon after Congress
granted Philippines independence.

"Ex Cathedra." WT, 17, no. 10 (May 10), 218.
    Notes on questionnaire answered by 20,000 ministers in America,
showing that "However badly the American Church is enmeshed in
bourgeois civilization, and however superficial may be some of
the radical opinion in it, no one can deny that it does harbor
a very healthy Left minority." In answers to international questions, there is more opposition to war and greater increase in
the number of pacifists over the 1931 survey. There is confusion
and a moralistic note in many answers. Answers show that "Henry
Ford is not yet completely debunked."

Other Writings by Reinhold Niebuhr

1934

"Ex Cathedra." WT, 17, no. 11 (May 24), 266.
Notes on the convention of New York Episcopal diocese and
their "resolution" which was little more than "pious wishes and
admonitions"; and on the moral confusion in Dr. Hugh Magill's
declaration that it is not wrong "that a man...defends his
property." States that the advantages of the New Deal are over-
balanced by disadvantages flowing from NRA policies; that continued kidnappings "Perhaps...merely reveal the complete moral
decay of our society"; and notes the furor caused by the European
nations' defaulting on token payments on the war debts.

"Ex Cathedra." WT, 17, no. 12 (June 14), 290.
Notes on the importance, the trials and tribulations of, and
the devotion of workers to, the Highlander Folk School.

"Ex Cathedra." WT, 17, no. 13 (June 28), 314.
Notes on "the insanity of private ownership in our age"; on
Walter Lippmann's judgment of Rexford Tugwell and the "idealism"
of his academic years; on the Socialist Convention and its pronouncements, concluding that "There is now a real possibility of
vitalizing the Socialist Party into a genuine instrument of labor"
and criticizing the Old Guard who are defecting because they fear
"an organization which contemplates illegal and unconstitutional
action"; and on the surfacing inner conflicts among Germany's
National Socialists.

"Ex Cathedra." WT, 17, no. 14 (July 12), 338.
Notes on recent conflict in the Nazi regime in which Hitler
suppressed those who expected a "real revolution"; on the New
York controversy between the Mayor and Police Commissioner over
whether police could "doff their coats on a hot day"; on the
Republican attack on Rexford Tugwell as a "reactionary" because
he believes in "government planning"; on another Roosevelt radio
address making promises of the security of everyone, saying that
he does not, however, indicate the source of funds for his pro-
grams; and on the establishment of a mediating board for the steel
industry. Organized labor fools itself with these boards, while
industry proceeds to organize company unions.

"Ex Cathedra." WT, 17, no. 15 (July 26), 362.
Notes on the pastor who said prayers for John D. Rockefeller,
Sr., on his 95th birthday, and for an old gatekeeper on the
Rockefeller estate: "Thus is the equalitarian ideal implicit in
the Christian ethic corrupted and sentimentalized in the hands of
foolish priests and a church which toadies to the wealthy."
Remarks further on Old Guard Socialists, concluding that "True
Socialism must neither be shocked by 'illegality' nor take a
prematurely negative attitude toward constitutional methods."
Attacks critics of the Socialist Party who harp on "the futility
of these discussions about what the Party might and ought to do

in the day of an ultimate crisis." Such discussions are "realistic" and not "academic."

"The Fellowship of Socialist Christians." WT, 17, no. 12 (June 14), 297-298.

"A Footnote on Religion." N, 139, no. 3612 (September 26), 358-359.
Review of John Dewey's A Common Faith.

"German Socialism Still Lives." N, 139, no. 3604 (August 1), 135-136.
Review of Socialism's New Beginning by "Miles" (a pseudonym).

"Historian, Poet--and Junker." WT, 17, no. 9 (April 26), 211.
Review of Oswald Spengler's The Hour of Decision.

"Militant Pacifism." N, 139, no. 3624 (December 19), 718.
Review of R. B. Gregg's The Power of Non-Violence.

"Optimism, Pessimism and Religious Faith." The Christian Register, 113, no. 22 (May), 379-381.
Also published in The Christian Leader, 37, nos. 22 and 23 (June 2 and 9), 685-687, 716-718. Reprinted as Chapters 14 and 15 of Christianity and Power Politics.

"Paul and the Graeco-Roman World." NYHT (September 2), p. 3.
Review of F. A. Spencer's Beyond Damascus.

"Perfect Revelation of Moral Confusion." WT, 17, no. 10 (May 10), 259.
Review of Roger Babson's Finding a Job.

"The Problem of Communist Religion." WT, 17, no. 15 (July 26), 378-379.

"Prophetic Religions." NYHT (August 12), p. 17.
Review of Nathan Soderblom's The Nature of Revelation.

"Religion as a Source of Radicalism." CCY, 51, no. 15 (April 11), 491-494.

"Shall We Seek World Peace or the Peace of America?" WT, 17, no. 6 (March 15), 132-133.

"Study in Black and White; A Reply." CCY, 51, no. 25 (June 20), 837.
A reply to an article by E. E. Voelkel with the title "Study in Black and White."

"Uncorrupted Optimism." WT, 17, no. 8 (April 12), 189-190.
Review of H. A. Overstreet's We Move in New Directions.

"When Will Christians Stop Fooling Themselves?" CCY, 51, no. 20 (May 16), 658-660.

"Why I Leave the F. O. R." CCY, 51, no. 1 (January 3), 17-19.
Reprinted in Love and Justice.

1935

"Angelo Herndon and Civil Liberties." RR, 1, no. 1 (Autumn), 10.

"Antidote to Optimism." NYHT (December 8), p. 25.
    Review of Barth and Thurneysen's God's Search for Man.

"A Catholic Liberal." N, 141, no. 3660 (August 28), 249.
    Review of R. W. Chambers's Thomas Moore.

"Christian Politics and Communist Religion," in Christianity and the
    Social Revolution. Edited by John Lewis, Karl Polanyi and D. K.
    Kitchin. London: Victor Gollancz, pp. 442–472.
    Reprinted by Scribner's in 1936.

"Christianity and its Relation to the Perennial and the Contemporary
    Man." Religion in Life, 4, no. 4 (Autumn), 551–558.

"Disinterested Intelligence." N, 140, no. 3645 (May 15), 580.
    Review of E. F. Carrit's Morals and Politics.

"Don't Preach Ideals in a Vacuum." The American Friend, NS 23
    (May 30), 208–209.

"Faith and Fact." NYHT (February 17), p. 15.
    Review of George Buttrick's The Christian Fact and Modern
    Doubt.

"George Lansbury: Christian and Socialist." RR, 1, no. 1 (Autumn),
    8–9.

"The German Church." The Saturday Review of Literature, 11, no. 41
    (April 27), 652–653.
    Review of Paul F. Douglas's God Among the Germans.

"Henri Bergson on the Nature of Morality and Religion." The New York
    Times Book Reviews (April 28), p. 3.
    Review of Henri Bergson's The Two Sources of Morality and
    Religion.

"The Historical Jesus." N, 141, no. 3677 (December 25), 747–748.
    Review of Charles Guidenbert's Jesus.

"Is Religion Counter-Revolutionary?" RR, 1, no. 1 (Autumn), 14–20.

"Is Social Conflict Inevitable?" Scribner's, 98, no. 3 (September),
    66–69.

"Marx, Barth and Israel's Prophets." CCY, 52, no. 5 (January 30),
    138–140.
        G. G. Atkins criticized this article in the February 27 issue
    of CCY. Niebuhr replied in "Mr. Niebuhr to Mr. Atkins." CCY,
    52, no. 12 (March 20), 369–370. Reprinted in Essays in Applied
    Christianity.

1936

"Mr. Laski Proceeds." N, 140, no. 3637 (March 20), 338-339.
    Review of H. J. Laski's The State in Theory and Practice.

"On the Ethiopian War." RR, 1, no. 1 (Autumn), 6-8.
    Reprinted in Love and Justice.

"Our Machine Made Culture." Christendom, 1, no. 1 (Autumn), 186-190.

"Our Romantic Radicals." CCY, 52, no. 15 (April 10), 474-476.

"The Pathos of Liberalism." N, 141, no. 3662 (September 11), 303-304.
    Occasioned by the publication of John Dewey's Liberalism and
    Social Action.

"The Philosophy of an Apostle." NYHT (December 29), p. 3.
    Review of Irwin Edman's The Mind of Paul.

"Plain Speaking and Fellowship." RR, 1, no. 1 (Autumn), 5-6.

"Radical Religion." RR, 1, no. 1 (Autumn), 3-5.

"The Revival of Feudalism." Harpers, 170 (March), 483-488.

"The Revolutionary Moment." The American Socialist Quarterly, 4,
    no. 2 (June), 8-13.

"Roosevelt and the Clergy." RR, 1, no. 1 (Autumn), 12-13.

"Salvation Through Education." RR, 1, no. 1 (Autumn), 11.

"Scared and Confused Liberals." N, 140, no. 3639 (April 3), 393-394.
    Review of E. D. Martin's Farewell to Revolution, along with
    R. C. Brooks's Deliver us From Dictators.

"Sects and Churches." CCY, 52, no. 27 (July 3), 885-887.
    Reprinted in Essays in Applied Christianity.

"Vital Modern Religion." NYHT (July 28), p. 15.
    Review of William Temple's Nature, Man and God.

"Who Pays the Piper Calls the Tune." RR, 1, no. 1 (Autumn), 11-12.

"Why a New Quarterly?" RR, 1, no. 1 (Autumn), 3-5.

1936

"An Analysis of Egotism." N, 142, no. 3702 (June 17), 787.
    Review of Phillip Leon's The Ethics of Power. Also reviewed
    in RR, 1, no. 3 (Spring), 40-41.

"Arrogance in the Name of Christ." CCY, 53, no. 36 (September 2),
    1157-1158.
    Reprinted in Essays in Applied Christianity.

"The Blindness of Liberalism." RR, 1, no. 4 (Autumn), 4-5.

1936

"Britain Bewildered." CCY, 53, no. 33 (August 12), 1081-1082.

"The British Labor Party." RR, 2, no. 1 (Winter), 7-8.

"The Catholic Worker." RR, 1, no. 3 (Spring), 3.
    Note applauding liberal Catholic journal.

"Catholicism and Communism." RR, 2, no. 1 (Winter), 4-6.

"Christian Politics and Communist Religion," in Christianity and the
    Social Revolution. Edited by John Lewis. New York: Scribner's,
    pp. 442-472.

"Christian Radicalism." RR, 2, no. 1 (Winter), 8-9.

"Christianity and Communism." The Spectator, 157, no. 5654
    (November 6), 802-803.

"Christianity and Society." NYHT (June 14), p. 18.
    Review of Christianity and the Social Revolution, edited by
    John Lewis, together with MacMurray's Creative Society and
    Matthew Spinka's Christianity Confronts Communism.

"The Church and the State," RR, 1, no. 3 (Spring), 7-8.
    About the German church and Hitler's government.

"The Church Speaks." RR, 1, no. 2 (Winter), 13.

"The Churches and the Social Security Act." RR, 1, no. 2 (Winter),
    12-13.

["Communism in Russia." Review of Sidney and Beatrice Webb's
    Soviet Communism, A New Civilization.] RR, 1, no. 3 (Spring),
    37-38.

"The Conflict in the Socialist Party." RR, 1, no. 2 (Winter), 9-10.

"Doom and Dawn." (with Sherwood Eddy.) New York: Kirby Page.

"Editor's Answer to a Letter." RR, 1, no. 3 (Spring), 45-46.
    An answer to Ross W. Anderson, who suggested the founding of
    a "Kingdom Fellowship" to bring religion to bear on contemporary
    problems.

"English and German Mentality--A Study in National Traits."
    Christendom, 1, no. 3 (Spring), 465-476.

"The English Church--An American View." The Spectator, 157, no. 5645
    (September 4), 373-374.

"The Failure of Sanctions." RR, 1, no. 4 (Autumn), 5-6.

"Fascism, Communism, Christianity." RR, 1, no. 2 (Winter), 7-8.

"The Freedom of Education." RR, 1, no. 3 (Spring), 3-4.

"From the Editorial Mailbag." RR, 1, no. 2 (Winter), 13-14.
    Reference to letters received from social-minded pastors who
    find rough going in their communities.

"George Lansbury." RR, 1, no. 3 (Spring), 10.

"The German Church Girds for Battle." CCY, 53, no. 35 (August 26),
    1129-1130.

"God and Piece Work." RR, 1, no. 3 (Spring), 5-6.
    About the Russian "League of Fighting Godless."

"Hilaire Belloc Looks at Zion." NYHT (April 5), p. 3.
    Review of Hilaire Belloc's The Battleground.

"Hitler and Buchman." CCY, 53, no. 41 (October 7), 1315-1316.
    Also published in Kirchliche Zeitschrift, 60: 695-697.
    Reprinted as Chapter XII of Christianity and Power Politics.

"The Idea of Progress and Socialism." RR, 1, no. 3 (Spring), 27-29.

"The International Situation." RR, 1, no. 3 (Spring), 8-9.

["The Interpretation of History." Review of Paul Tillich's The
    Interpretation of History.] RR, 2, no. 1 (Winter), 41-42.

"The Jerome Davis Case." RR, 2, no. 1 (Winter), 6-7.

["The Last Puritan." Review of George Santayana's The Last Puritan.]
    RR, 1, no. 3 (Spring), 41.

["The Meaning of History." Review of Nicholas Berdyaev's The Meaning
    of History.] RR, 2, no. 1 (Winter), 42-43.

"Modern Utopians." Scribner's, 100, no. 3 (September), 142-145.
    Reprinted as Chapter XI of Christianity and Power Politics.

"Moralistic Preaching." CCY, 53, no. 29 (July 15), 985-987.
    Also published in Kirchliche Zeitschrift, 60: 569-573.

"Morals and Mechanism." RR, 1, no. 2 (Winter), 11-12.

"Must Radicals be Atheists?" Common Sense, 5, no. 7 (July), 11-13.

"The National Election." RR, 2, no. 1 (Winter), 3-4.

"The National Manufacturers Association." RR, 1, no. 2 (Winter),
    10-11.

"Nationalism and Religion." RR, 1, no. 3 (Spring), 6.

"On the Arrogance of the Minor Prophets." NYHT (October 25), p. 7.
    On Stefan Zweig's The Right to Heresy.

"Our Labor Church Fund." RR, 2, no. 1 (Winter), 9.

"Our World," in Students and the Christian World. Edited by Jesse R.
    Wilson. New York: Student Volunteer Movement for Foreign
    Missions, pp. 7-14.

1936

"Pacifism Against the Wall." The American Scholar, 5 no. 2 (Spring),
133-141.
Reprinted in Love and Justice.

"Pacifism and Sanctions." RR, 1, no. 2 (Winter), 27-30.
A Symposium by J. N. Sayre and Reinhold Niebuhr.

"The Political Campaign." RR, 1, no. 3 (Autumn), 4-5.

"The Political Confusions of Dr. Kagawa." RR, 1, no. 2 (Winter), 6-7.

"The Political Opinion of the 'Enlightened.'" RR, 2, no. 1 (Winter),
4.

"The Pope." RR, 1, no. 4 (Autumn), 3-4.

"Prosperity." RR, 1, no. 2 (Winter), 12.

"The Racial Will." N, 143, no. 1 (July 4), 26-27.
A letter to the Editor.

"The Radical Minister and His Church." RR, 2, no. 1 (Winter), 25-27.

"Radicalism in British Christianity." RR, 1, no. 4 (Autumn), 7-9.

"Secret of Creative Action." NYHT (October 25), p. 22.
Review of Etienne Gilson's The Spirit of Medieval Philosophy,
together with Karl Barth's Credo.

"The Secular and the Religious." CCY, 53, no. 45 (November 4),
1452-1454.

["Sharecroppers' Revolt." Review of Howard Kester, Revolt of the
Sharecroppers (a pamphlet).] RR, 1, no. 3 (Spring), 40.

"Sidelights on England." RR, 1, no. 4 (Autumn), 10, 18.

"The Spanish Counter-Revolution." RR, 1, no. 4 (Autumn), 9.

"Stupidity or Dishonesty." RR, 1, no. 3 (Spring), 6-7.
Comment on various explanations for the causes of the
depression.

"Sunday Morning Debate." CCY, 53, no. 17 (April 22), 595-597.
Reprinted in Essays in Applied Christianity.

"The Supreme Court Decision." RR, 1, no. 2 (Winter), 8-9.
The Court declared AAA unconstitutional.

"Taxation and Equality." RR, 1, no. 3 (Spring), 4-5.

"Thomism and Mysticism." The Saturday Review of Literature, 14,
no. 15 (August 8), 16.
Review of Jacques Maritain's Freedom in the Modern World,
together with Nicholas Berdyaev's Freedom and the Spirit.

"The Ultimate Issues." NYHT (September 27), p. 17.
Review of Emil Brunner's The Doctrine of the Word of God,
together with Karl Heim's God Transcendent.

"The United Christian Council for Democracy." RR, 2, no. 1 (Winter), 9-10.

"The United Front." RR, 1, no. 2 (Winter), 3-6.

"Which Way, Great Britain?--Will it be France or Germany?" Current History, 45, no. 2 (November), 35-39.

1937

"The Administration and the Depression." RR, 3, no. 1 (Winter), 7-8.

"Against Earl Browder." NR, 91, no. 1175 (June 9), 132.
   A letter to the Editor.

"Aldous Huxley's Apologia." RR, 3, no. 1 (Winter), 35-36.
   Review of Aldous Huxley's Ends and Means. Also in Christendom, 3, no. 2 (Spring, 1938), 286-289.

"America and the War in China." CCY, 54, no. 39 (September 29), 1195-1196.

["American Jungle." Review of Waldo Frank's In An American Jungle.]
   RR, 2, no. 3 (Summer), 42-44.

"Bishop McConnell." RR, 2, no. 3 (Summer), 5.

"The Boycott." RR, 3, no. 1 (Winter), 4.
   Boycott of Japanese goods by The United Christian Council for Democracy.

"Brief Comments." RR, 2, no. 2 (Spring), 5-7.
   Comments on Stalinism; the British Monarchy; opposition to child labor amendment; G.M. and the sit-down strike; LaFollette Committee's findings; Hitler and the church; European nonintervention committee; desirability of neutrality legislation.

"Brief Comments." RR, 2, no. 3 (Summer), 6-8.
   Notes on Catholic anti-communist campaign; sit-down strike; Henry Ford's views on labor organization and international bankers; French government troubles; English Monarchy; growth of British military strength; Link's Return to Religion; proposed incorporation of labor unions.

"Brief Comments." RR, 3, no. 1 (Winter), 8-9.
   Notes on a New York sermon; Hitler's Germany; LaGuardia's victory and labor support; an attack on the war problem through prayer; Southern Congressmen and the anti-lynching bill; British paper on Japan's ability to wage war being tied to oil-producing nations; Delta Cooperative Farm and land purchase.

"The Catholic Heresy." CCY, 54, no. 49 (December 8), 1524-1525.
   Reprinted in Essays in Applied Christianity.

1937

"Catholicism and Anarchism in Spain." RR, 2, no. 2 (Spring), 25–28.
    Reprinted in Love and Justice.

"Christian Perfectionism." RR, 2, no. 3 (Summer), 1–2.

"Christianity Without the Cross." RR, 2, no. 3 (Summer), 8–9.
    A note on a sermon by Dr. Ralph Sockman.

"The Contribution of Paul Tillich." Religion in Life, 6, no. 4
    (Autumn), 574–581.

"Defense of the Spanish Hierarchy." RR, 2, no. 4 (Autumn), 7–8.

"Disillusionment." RR, 3, no. 1 (Winter), 44–45.
    Review of Fred E. Beal's Proletarian Journey, along with
    Eugene Lyons's Assignment in Utopia and Victor Serge's Russia
    Twenty Years After.

"Do the State and the Nation Belong to God or the Devil?" (Burge
    Memorial Lecture). London: S. C. M. Press.
    Reprinted in Faith and Politics.

"Editor's Answer." RR, 2, no. 2 (Spring), 47–48.
    Answer to a letter by Maurice B. Reckitt, leader of the
    British group publishing Christendom. Niebuhr repeats an earlier
    statement that he sees similarity in the publication to the Amer-
    ican Social Gospel.

"The Eternal and History." RR, 2, no. 3 (Summer), 4–5.

"European Impressions." RR, 2, no. 4 (Autumn), 31–33.

"Facts Without Insight." RR, 3, no. 1 (Winter), 42–43.
    Review of Ferdinand Lundberg's America's Sixty Families.

"Faith in Man." RR, 3, no. 1 (Winter), 4–5.

"The International Situation." RR, 3, no. 1 (Winter), 2–3.

"Japan and the Christian Conscience." CCY, 54, no. 45 (November 10),
    1390–1391.

"Law and Peace." RR, 3, no. 1 (Winter), 1.

["The Life of Jesus." Review of Conrad Noel's The Life of Jesus,
    along with Toward a Christian Revolution, edited by R. B. Y.
    Scott and Gregory Vlastos.] RR, 2, no. 2 (Spring), 42–44.

"Meditations From Mississippi." CCY, 54, no. 6 (February 10),
    183–184.

"The Moscow Trials." RR, 2, no. 2 (Spring), 1–2.

"The National Preaching Mission." RR, 2, no. 2 (Spring), 2–3.

"The New Horrors of War." RR, 2, no. 4 (Autumn), 4.

"A New Party?" RR, 2, no. 4 (Autumn), 6–7.

["On Journey." Review of Vida Scudder's On Journey.] RR, 2, no. 3
    (Summer), 43-44.

"Our Labor Church Fund." RR, 2, no. 2 (Spring), 4-5.

"The Oxford Conference on Church and State." RR, 2, no. 4 (Autumn),
    1-2.
        Reprinted in Essays in Applied Christianity.

"Paraphrase of Gospel." The Saturday Review of Literature, 15,
    no. 24 (April 10), 17.
        Review of F. Mauriac's Life of Jesus.

"Pawns for Fascism--Our Lower Middle Class." The American Scholar,
    6, no. 2 (Spring), 145-152.

"Pedestrian Christianity." RR, 2, no. 3 (Summer), 9.
        Note on a sermon by Dean Milo Gates.

"Pius XI and His Successor." N, 144, no. 5 (January 30), 120-122.

"The Pope and Politics." N, 145, no. 24 (December 11), 662-663.
        Review of Willing Teeling's Pope Pius XI and World Affairs.

"The Price of Courage." RR, 2, no. 2 (Spring), 4.

"Product of the Classroom." NYHT (April 11), p. 17.
        Review of Vergilius Ferm's First Chapters in Religious
    Philosophy.

"Quaker Strategy." RR, 2, no. 4 (Autumn), 8.

"The Relief Situation." RR, 2, no. 3 (Summer), 5-6.

"Religion and Marxism." Modern Monthly, 8, no. 12 (February), 712-714.

"Roosevelt and the Sharecroppers." RR, 2, no. 2 (Spring), 3-4.

"The Russian Mystery." RR, 2, no. 4 (Autumn), 4-6.

["The Russian Revolution Betrayed." Review of Leon Trotsky's The
    Russian Revolution Betrayed.] RR, 2, no. 3 (Summer), 39-40.

"Sanctification." RR, 2, no. 3 (Summer), 9.
        Note on a sermon by Sam Shoemaker.

"Schleiermacher to Barth." NYHT (December 12), p. 24.
        Review of H. R. Mackintosh's Types of Modern Theology.

"Social Justice," in Christianity and Communism. Edited by Henry W.
    Harris. Oxford: Basil Blackwell, pp. 62-69.

"The Socialist Party and the Labor Movement." RR, 3, no. 1
    (Winter), 3.

"Socialists and Communists." RR, 2, no. 3 (Summer), 3.

1937

"The Sources of Religion." NYHT (July 11), p. 6.
    Review of E. R. Goodenough's Religious Tradition and Myth.

"Spanish Problems." RR, 2, no. 4 (Autumn), 6.

"The Supreme Court." RR, 2, no. 2 (Spring), 2.

"The Supreme Court Issue." RR, 2, no. 3 (Summer), 2-3.

"Temporal and Spiritual." NYHT (May 23), p. 17.
    Review of Adolph Keller's Church and State on the European
    Continent, along with Eckhardt's The Papacy and World Affairs.

"A Theology of Revelation." NYHT (May 16), p. 20.
    Review of Emil Brunner's The Divine Imperative, along with
    The Philosophy of Religion and God and Man.

"Thoughts on Immortality." NYHT (June 20), p. 8.
    Review of W. E. Hocking's Thoughts on Life and Death.

"The Truth in Myths," in The Nature of Religious Experience. Essays
    in Honor of D. C. Macintosh. New York: Harper & Brothers,
    pp. 117-135.
        Reprinted several times: in Philosophic Problems, edited by
    Mandelbaum, Gramlich and Anderson. New York: The Macmillan Co.,
    1957. Also in Evolution and Religion, edited by Gail Kennedy.
    Boston: D. C. Heath. Also reprinted in Faith and Politics.
    Dr. Macintosh wrote a series of articles in The Review of Reli-
    gion replying to criticims of his thought in this book dedicated
    to him. He discusses Dr. Niebuhr's chapter in an article en-
    titled "Is Theology Reducible to Mythology?" The Review of
    Religion, 4, no. 2 (January), 140-158.

"Unhappy Spain." RR, 2, no. 3 (Summer), 3-4.

"United Christian Council for Democracy." RR, 2, no. 2 (Spring),
    47-48.
        A discussion of the Council's rejection of the Catholic appeal
    for a united front against Communism and also a declaration of
    belief in the right of labor to strike.

"Viewing Human Nature." NYHT (October 17), p. 18.
    Review of Nicholas Berdyaev's The Destiny of Man.

"The War in China." RR, 2, no. 4 (Autumn), 2.

"Worship and the Social Conscience." RR, 3, no. 1 (Winter), 5-7.

"Youth in Conference." RR, 2, no. 4 (Autumn), 3-4.
    Youth meetings in Milwaukee and at Oxford.

1938

"After Munich." RR, 4, no. 1 (Winter), 1-2.

"Aldous Huxley's Apologia." Christendom, 3, no. 2 (Spring), 286-289.
Review of Aldous Huxley's Ends and Means.

"Anatomy of Power." N, 147, no. 14 (October 1), 326-327.
Review of Bertrand Russell's Power, A New Social Analysis.
Also in RR, 3, no. 4 (Fall), 37-38.

"Anti-Semitism." RR, 3, no. 3 (Summer), 5.

"An Appeal." RR, 4, no. 1 (Winter), 33.

"The Bible's Own Story." NYHT (February 27), p. 4.
Review of E. S. Bates's A Biography of the Bible.

"Brief Comments." RR, 3, no. 4 (Fall), 9-10.
Notes on Dombroski report of anti-labor support for travelling
evangelists; Roger Babson; Mexican oil expropriation; a sermon by
F. K. Shepherd; Hitler's "Cultural Prize."

"Brief Comments." RR, 4, no. 1 (Winter), 7-9.
Notes on religious services in Russia; Roosevelt's foreign
policy; loss of democracy in Czechoslovakia and France; Russia
and the "perishing away of the state"; split in labor ranks;
conflict between farmers and workers.

"Brief Notes." RR, 3, no. 2 (Spring), 6-8.
Notes on Glenn Frank's political pronouncements; the Van
Zeeland plan for peace; Roosevelt's defense budget; boycott
against Japan; labor-saving devices in steel industry and the
problem of jobs; Mayor Hague of Jersey City buying off his enemies; Roosevelt and high finance ("If that man could only make up
his mind to cross the Rubicon! A better metaphor is that he is
like Lot's wife. Let him beware, lest he turn into a pillar of
salt"); sentimental talk about church unity from the Oxford and
Edinburgh conferences.

"Brief Notes." RR, 3, no. 3 (Summer), 12-13.
Notes on Mr. Schwab of Bethlehem Steel; Henry Ford on unemployment; E. T. Stotesbury, a millionaire; Spain and the neutrality
act; Hitler and "elections"; Catholic surrender to Hitler in
Austria.

"Buchmanism and World Peace." RR, 3, no. 4 (Fall), 7-8.

"Chastisement for Missions." NYHT (June 26), p. 13.
Review of Hendrick Kraemer's The Christian Message in a Non-
Christian World.

"Christian Faith and the Common Life," in Christian Faith and the
Common Life. New York: Willett, Clark & Co., pp. 69-97.

"Christian Socialism." RR, 3, no. 4 (Fall), 3-4.

"Christian Testimony in Japan." RR, 3, no. 2 (Spring), 3-4.

1938

"Church and Governments." NYHT (October 16), p. 22.
     Review of Albert Hyma's Christianity and Politics.

"The Creed of Modern Christian Socialists." RR, 3, no. 2 (Spring),
     13-18.

"Culture Religions." RR, 3, no. 3 (Summer), 9-10.

["The Defense of Democracy." Review of F. E. Jones's The Defense of
     Democracy.] RR, 3, no. 4 (Fall), 41.

"The Delta Cooperative Farm." RR, 4, no. 1 (Winter), 7.

"Denomination." NYHT (October 30), p. 18.
     Review of Clarence P. Shedd's The Church Follows the Students.

"Descent into War." N, 146, no. 17 (April 23), 479-480.
     Review of C. C. Tansill's America Goes to War.

"Distribution of National Income." RR, 3, no. 4 (Fall), 6.

"The Domestic Situation." RR, 3, no. 3 (Summer), 3-4.

"Early Christianity." The Saturday Review of Literature, 18, no. 8
     (June 18), 19.
     Review of Johannes Weiss's The History of Primitive Christian-
     ity, along with K. Latourette's The First Five Centuries and The
     Thousand Years of Uncertainty.

"Europe and America." RR, 4, no. 1 (Winter), 6-7.

"The Future of Europe." RR, 3, no. 3 (Summer), 4-5.

"Greek Tragedy and Modern Politics." N, 146, no. 1 (January 1),
     740-744.
     Reprinted as Chapter 7 of Christianity and Power Politics.

"Heretics." RR, 3, no. 3 (Summer), 12.

["Heroes of Thought." Review of J. M. Murry's Heroes of Thought.]
     RR, 4, no. 1 (Winter), 39-41.

"Hope of Church Union." NYHT (October 30), p. 25.
     Review of Kenneth MacKenzie's Union of Christendom.

"If Winter Comes, Can Spring be far Behind?" RR, 4, no. 1 (Winter),
     3.
     Reference to possible signs of Nazi collapse.

"The Inept Middle Class." RR, 3, no. 4 (Fall), 6.

"The International Situation." RR, 3, no. 3 (Summer), 1-2.

"The International Situation." RR, 3, no. 4 (Fall), 1-3.

"Jerome Frank's Way Out." N, 147, no. 2 (July 9), 45-46.
     Review of Jerome Frank's Save America First.

"Karl Barth and Democracy." RR, 4, no. 1 (Winter), 4–5.
      Reprinted in Essays in Applied Christianity.

"LaFollette's Third Party." RR, 3, no. 3 (Summer), 6–7.

"The London Times and the Crisis." RR, 4, no. 1 (Winter), 29–32.

"Nicholas Murray Butler." RR, 3, no. 4 (Fall), 7.

"On the International Situation." RR, 3, no. 2 (Spring), 4–5.

["The Origin of Russian Communism." Review of Nicholas Berdyaev's
      The Origin of Russian Communism.] RR, 3, no. 2 (Spring), 46–47.

"Our Mad World." RR, 3, no. 2 (Spring), 2–3.

"Our Name." RR, 3, no. 2 (Spring), 6.
      Reference to desirability of changing name of journal from
      Radical Religion possibly to "Prophetic Religion." [Name changed
      in 1940 to Religion and Society.]

["Out of Revolution." Review of Eugen Rosenstock-Huessy's Out of
      Revolution, Autobiography of Western Man.] RR, 4, no. 1 (Winter),
      37.

"The Peril of Western Democracies." RR, 4, no. 1 (Winter), 2–3.

"The Plight of the Jews." RR, 3, no. 4 (Fall), 8–9.

"The Professional Union." RR, 3, no. 3 (Summer), 6.

"The Protestant Opposition Movement in Germany, 1934–1937." New
      York: Friends of Europe.

["Rebel." Review of Angelica Balabanoff's My Life as a Rebel.]
      RR, 3, no. 4 (Fall), 38–39.

"The Recent Election." RR, 4, no. 1 (Winter), 5–6.

"The Red Army Purge." RR, 3, no. 3 (Summer), 11.

"Religion and Patent Medicine." RR, 3, no. 2 (Spring), 5–6.

"The Return to Primitive Religion." Christendom, 3, no. 1 (Winter),
      1–8.
      Nazi aberrations and Communism as a religion.

"The Revised Communist Faith." N, 146, no. 9 (February 26), 247–249.
      Review of Earl Browder's The People's Front. Also reviewed in
      RR, 3, no. 2 (Spring), 47.

["Revolutionary Religion." Review of Roger Lloyd's Revolutionary
      Religion.] RR, 3, no. 3 (Summer), 39–40.

"The Roosevelt Purge." RR, 3, no. 4 (Fall), 5.

"Roosevelt's Merry-Go-Round." RR, 3, no. 2 (Spring), 4.

"Russia and Japan." RR, 3, no. 3 (Summer), 2–3.

1938

"Russia and Karl Marx." N, 146, no. 19 (May 7), 530-531.

"The Socialist Convention." RR, 3, no. 3 (Summer), 8-9.

"The Socialist Decision and Christian Conscience." RR, 3, no. 2 (Spring), 1-2.

"The Socialist Party." RR, 4, no. 1 (Winter), 6.

"Spain and the Catholic Church." RR, 4, no. 1 (Winter), 3-4.

"Spiritual Pilgrimage." The Saturday Review of Literature, 17, no. 11 (January 8), 19.
    On P. E. More's Pages From an Oxford Diary.

"Stuffed Shirts." RR, 3, no. 3 (Summer), 10-11.

"Taxation." RR, 3, no. 3 (Summer), 5-6.

["This Peace." Review of Thomas Mann's This Peace.] RR, 4, no. 1 (Winter), 41.

"Tract for the Times." N, 146, no. 21 (May 21), 594-595.
    Review of Hubert Herring's And So to War.

"Trials on Trial." N, 147, no. 5 (July 30), 112-113.
    Report of the Commission of Inquiry into the Charges Against Leon Trotsky in the Moscow Trials.

"True Martyr." NYHT (February 20), p. 21.
    Review of J. F. Mozley's William Tyndale.

["The War Against the West." Review of Aurel Kolnai's The War Against the West.] RR, 4, no. 1 (Winter), 37-39.

"Will of God and the Van Zeeland Report." CCY, 55, no. 50 (December 14), 1549-1550.
    Reprinted in Love and Justice.

1939

"The Ambiguity of Human Decisions." RR, 4, no. 3 (Summer), 3-4.

"Barcelona." RR, 4, no. 2 (Spring), 9-10.

"Bishop Paddock." RR, 4, no. 4 (Fall), 5-6.

"Bourgeois and Christian." RR, 4, no. 2 (Spring), 4.

"Boycott," RR, 4, no. 2 (Spring), 12-13.
    Boycott of German ships and goods.

"The British Conscience." N, 149, no. 9 (August 26), 219-221.

"Catholic Individualism." RR, 4, no. 2 (Spring), 12.

"Christian Fascism." RR, 4, no. 4 (Fall), 5.

Other Writings by Reinhold Niebuhr

"A Christian Peace Policy." RR, 4, no. 2 (Spring), 10–12.

"The Clue to History." Modern Churchman, 29, no. 2 (May), 75–81.
　　Review of John MacMurray's Clue to History.

"The Coming Presidential Election." RR, 4, no. 4 (Fall), 3–4.

"Communists and the United Front." RR, 4, no. 3 (Summer), 8–9.

"Crisis in Washington." RR, 4, no. 2 (Spring), 9.

"A Cry From Czechoslovakia." RR, 4, no. 2 (Spring), 10.

["The Dragon Wakes." Review of E. A. Mowrer's The Dragon Wakes.]
　　RR, 4, no. 2 (Spring), 47–48.

"The Ethics of Taxation." RR, 4, no. 3 (Summer), 9–10.

"Faith and the Intellect." NYHT (December 3), p. 26.

"Father Grosser." RR, 4, no. 4 (Fall), 4–5.

["Fighting Years." Review of O. G. Villard's Fighting Years.] RR,
　　4, no. 3 (Summer), 33–34.

"Germans and Nazis." Spectator, 163, no. 5804 (September 22),
　　401–402.

"The Good People of Britain." RR, 4, no. 3 (Summer), 6–8.

"A History of Missions." NYHT (December 10), p. 27.
　　Review of K. S. Latourette's Three Centuries of Advance, 1500–
　　1800, A History of the Expansion of Christianity.

"The Hitler-Stalin Pact." RR, 4, no. 4 (Fall), 1–3.
　　Reprinted in Love and Justice.

"Ideology and Pretense." N, 149, no. 24 (December 9), 645–646.
　　Reprinted as Chapter 8 of Christianity and Power Politics.

"The Internal Condition in Germany." RR, 4, no. 3 (Summer), 2–3.

"The International Situation." RR, 4, no. 3 (Summer), 1–2.

"Jews in China." RR, 4, no. 2 (Spring), 13.

["Jobs For All." Review of Mordecai Ezekiel's Jobs For All.] RR,
　　4, no. 2 (Spring), 42–44.

"Karl Barth on Politics." RR, 4, no. 2 (Spring), 3–5.
　　Reprinted in Essays in Applied Christianity.

"Leaves From the Notebook of a War-Bound American." CCY, 56, no. 43
　　(October 25), 1298–1299; no. 46 (November 15), 1405–1406; no. 49
　　(December 6), 1502–1503; no. 52 (December 27), 1607–1608.

["The Marxist Philosophy and the Sciences." Review of J. B. S.
　　Haldane's The Marxist Philosophy and the Sciences.] RR, 4,
　　no. 3 (Summer), 32–33.

1939

["Men Must Act." Review of Lewis Mumford's Men Must Act.] RR, 4, no. 2 (Spring), 44-45.

"Mr. Niebuhr's Rebuttal." N, 148, no. 7 (February 11), 187.
A letter discussing Bertrand Russell's article, "Must Democracy Use Force?," in the same issue.

"Moral Rearmament." RR, 4, no. 2 (Spring), 13-14.

"Moral Rearmament." RR, 4, no. 4 (Fall), 9-11.

"New Deal Medicine." RR, 4, no. 2 (Spring), 1-3.

"A New Sharecropper Crisis." RR, 4, no. 2 (Spring), 8-9.

"Notes on the World Crisis." RR, 4, no. 4 (Fall), 6-8.

"Peace and the Liberal Illusion." N, 148, no. 5 (January 28), 117-119.
Second in a series called "Must Democracy Use Force?" Reprinted as Chapter 6 of Christianity and Power Politics.

"Prisoners of Destiny." RR, 4, no. 3 (Summer), 4-6.
Man neither master nor slave of historic destiny.

["Reaching for the Stars." Review of Nora Waln's Reaching for the Stars.] RR, 4, no. 3 (Summer), 32.

"Returning to Orthodoxy." The British Weekly, 106, no. 2757 (September 14), 391.
Review of D. R. Davies's On To Orthodoxy.

["The Revolution of Nihilism." Review of Herman Rauschning's The Revolution of Nihilism.] RR, 4, no. 4 (Fall), 41-42.

"Some Reflections on the Retreat of Democracy." RR, 4, no. 2 (Spring), 5-8.

"Synthetic Barbarism." New Statesman and Nation, 18, no. 446 (September 9), 368-369.
Reprinted as Chapter 9 of Christianity and Power Politics.

"Ten Years That Shook My World." CCY, 56, no. 17 (April 26), 542-546.
Fourteenth in a series on "How My Mind Has Changed in This Decade." An editorial summary of Niebuhr's position in the October 25 issue, p. 1302.

"Transcending Conflict." NYHT (April 9), p. 15.
Also in RR, 4, no. 2 (Spring), 45.

["True Humanism." Review of Jacques Maritain's True Humanism.] RR, 4, no. 2 (Spring), 45.

"Tyranny and War." RR, 4, no. 4 (Fall), 8-9.

1940

"American Creeds." N, 150, no. 15 (April 13), 484.
   Review of E. S. Bates's American Faith. Also in The Union
   Review, 1, no. 3 (May), 30.

"American Foreign Policy." N, 150, no. 21 (May 25), 656-658.
   Review of Charles Beard's A Foreign Policy for America, along
   with R. L. Buell's Isolated America. Also reviewed in RR, 5,
   no. 3 (Summer), 35-36.

"American Neutrality." CS, 5, no. 3 (Summer), 5-7.

"Answering the Humanist." NYHT (February 4), p. 12.
   Review of A. H. Dakin's Man the Measure.

["Beyond Tears." Review of Irmgard Litten's Beyond Tears.] CS, 5,
   no. 4 (Fall), 45.

"Catholic Defense of Christianity." RR, 5, no. 1 (Winter), 6-7.

"Catholicism and Fascism." CS, 5, no. 4 (Fall), 9-10.
   Delivered as an address to the Oxford Conference on Church,
   Community and State. Published in The Student World, organ of
   the World Student Christian Federation. Reprinted as Chapter 16
   of Christianity and Power Politics.

"Christian Faith and Natural Law." Theology, 40, no. 236 (February),
   86-94.
   Reprinted in Love and Justice.

"Christian Moralism in America." CS, 5, no. 2 (Spring), 1.
   First issue under the title Christianity and Society. Previous
   title was Radical Religion.

"Christianity and the World Crisis." CS, 5, no. 4 (Fall), 2-5.

["The Creed of Christ." Review of Gerald Heard's The Creed of Christ.]
   RR, 6, no. 1 (Winter), 46-47 (Printed erroneously as vol. 5,
   no. 5).

"Defending Democracy." CS, 5, no. 4 (Fall), 10-11.

["Democracy and Social Change." Review of Harry F. Ward's Democracy
   and Social Change.] The Union Review, 2, no. 1 (November), 36.

"The Domestic Political Situation." CS, 5, no. 2 (Spring), 7-8.

"Editorial Notes." CS, 5, no. 2 (Spring), 9-11.
   Notes on Finland; The Christian Century; sickness of Western
   civilization; prayer for those in need; conscientious objectors.

"Editorial Notes." CS, 5, no. 3 (Summer), 9-11.
   Notes on Wendell Willkie; Norway and the big lie in Germany; a
   student peace pronouncement.

1940

"Editorial Notes." CS, 6, no. 1 (Winter), 8-10.
　　Notes on Germans and Nazis; labor issues; Catholicism and
　　Fascism.

"An End to Illusions." N, 150, no. 26 (June 29), 778-779.
　　Reprinted as Chapter 13 of Christianity and Power Politics.

"Europe's Catastrophe and the Christian Faith." London: Nisbet and
　　Company, 46 pp.

"Feeding the Oppressed Nations." CS, 6, no. 1 (Winter), 7-8.

"Fellow Travellers." RR, 5, no. 1 (Winter), 7-8.

"Force and Reason in Politics." N, 150, no. 6 (February 10),
　　216-217.
　　Review of C. E. Merriam's Prologue to Politics.

"Foreword," to Forgiveness: Decisive Issue in Protestant Thought.
　　By Paul H. Lehmann. New York: Harper and Brothers, pp. ix-x.

["Freedom's Battle." Review of J. A. Del Vayo's Freedom's Battle.]
　　RR, 5, no. 3 (Summer), 36-37.

["From England to America." Review of H. N. Brailsford's From England
　　to America.] RR, 5, no. 4 (Fall), 40.

"George Lansbury." CS, 5, no. 3 (Summer), 2-3.

"Heywood Broun." RR, 5, no. 1 (Winter), 8-9.

["I Have Seen God Do It." Review of Sherwood Eddy's I Have Seen God
　　Do It.] RR, 5, no. 3 (Summer), 35.

"Idealists as Cynics." N, 150, no. 3 (January 20), 72-74.
　　Reprinted as Chapter 5 in Christianity and Power Politics.

["Idle Money, Idle Men." Review of Stuart Chase's Idle Money, Idle
　　Men.] RR, 5, no. 4 (Fall), 44.

"If America is Drawn into the War, Can You, as a Christian, Partici-
　　pate in it or Support it?" CCY, 57, no. 51 (December 18),
　　1578-1580.
　　Reprinted in Love and Justice.

"Individualism and Civilization." CS, 5, no. 4 (Fall), 7-9.

"International Relations." NYHT (April 14), p. 22.
　　Review of L. J. Shafer's The Christian Alternative to World
　　Chaos.

"The International Situation." CS, 5, no. 4 (Fall), 1-2.

"The International Situation." RR, 5, no. 1 (Winter), 1-4.

"The Issue of a Just Peace." CS, 5, no. 2 (Spring), 1-5.

"J. B. Matthews." RR, 5, no. 1 (Winter), 5-6.

1940

"The Japanese Pact." CS, 5, no. 4 (Fall), 11-12.

"Let Him Who is Without Sin." The Union Review, 1, no. 2 (March), 9-11, 25.
    The war and common guilt.

"Lewis and the CIO." CS, 6, no. 1 (Winter), 6-7.

"Liberal Christianity." NYHT (September 15), p. 18.
    Review of Georgia Harkness's The Faith by Which the Church Lives, together with Albert Day's The Faith We Live By, and F. C. Grant's The Gospel of the Kingdom.

"Marked Men." N, 150, no. 26 (June 29), 787-788.
    Writing as Chairman of the American Friends of German Freedom, Niebuhr appeals for funds to aid anti-Nazi Germans.

"Marxists are Taking Stock." CS, 5, no. 2 (Spring), 8-9.

"National Defense." CS, 5, no. 2 (Summer), 10-12.

"Nature of the Divine." NYHT (October 6), p. 29.
    Review of E. S. Brightman's A Philosophy of the Divine.

"A New Name." RR, 5, no. 1 (Winter), 4-5.
    For the journal and for the group.

"Notes." CS, 5, no. 4 (Fall), 12-13.
    Notes on The Christian Century's defense of Lindbergh; isolationists; treason and hysteria; lay Catholicism.

"An Open Letter to Richard Roberts." CS, 5, no. 3 (Summer), 30-33.
    Reprinted in Love and Justice.

"Politics and the Christian Ethic." CS, 5, no. 2 (Spring), 24-28.

"A Prayer." CS, 5, no. 2 (Spring), 40.

"A Prayer." CS, 5, no. 3 (Summer), 29.

"A Prayer Against Tyrants." CS, 6, no. 1 (Winter), 48 (Published erroneously as vol. 5, no. 5).

"The Presidential Election." CS, 5, no. 3 (Summer), 7-8.

"The Presidential Election." RR, 5, no. 1 (Winter), 9-11.

"The Rationalist Rearguard." CS, 5, no. 2 (Spring), 5.

"Religious Books of Distinction." NYHT (November 17), p. 30.
    Review of D. C. Macintosh's The Problem of Religious Knowledge, along with Edwin Lewis's A Philosophy of Christian Revelation and D. R. Davies's The Two Humanities.

"A Reply to Professor Macintosh." The Review of Religion, 4, no. 3 (March), 304-308.

1940

"Roosevelt and Willkie." CS, 5, no. 4 (Fall), 5-7.

"Roosevelt's Election." CS, 6, no. 1 (Winter), 4-5 (Erroneously printed as vol. 5, no. 5).

["Russia and France." Review of Arnold Wolfers's Russia and France Between the Wars.] CS, 5, no. 4 (Fall), 44.

"Saving Liberty at Home." RR, 5, no. 1 (Winter), 11.

"Sin in Politics." CS, 5, no. 2 (Spring), 6-7.

"The Sino-Japanese War." CS, 5, no. 2 (Spring), 5-6.

["The Social Function of Religion." Review of E. O. James's The Social Function of Religion.] The Union Review, 2, no. 1 (November), 36.

"The Social Struggle and the Roosevelt Victory." CS, 6, no. 1 (Winter), 5-6.

"The Socialist Campaign." CS, 5, no. 3 (Summer), 3-5.

["Springs of Creative Living." Review of Rollo May's Springs of Creative Living.] CS, 6, no. 1 (Winter), 47-48.

"The Threat of Reaction." CS, 5, no. 3 (Summer), 8-9.

["To the Finland Station." Review of Edmund Wilson's To the Finland Station.] N, 151, no. 13 (September 28), 274-276. Also in CS, 5, no. 4 (Fall), 44.

"Too Late for This War." CCY, 57, no. 22 (May 29), 706-707. A letter to the editors. Reply to the editors, p. 707.

"The Total War is Here." CS, 5, no. 3 (Summer), 1-2.

"Waldo Frank: Pilot." N, 150, no. 19 (May 11), 600-601. Review of Waldo Frank's Chart for Rough Waters: Our Role in a New World. Also in RR, 5, no. 3 (Summer), 42-44.

"War Aims and a Just Peace." CS, 6, no. 1 (Winter), 1-3.

"The War Situation." CS, 6, no. 1 (Winter), 3-4.

"Why the Christian Church is Not Pacifist." London: S. C. M. Press, 47 pp. Reprinted as Chapter 1 of Christianity and Power Politics.

1941

"The Aftermath." CS, 6, no. 4 (Fall), 1-3.

"Allied Peace Aims." CC, 1, no. 11 (June 30), 1-2. Reprinted in Love and Justice.

"America and the Enslaved Nations." CC, 1, no. 17 (October 6), 1-2.

"America and the Peace After the War." CC, 1, no. 4 (March 24), 1-2.

"America in the Hour of Decision." CS, 6, no. 3 (Summer), 1-3.

"American Doldrums." CC, 1, no. 16 (September 22), 1-2.

"American Political Theory." N, 153, no. 19 (November 8), 460.
> Review of D. W. Brogan's Politics and Law in the United States,
> along with T. V. Smith's The Democratic Tradition in America.
> Also reviewed, along with Becker's New Liberties for Old, in
> CS, 7, no. 1 (Winter), 44-45.

"American Response to the World Crisis." CS, 6, no. 2 (Spring), 4-5.

"America's Last Chance." CC, 1, no. 12 (July 14), 1-2.
> May be last chance to join effectively in crushing the Nazi
> tyranny.

"Armistice Day 1941." CC, 1, no. 20 (November 17), 1-2.

"Britain's Atonement." CS, 6, no. 4 (Fall), 5-7.

"British Churchmen and Peace Aims." CC, 1, no. 1 (February 10), 3.

"Calling all Prophets." CC, 1, no. 2 (February 24), 2.

"A Charitable Opponent." CC, 1, no. 6 (April 21), 3.

"Christ and Ceasar." CC, 1, no. 5 (April 7), 2.

"Christ and our Political Decisions." CC, 1, no. 14 (August 11), 1-2.

"The Christian Faith and the World Crisis." CC, 1, no. 1
> (February 10), 4-6.
> Reprinted in Love and Justice.

"Christianity and Classical Culture." The University of Toronto
> Quarterly (July).
> Review of C. N. Cochrane's Christianity and Classical Culture:
> A Study of Thought and Action from Augustus to Augustine.

"Church and State in America." CC, 1, no. 22 (December 22), 1-2.
> Reprinted in Essays in Applied Christianity.

"The Church Speaks on Labor." CS, 6, no. 3 (Summer), 6.

"The City of Man: A Declaration on World Democracy." Committee of
> Fifteen--Reinhold Niebuhr, H. Agar, F. Aydelotte, G. A. Borgese
> et al. New York: Viking Press, 113 pp.

"The Claims Men Make." CS, 7, no. 1 (Winter), 8-9.

"Communists and Unions." N, 152, no. 11 (March 15), 307.
> Letter to the Editor.

"Conscription of Labor in Britain." CS, 6, no. 2 (Spring), 5-6.

Other Writings by Reinhold Niebuhr

1941

"The Crisis." CC, 1, no. 1 (February 10), 1-2.

"The Crisis Deepens." CC, 1, no. 7 (May 5), 1-2.

"The Crisis in the Far East." CC, 1, no. 3 (March 10), 1-2.

"Critical Loyalty." CC, 1, no. 11 (June 30), 2.

"Croce on History." N, 152, no. 24 (June 14), 699-700.
Review of B. Croce's History as the Story of Liberty.

"Dr. Press and Evangelical Theology."
An address delivered on the occasion of the retirement of
Dr. Press at Eden Seminary. Unpublished copy in Eden Theological
Seminary Library.

"Editorial Notes." CS, 6, no. 2 (Spring), 7-8.
Notes on false explanations for the causes of the war; Henry
Luce's article on the "American Century"; and an article in a
Catholic magazine laying the world's troubles to the Reformation.

"Editorial Notes." CS, 7, no. 1 (Winter), 9-10.
Notes on misreading history; the approach to the war in sermons; the correctness of earlier proposals of collective action;
and the possibility of avoiding hating the enemy.

"Equality of Sacrifice." CS, 7, no. 1 (Winter), 7.

"Essays by MacLeish." N, 152, no. 17 (April 26), 506.
Review of Archibald MacLeish's The American Cause, along with
A Time to Speak: The Selected Prose of Archibald MacLeish.

"Ethical Norm of Action." NYHT (September 14), p. 16.
Review of I. G. Whitchurch's An Enlightened Conscience.

"The Ethical Resources of the Christian Religion," in Contemporary
Religious Thought. Edited by Thomas S. Kepler. New York:
Abingdon-Cokesbury, pp. 51-59.
Footnote says "From Education Adequate for Modern Times. New
York: Association Press, 1931, pp. 54-66."

"Evangelical Liberalism." NYHT (February 23), p. 22.
Review of H. F. Rall's Christianity, An Inquiry Into Its Nature
and Truth.

"Fighting Chance for a Sick Society." N, 152, no. 12 (March 22),
357-360.

"The Fulfillment of Life," in Contemporary Religious Thought. Edited
by Thomas S. Kepler. New York: Abingdon-Cokesbury, pp. 373-380.
From Niebuhr's Beyond Tragedy, pp. 289-306.

"Geography, Christianity and Politics." CC, 1, no. 10 (June 16), 5-6.

"Germans and Nazis." CS, 6, no. 2 (Spring), 3.

"Hero and Martyr." N, 153, no. 21 (November 22), 519.
     Review of Martin Niemoeller's God is My Fuehrer.

"History (God) Has Overtaken Us." CS, 7, no. 1 (Winter), 3-5.
     Reprinted in Love and Justice.

"Holy Wars." CC, 1, no. 1 (February 10), 2-3.

"Imperialism and Irresponsibility." CC, 1, no. 2 (February 24), 6.

"An Ineffectual Sermon on Love." CC, 1, no. 22 (December 22), 2-3.

"Japan and Economic Sanctions." CC, 1, no. 15 (August 25), 2.

"Just or Holy." CC, 1, no. 19 (November 3), 1-2.
     Discussion of The Christian Century article calling the dis-
     tinction between a just and a holy war "theological dust."

["Kierkegaard." Review of David Swenson's Something About Kierkegaard,
     along with Kierkegaard's Thoughts on Crucial Situations in Life.]
     CS, 7, no. 1 (Winter), 41-43.

"Kierkegaard's Message." NYHT (November 30), p. 33.
     Review of Kierkegaard's Concluding Unscientific Postscript.
     Also in CS, 6, no. 4 (Fall), 44-45.

"Knowledge is Not Enough." CS, 6, no. 3 (Summer), 9-10.

"Labor and Defense." CC, 1, no. 6 (April 21), 1-2.

"The Lend-Lease Bill." CC, 1, no. 1 (February 10), 2.

"The Lend-Lease Bill Passed." CC, 1, no. 3 (March 10), 2.

"Lessons From Russian Resistance." CS, 6, no. 4 (Fall), 3-5.

"Let us Reason More Carefully." CC, 1, no. 6 (April 21), 2.
     No analogy between soldiers and workers in industrial strife.

"Literature and Democracy." N, 153, no. 23 (December 6), 572-574.
     Review of Edman and Schneider's Fountainheads of Freedom.

"Literature on the International Situation." CC, 1, no. 8 (May 19),
     2-3.

"The Long and the Short Range of History." CS, 7, no. 1 (Winter),
     7-8.

"The Malvern Conference." CS, 6, no. 2 (Spring), 3-4.

"The Mirage of Mediation." CC, 1, no. 13 (July 28), 1-2.

"Mr. Hoover Appeals to Reason." CC, 1, no. 12 (July 14), 2.

"Momentous Decision By Narrow Margin." CC, 1, no. 21 (December 1),
     1-2.
     House votes to amend the Neutrality Act.

1941

"The Necessity of Decision." CC, 1, no. 9 (June 2), 1-2.
   On the necessity of American choice between allowing a Nazi
   victory and risking war.

"A Negotiated Peace." CC, 1, no. 5 (April 7), 1-2.
   Reprinted in Love and Justice.

"New Allies, Old Issues." N, 153, no. 3 (July 19), 50-52.

"On a Certain Christian Defeatism." CC, 1, no. 7 (May 5), 2.

"Onward Then Ye Faithful." NYHT (June 1), p. 11.
   Review of E. R. Hardy's Militant in Earth.

"Pacifism and America First." CC, 1, no. 10 (June 16), 2-5.
   Reprinted in Love and Justice.

"The Paradox of Peace." CC, 1, no. 2 (February 24), 2.

"Present Times Anticipated." CS, 7, no. 1 (Winter), 5-7.
   Note about Christian Socialism's separation from Christian
   Liberalism.

"The President and the People." CC, 1, no. 10 (June 16), 1-2.

"The Problem Stated." N, 152, no. 15 (April 12), 441.
   Review of Carl Becker's Modern Democracy.

"The Providence of God and the Defense of Civilisation." The Christian News-Letter (May 21), Supplement 82.

"A Quaker View of Political Pacifism." CC, 1, no. 18 (October 22),
   2.

"Quest Not Conflict." CC, 1, no. 3 (March 10), 2.

"The Red Thirties." CS, 6, no. 4 (Fall), 42.
   Review of Eugene Lyons's The Red Decade. Also in N, 153,
   no. 12 (September 20), 256-257.

"Reflections on the World Situation." CC, 1, no. 6 (April 21), 2-3.

"Religion and Action," in Religion and the Modern World. Philadel-
   phia: University of Pennsylvania Press, pp. 89-108.
   Reprinted in Science and Man, edited by Ruth N. Anshan. New
   York: Harcourt, Brace and Company, 1942, pp. 44-64.

"Repeal the Neutrality Act." CC, 1, no. 18 (October 20), 1-2.
   Reprinted in Love and Justice.

"The Role of Reason." N, 153, no. 18 (November 1), 430-431.
   Review of Carl L. Becker's New Liberties for Old.

"Roosevelt's Opportunity." CC, 1, no. 12 (July 14), 2.

"The Russian Situation." CC, 1, no. 19 (November 3), 2.

"The Russian Venture." CC, 1, no. 11 (June 30), 2-3.

1941

"The Russians and Our Interdependence." CC, 1, no. 15 (August 25), 1-2.

"The Scylla and Charybdis of Society." CC, 1, no. 20 (November 17), 2.
    War on the one hand and tyranny on the other.

"A Sermonette." CC, 1, no. 5 (April 7), 2.

"Social Justice in Defense Economy." CS, 6, no. 2 (Spring), 6-7.

"Sorokin on Culture." N, 153, no. 25 (December 20), 648.
    Review of P. A. Sorokin's The Crisis of Our Age. Also in CS, 7, no. 1 (Winter), 39.

"Statement." The New York Times (January 23), p. 8.
    Statement opposing Norman Thomas's stand against lend-lease by Niebuhr along with A. B. Lewis, Jack Altman and Gus Tyler.

"A Statement of Belief." NYHT (October 5), p. 26.
    Review of J. B. Pratt's Can We Keep the Faith?

"The Story of a False Religion." CS, 6, no. 3 (Summer), 6-8.
    Notes on Communism.

"Strikes in Industry." CS, 6, no. 3 (Summer), 5-6.

"The Supreme Court and Jim Crowism." CS, 6, no. 3 (Summer), 8-9.

"Taxation and Defense Economy." CS, 6, no. 4 (Fall), 4-5.

"A Theologian's Career." NYHT (January 26), p. 17.
    Review of Kierkegaard's Stages on Life's Way.

"Union for Democratic Action." CS, 6, no. 3 (Summer), 6.

"The War Comes Closer." CC, 1, no. 20 (November 17), 2.

"We Are At War." CC, 1, no. 23 (December 29), 2-3.

["We Are Not Divided." Review of John Hutchison's We Are Not Divided.]
    CS, 6, no. 4 (Fall), 43.

"What is at Stake?" CC, 1, no. 8 (May 19), 1-2.

"What is the Alternative?" CC, 1, no. 8 (May 19), 6.

"Where do we go From Here?" N, 153, no. 17 (October 25), 403-405.
    Review of I. D. Talmadge's Whose Revolution?

"Whether we Live or Die." CC, 1, no. 7 (May 5), 2.

"White Man's Burden." CS, 6, no. 3 (Summer), 3-5.
    Further on Henry Luce's article in Life on "The American Century."

"Whosoever Will Save His Life." CC, 1, no. 2 (February 24), 1-2.

"Woe Unto Them That Are at Ease!" CS, 6, no. 2 (Spring), 1-2.

Other Writings by Reinhold Niebuhr

1941

"The World After the War." CC, 1, no. 1 (February 10), 3.

1942

["Agenda of Post-War World." Review of J. B. Condliffe's Agenda of
   Post-War World.] CS, 8, no. 1 (Winter), 45-46.

"American Dream vs. Nightmare." N, 154, no. 8 (February 21), 230.
      Review of John MacCormac's America and World Mastery. Also
   in CS, 7, no. 2 (Spring), 42.

"Amidst Encircling Gloom." CC, 2, no. 3 (March 9), 1-2.

"The Anglo-Russian Pact." CC, 2, no. 11 (June 29), 2-3.

"The Art of Government." N, 154, no. 11 (March 14), 317-318.
      Review of C. J. Friedrich's Constitutional Government and
   Democracy.

"Authority and Liberty." N, 154, no. 12 (March 21), 347.
      Review of C. E. Merriam's On the Agenda of Democracy.

"Bergson and Maritain." The Union Review, 3, no. 2 (March), 28-29.
      Review of Jacques Maritain's Ransoming the Time, along with
   J. M. and Raisa Maritain's We Have Been Friends Together.

"Better Government Than we Deserve." CS, 7, no. 2 (Spring), 10.

"Chastisement Unto Repentance or Death." CS, 7, no. 2 (Spring), 3-5.
      Punishments of war can bring to us repentance or degradation.

"The Christian and the War." CCY, 59, no. 51 (November 16), 5-7.
      Review article of C. C. Morrison's The Christian and the War.
   Discussion concluded in "The Christian and the War--Concluding
   the Reply to Dr. Niebuhr." CCY, 59, no. 52 (December 30), 1620-
   1623. Also in CCY, 59, no. 51 (December 23), 1589-1590, and CS,
   7, no. 4 (Autumn), 43-44.

["The Christian Interpretation of Sex." Review of Otto Piper's The
   Christian Interpretation of Sex.] CS, 7, no. 2 (Spring), 40-41.

"The Churches and the War." Town Meeting of the Air, August 27.

"Churchill, Democratic Tory." N, 154, no. 5 (January 31), 122.
      Review of Phillip Guedalla's Mr. Churchill.

"Civil Liberties in Wartime." CC, 2, no. 16 (February 23), 1-2.

"Common Council for United Nations." CC, 2, no. 16 (December 5), 1-2.

["The Destiny of Western Man." Review of W. T. Stace's The Destiny
   of Western Man.] CS, 7, no. 2 (Spring), 42-43.

"Does the Church Pray?" CC, 2, no. 10 (June 15), 3-4.

1942

"The End of the Beginning." CC, 2, no. 20 (November 30), 1-2.

"The Evacuation of Japanese Citizens." CC, 2, no. 8 (May 18), 2-5.

"A Faith for History's Greatest Crisis." Fortune, 26, no. 1 (July), 99-100, 122, 125-126, 128, 131.

"The German Tragedy." NR, 107, no. 23 (December 7), 763-766.
    Review of L. P. Lochner's What About Germany? along with Curt Reiss's The Self-Betrayed, Hubertus zu Loewenstein's On Borrowed Peace, Prince Starhemberg's Between Hitler and Mussolini and Ladislas Farago's German Psychological Warfare.

"The Germans and the Nazis." N, 154, no. 14 (April 4), 398-400.
    Review article on several discussions of the subject.

"The Goals of Democracy." N, 154, no. 15 (April 11), 428, 430.
    Review of J. D. Kingsley's Strategy for Democracy.

["Grey Eminence." Review of Aldous Huxley's Grey Eminence.] CS, 7, no. 3 (Summer), 45-46.

"In the Battle and Above It." CS, 7, no. 4 (Autumn), 3-4.

"Jews After the War." N, 154, nos. 8 and 9 (February 21 and 28), 214-216, 253-255.
    Published in England by the Inter-University Jewish Federation of Great Britain; also by the Common Council for American Unity, Inc., New York. Reprinted in Love and Justice.

"Jews and Gentiles." N, 154, no. 23 (June 6), 659-660.
    Review of Jews in a Gentile World, edited by Graeber and Britt.

"Labor and the Future." CS, 7, no. 4 (Autumn), 4-5.

["Liberal Theology." Review of Liberal Theology, An Appraisal, Essays in Honor of Eugene Lyman.] CS, 8, no. 1 (Winter), 43-44.

"The Limits of Liberty." N, 154, no. 4 (January 24), 86-88.

"Love Your Enemies." CS, 7, no. 4 (Autumn), 35-37.
    Reprinted in Love and Justice.

"Man Proposes But God Disposes." CS, 7, no. 4 (Autumn), 9-10.

"Mann's Political Essays." N, 155, no. 22 (November 28), 582-584.
    Review of Thomas Mann's Order of the Day.

["Man's Vision of God." Review of Charles Hartshorne's Man's Vision of God.] CS, 7, no. 2 (Spring), 43-44.

"The Middle Ground." N, 155, no. 23 (December 5), 627-628.
    Review of A. M. Bingham's The Techniques of Democracy.

"Military Victory and Political Defeat." CS, 8, no. 1 (Winter), 3-4.

1942

"The Mind of Nehru." N, 155, no. 6 (August 8), 117.
    Review of J. Nehru's Glimpses of World History.

"Mr. Hoover on Peace." N, 155, no. 2 (July 11), 36–37.
    Review of Hoover and Gibson's The Problems of Lasting Peace.

"No Adequate Blueprint." N, 154, no. 4 (January 24), 103.
    Reply to F. L. Schuman's criticism of Niebuhr's review of
    Schuman and Brodsky's Design for Power.

"Notes on the World Conflict." CS, 7, no. 4 (Autumn), 10–11.
    Notes on developments in India and the Russian resistance.

"Nothing But the Truth." CS, 7, no. 3 (Summer), 9–10.

"Our Inadequate Congress." CS, 7, no. 2 (Spring), 7–8.

"Our Responsibilities in 1942." CC, 1, no. 24 (January 12), 1–2.
    Speaking for the editorial board of CC.

"The Peril of Inflation." CS, 7, no. 4 (Autumn), 5–6.

"The Perils of Sainthood." CS, 7, no. 4 (Autumn), 8–9.

["Personal Religion." Review of D. C. Macintosh's Personal Religion.]
    CS, 8, no. 1 (Winter), 44–45.

"Plans for World Organization." CS, 7, no. 3 (Summer), 6–7.

"Plans for World Reorganization." CC, 2, no. 17 (October 19), 3–6.
    Reprinted in Love and Justice.

"Politics and Economics." CS, 7, no. 4 (Autumn), 7–8.

"The Pope and God." CS, 7, no. 3 (Summer), 5–6.

"The Pope's Christmas Message." CS, 8, no. 1 (Winter), 4–6.
    Reprinted in Essays in Applied Christianity.

"Power and Freedom." N, 155, no. 18 (October 31), 454.
    Review of Peter Drucker's The Future of Industrial Man.

"Power and Justice." CS, 8, no. 1 (Winter), 9–10.

"Power and Politics." N, 154, no 17 (April 25), 495.
    Review of L. Gelber's Peace by Power.

"A Prayer." CS, 7, no. 1 (Spring), 12.

"A Prayer." CS, 7, no. 3 (Summer), 11.

"Preaching in War-Time." CC, 1, no. 26 (February 9), 1–2.

"The Probable End of the New Deal." CS, 8, no. 1 (Winter), 6–7.

"The Problem of Power." N, 154, no. 2 (January 10), 42–44.
    Review of F. L. Schuman's Design for Power. Schuman's reply
    and Niebuhr's rejoinder in N (January 24), p. 103.

"The Problem of Sovereignty." N, 155, no. 12 (September 19), 240-241.
    Review of G. Ferrero's The Principles of Power. Also in CS,
    8, no. 1 (Winter), 46.

"The Race Problem." CS, 7, no. 3 (Summer), 3-5.
    Reprinted in Love and Justice.

"Rationing and Democracy." CS, 8, no. 1 (Winter), 8-9.
    Reprinted in Love and Justice.

"Restraint and Modesty in the Pulpit." CC, 1, no. 25 (January 26),
    1-2.

"The Role of Prophetic Religion in the World Crisis," in Men of
    Tomorrow. Edited by T. H. Johnson. New York: G. P. Putnam's
    Sons, pp. 105-124.

"Roots of the Conflict." N, 154, no. 16 (April 18), 464-465.
    Review of Raoul de Roussy de Sales's The Making of Tomorrow.

"Russia and the Peace." CS, 7, no. 2 (Spring), 8-9.

"Russia and the Western World." CS, 7, no. 3 (Summer), 7-9.

"Russia's Partnership in War and Peace." CC, 2, no. 2 (February 23),
    2-3.

["Sickness Unto Death." Review of Kierkegaard's Sickness Unto Death.]
    CS, 7, no. 2 (Spring), 41-42.

"Social Security in Britain." CS, 8, no. 1 (Winter), 7-8.

"The Spirit and the Body in War." CC, 2, no. 14 (August 10), 1-2.

"Stafford Cripps and India." CS, 7, no. 2 (Spring), 9-10.

"The Tax Problem." CS, 7, no. 4 (Autumn), 6-7.

"Taxation and Inflation." CS, 7, no. 2 (Spring), 10-11.

"Taxation and Inflation." CS, 7, no. 3 (Summer), 10-11.

"Thoughts on 'World War III?'" N, 155, no. 2 (July 11), 32.
    One of several responses to an article by J. Alvarez del Vayo
    in The Nation (June 20).

"A Too Sudden Change." CC, 1, no. 24 (January 12), 2.

"The Unity of History." CC, 2, no. 7 (May 4), 1-2.

["Virgin Spain." Review of Waldo Frank's Virgin Spain.] CS, 7,
    no. 2 (Spring), 44.

"We Recommend St. Augustine to The Christian Century." CS, 7, no. 2
    (Spring), 5-7.

["A Week With Gandhi." Review of L. Fischer's A Week With Gandhi.]
    CS, 8, no. 1 (Winter), 43-44.

1942

"Workers and Soldiers." CS, 7, no. 2 (Spring), 11.

["The World After the War." Review of H. B. Parkes's The World After
the War.] CS, 8, no. 1 (Winter), 41.

1943

"American Power and World Responsibility." CC, 3, no. 5 (April 5),
2-4.
Reprinted in Love and Justice.

"American Trends." The Spectator, 171, no. 6025 (December 17), 573.

"Anglo-Saxon Destiny and Responsibility." CC, 3, no. 16 (October 4),
2-4.
Reprinted in Love and Justice.

"Blind Anger." N, 157, no. 11 (September 11), 300-302.
Review of Lin Yutang's Between Tears and Laughter.

"The Bombing of Germany." CS, 8, no. 3 (Summer), 3-4.
Reprinted in Love and Justice.

"British Labor Marks Time." N, 156, no. 26 (June 26), 880.

"Caste and Vocation." N, 156, no. 5 (January 30), 180.
A letter answering criticism of his review of Shridharani's
Warning to the West.

"Champion of Zionism." N, 157, no. 26 (December 25), 766.
Review of Pierre van Paassen's The Forgotten Ally.

"Chaos in Congress." CS, 9, no. 1 (Winter), 8-10.

"Christian Otherworldliness." CS, 9, no. 1 (Winter), 11-12.

"Christianity and Politics in Britain." CS, 8, no. 3 (Summer), 6-7.
Reprinted in Love and Justice.

"Churchill's View of the Future." CS, 8, no. 2 (Spring), 4-5.

"Comments." N, 156, no. 15 (April 10), 537.
A letter commenting on R. Bates's review of "America, Russia,
and the Communist Party in the Post-War World."

"Confessions in Order." CS, 9, no. 1 (Winter), 13.
Question of whether the prophets of doom about deficit spend-
ing have confessed their error; Niebuhr's own concern about the
national debt in "Ex Cathedra," March 15 and July 12, 1934.

"Conflict in the Democratic Cause." CS, 8, no. 4 (Fall), 7.

["Editorial Paragraph." N, 156, no. 23 (June 5), 793.
About French resurgence under de Gaulle's leadership.

Other Writings by Reinhold Niebuhr

"Editor's Note." CC, 3, no. 19 (November 15), 6.
     Comment on a letter by Chaplain C. C. Kilde.

"The Editor's Report on Britain." CC, 3, no. 11 (June 28), 4-6.

"Educational and Religious Barrenness." CC, 3, no. 14 (August 9),
     1-2.
     Comparison of our Army educational program with that of the
     British.

"England Teaches its Soldiers." N, 157, no. 8 (August 21), 208-210.

"Factors of Cohesion." The Spectator, 170, no. 5999 (June 18),
     562-563.
     A meld of idealism and realism for world beyond the war.

"The Fires of History." CS, 8, no. 2 (Spring), 7-9.

"Foreword," to Liberty Through Power. By Eduard Heimann. New York:
     Union For Democratic Action Educational Fund.

"A Fourth Term for Roosevelt." The New Statesman and Nation, 25,
     no. 638 (May 15), 315-316.

["From Victory to Peace." Review of Paul Hutchinson's From Victory
     to Peace.] CS, 9, no. 1 (Winter), 36-38.

"From Wilson to Roosevelt." CS, 8, no. 4 (Fall), 3-5.

"Great Britain's Post-War Role." N, 157, no. 2 (July 10), 39-40.

["The Growth of American Thought." Review of Merle Curti's The Growth
     of American Thought.] CS, 8, no. 4 (Fall), 36.

"The Historian as Prophet." N, 156, no. 15 (April 10), 530-531.
     Review of Jacob Burckhardt's Force and Freedom: Reflections
     on History.

["The Historic Church and Modern Pacifism." Review of Umphrey Lee's
     The Historic Church and Modern Pacifism.] CS, 8, no. 2 (Spring),
     39.

["In Search of Maturity." Review of Fritz Kunkel's In Search of
     Maturity.] CS, 8, no. 4 (Fall), 38-39.

"The Intelligent Man's Burden." N, 156, no. 1 (January 2), 25-26.
     Review of Shridharani's Warning to the West.

"The International Situation." CS, 8, no. 2 (Spring), 5-7.

"Introduction," to The Silent War, The Underground Movement in
     Germany. By J. B. Jansen and Stefan Weyl. New York: J. B.
     Lippincott, pp. 9-10.

"Job's Problem and St. Paul's." CCY, 60, no. 45 (November 10),
     1298-1300.
     Review of A. C. Garnett's A Realistic Philosophy of Religion.

1943

"A Just World Power." Current Religious Thought, 3, no. 8 (October), 11-13.

"Labor Has Lost its Driving Force." CS, 8, no. 2 (Spring), 3-4.

"Letter From Britain." CC, 3, no. 12 (July 12), 2.
    Impressions of the religious and political situation in Britain.

"Mann Speaks on Germany." N, 156, no. 7 (February 13), 244.
    Review of Thomas Mann's Listen, Germany!

"Marxism in Eclipse." The Spectator, 170, no. 5997 (June 4), 518-519.

"Mr. Willkie's Two Odysseys." N, 156, no. 17 (April 24), 604-606.
    Review of Wendell Willkie's One World.

"National Power and the Organization of Peace." The American Teacher, 27, no. 7 (April), 23-26.

"Nationalism and the Possibilities of Internationalism." CS, 8, no. 4 (Fall), 5-7.

"Negroes and the Railroads." CS, 9, no. 1 (Winter), 11.

"Notes." CS, 8, no. 2 (Spring), 11.
    Notes on the inflationary spiral.

"Oriental Self-Righteousness." N, 156, no. 4 (January 23), 142-143.
    A letter answering Louis Fischer's criticism of Niebuhr's review of Shridharani's Warning to the West. Answer to another critic in the issue of January 30, p. 180.

"Our Ministry to the Armed Forces." CC, 3, no. 18 (November 1), 2.

"The Perils of Being the Judge." CS, 9, no. 1 (Winter), 10-11.

"The Perils of Our Foreign Policy." CS, 8, no. 2 (Spring), 18-21.

"Pillars of Peace." The Spectator, 171, no. 6017 (October 22), 378-379.

"Politics and Religion in Britain." CC, 3, no. 13 (July 26), 2-3.

"Politics and the Children of Light." CC, 3, no. 20 (November 29), 2.

"Politics and the Pursuit of 'Goodness.'" N, 156, no. 8 (February 20), 281-282.
    Review of T. V. Smith's Disciplines for Democracy.

"The Politics of North Africa." CC, 3, no. 2 (February 22), 2.

"The Possibility of a Durable Peace." CS, 8, no. 3 (Summer), 9-12.
    Reprinted in Love and Justice.

"Power and Justice." N, 156, no. 10 (March 6), 353-354.
    Review of H. B. Parkes's The World After the War.

1943

"Power Politics and Justice." CS, 9, no. 1 (Winter), 5-8.

["The Principles of Christian Ethics." Review of A. C. Knudson's
The Principles of Christian Ethics.] CS, 8, no. 4 (Fall), 36-37.

"The Probable and the Actual Defeat." CS, 8, no. 2 (Spring), 10-11.

"The Problems of Bourgeois Society." CS, 8, no. 2 (Spring), 9-10.

"Rationing and Food Subsidies." CS, 8, no. 3 (Summer), 5-6.

"Republican Internationalism." CS, 8, no. 4 (Fall), 7.

"Revelation and the Meaning of History." The Dudleian Lecture,
Harvard University, April 14, 1942. Harvard Divinity School
Bulletin.
    Lecture is in four parts: I. Where a Christ is not expected,
II. Where a Christ is expected, III. Jesus' Reinterpretation of
Messianism, IV. The Church's Acceptance of this Messianism.

"Roosevelt and the New Deal." CS, 8, no. 3 (Summer), 4-5.

"Russia and the Christian World." Christian News-Letter (August 25),
Supplement 189.

"Russia and the Communist Party." N, 156, no. 15 (April 10), 537.

"Russia and the West, Part I." N, 156, no. 3 (January 16), 82-84.

"Russia and the West, Part II." N, 156, no. 4 (January 23), 124-125.

"Russia as an Ally in War and Peace." A radio discussion by Reinhold
Niebuhr, Walter Duranty and Louis Gotteschalk. "The University
of Chicago Roundtable," No. 257 (February 21), 16 pp.

"The Shape of Things." N, 156, no. 23 (June 5), 793.

"Study in Cynicism." N, 156, no. 18 (May 1), 636-638.
    Review of James Burnham's The Machiavellians: Defenders of
Freedom.

"Taxation and Inflation." CS, 8, no. 4 (Fall), 7-8.

"Tensions in British Politics." N, 156, no. 26 (June 26), 889-890.

"They Died for Free Enterprise." CS, 9, no. 1 (Winter), 12-13.

"The Timeless Christian Message and its Immediate Meaning." Current
Religious Thought, 3, no. 3 (March), 10-14.

["Total Peace." Review of Ely Culbertson's Total Peace.] CS, 9,
no. 1 (Winter), 42.

["Towards an Abiding Peace." Review of R. M. McIver's Towards an
Abiding Peace.] CS, 8, no. 3 (Summer), 50.

["The Tragedy of European Labor." Review of Adolph Sturmthal's The
Tragedy of European Labor.] CS, 8, no. 2 (Spring), 39-40.

1943

"Understanding England." N, 157, no. 7 (August 14), 175-177.

"The United Nations and World Organization." CC, 2, no. 24
(January 25), 1-2.

"The Vatican and the Soviet Union." CC, 3, no. 18 (November 1), 2.

"We Are in Peril." CC, 3, no. 17 (October 18), 2-3.

"What to do With Germany." N, 157, no. 20 (November 13), 559-560.
Review of Heinz Pol's The Hidden Enemy.

"When Freedom is Forgotten." N, 157, no. 25 (December 18), 738.
Review of Helmut Kuhn's Freedom, Forgotten and Remembered.
Also reviewed in CS, 8, no. 4 (Fall), 39-40, along with Heinz
Pol's The Hidden Enemy.

"Who Wants the Hapsburg Monarchy?" CC, 2, no. 23 (January 11), 2-3.

["World Federation Plan." Review of Ely Culbertson's Total Peace.]
CS, 8, no. 2 (Spring), 45.

1944

"Airplanes Are Not Enough." CC, 4, no. 1 (February 7), 1-2.
Reprinted in Love and Justice.

["An American Dilemma." Review of Gunnar Myrdal's An American
Dilemma.] CS, 9, no. 3 (Summer), 42.
Also in CC, 4, no. 15 (September 18), 2.

"America's Foreign Policy and World Peace."
Excerpts from an address at the Conference on America's
Opportunity to Create and Maintain Lasting Peace, October 7.
New York: News From The Nations Associates. Reproduced from
typewritten copy. Copy at Union Theological Seminary Library,
New York.

"Archbishop Temple." CC, 4, no. 19 (November 13), 1.

"The Basis of World Order." N, 159, no. 17 (October 21), 489.

"The Christian Faith and the German Problem." The Student Movement,
47, no. 1 (October), 6-8.
Head of the title: "The Battle of the Peace, II."

"The Christian Perspective on the World Crisis." CC, 4, no. 7
(May 1), 2-5.

"The Church's Support of the Chaplains." CC, 4, no. 3 (March 6),
1-2.

"The Climax of the War." CC, 4, no. 9 (May 29), 1-2.

Other Writings by Reinhold Niebuhr

["The Clue to Pascal." Review of Emile Caillet's The Clue to Pascal.]
The Union Review, 5, no. 1 (March), 28.

"The Collectivist Bogey." N, 159, no. 17 (October 21), 478, 480.
Review of F. Hayek's The Road to Serfdom, along with
M. Gordon's How to Tell Progress From Reaction.

"The Communist Party and Russia." CS, 9, no. 2 (Spring), 8-9.

"Critical Analysis of Dumbarton Oaks Proposals." Post War World,
2, no. 1 (December 15), 1, 3.

["The Crucifixion." Review of Mary B. Miller's The Crucifixion: A
Poem.] CS, 9, no. 3 (Summer), 45.

"Democratic Goals and World Order." NL, 27, no. 29 (September 23),
4-5.

"Dr. William Temple." CS, 10, no. 1 (Winter), 10.

"Dr. William Temple and His Britain." N, 159, no. 20 (November 11),
584-586.

"Dumbarton Oaks." CS, 10, no. 1 (Winter), 3-4.

"Editorial Notes." CC, 4, no. 4 (March 20), 2.
Notes on dismemberment of Germany; international penology;
obliteration bombing; domestic party conflict; heightened racial
tension; and the education program in the Army.

"Editorial Notes." CC, 4, no. 5 (April 3), 2.
Notes on Mary B. Miller's The Crucifixion; a book on the
Palestinian problem; "White Paper" restrictions on immigration
to Palestine; Russian recognition of the Badoglio government; and
The Holy Name Journal attack upon Christianity and Crisis and
members of the editorial board.

"Editorial Notes." CC, 4, no. 6 (April 17), 2.
Notes on "Foxhole religion"; reaction of military officers to
Christianity and Crisis article on chaplains; chaplains and
doctors and the sex problem in the Army; and obliteration bombing.

"Editorial Notes." CC, 4, no. 8 (May 15), 2.
Notes on LaGuardia's expression of alarm over the few thousand
Japanese-Americans in New York; Selective Service cancellation of
exemption of pre-theological students; and the possibility of
bringing military chaplains under some civilian agency.

"Editorial Notes." CC, 4, no. 9 (May 29), 2.
Notes on the poverty of worship in American Protestantism
revealed by chaplains' experiences in Army work; and Catholicism
and Russia.

"Editorial Notes." CC, 4, no. 11 (June 26), 2.
Notes on a "Society for the Prevention of World War III"; further notes on chaplains and religion in the armed forces.

1944

"Editorial Notes." CC, 4, no. 13 (July 24), 2.
Notes on technical development and modern war; answer to protest that American Protestantism is not impoverished in its
worship life.

"Editorial Notes." CC, 4, no. 14 (August 7), 2.
Notes on the difficulty the Army faces in its educational
work; difficulties Protestant military men have getting to worship services as compared to Catholics; killing German civilians;
and the disintegration of Nazi authority.

"Editorial Notes." CC, 4, no. 15 (September 18), 2.
Notes on Myrdal's An American Dilemma; Welles's The Time for
Decision; and Dumbarton Oaks.

"Editorial Notes." CC, 4, no. 16 (October 2), 2.
Notes on the German military defeat; fanaticism of the Nazis;
Bretton Woods and Dumbarton Oaks; and the puzzling Russian policy.

"Editorial Notes." CC, 4, no. 22 (December 25), 2.
Notes on evidence of political maturity; Dumbarton Oaks; and
the Army policy against fraternization in Germany.

"Election Insights on Our Civilization." CS, 10, no. 1 (Winter),
6-7.

"The End of Total War." CS, 9, no. 4 (Fall), 3-4.

"Foreword," to The University and the Modern World. By Arnold N.
Nash. New York: The Macmillan Co., pp. xi-xii.

"The Future of Imperialism." NL, 27, no. 24 (June 10), 11.
Review of Louis Fischer's Empire.

"The German Problem." CC, 3, no. 23 (January 10), 2-4.
Reprinted in Love and Justice.

"The German Question." N, 159, no. 19 (November 4), 563, 566.
Review of Moulton and Marlio's The Control of Germany, along
with Brailsford's Our Settlement With Germany and Chatham House
Study Group's The Problem of Germany.

["The Great Transformation." Review of Karl Polanyi's The Great
Transformation.] CS, 9, no. 2 (Spring), 44-45.

"International Ideals and Realities." CS, 9, no. 3 (Summer), 3-5.

"Introduction," to The Jew in Our Day. By W. Frank. New York:
Duell, Sloan and Pearce, pp. 3-14.

"Is the Bombing Necessary?" CC, 4, no. 5 (April 3), 1-2.

"The Janus-Faced Republicans." CS, 9, no. 3 (Summer), 10-11.

"The Japanese Atrocities." CC, 4, no. 2 (February 21), 1-2.

"Judgment and Forgiveness." CS, 9, no. 3 (Summer), 8-10.

Other Writings by Reinhold Niebuhr

"Justice for the Enemy." CS, 9, no. 4 (Fall), 5-6.

"Labor and Foreign Policy." CS, 9, no. 3 (Summer), 11.

"Law and Humility." CS, 10, no. 1 (Winter), 5-6.

"Man: Real and Ideal." Religion in Life, 13, no. 2 (Spring), 296-298.
　　Review of E. G. Conklin's Faith, Reason, and Civilization: An Essay in Historical Analysis. Also in CS, 9, no. 3 (Summer), 42-43.

"My Choice for President." NR, 110, no. 8 (February 21), 245.

["My Life in Russia." Review of Markoosha Fischer's My Life in Russia.] CS, 9, no. 3 (Summer), 41.

"The Negro Issue in America." CS, 9, no. 3 (Summer), 5-7.
　　Reprinted in Love and Justice.

"Our Foreign Policy and the Peace." The Committee for a Democratic Foreign Policy. Lecture Number 1, In-Service Course (Spring). Mimeographed.

"Peace Beyond Our Time." N, 158, no. 23 (June 3), 658-659.
　　Review of M. J. Adler's How to Think About War and Peace.

"The Perspective of Faith Upon History." CS, 9, no. 2 (Spring), 4-7.

"Political Wisdom in Advertising." CS, 10, no. 1 (Winter), 9-10.
　　Reference to manufacturing companies buying space to preach "a completely discredited and impossible laissez faire political philosophy."

"The Pope on Property." CS, 9, no. 4 (Fall), 6-8.
　　Reprinted in Essays in Applied Christianity.

"Prayer and a Global Civilization." CC, 4, no. 15 (September 18), 1-2.

"The Presidential Election and American Politics." CS, 9, no. 2 (Spring), 3-4.

"Realistic Internationalism." CS, 9, no. 4 (Fall), 4-5.

"Realist's Eye View." N, 159, no. 4 (July 22), 105-107.
　　Review of Leopold Schwarzschild's Primer of the Coming World.

"Reason and Interest in Politics." CS, 10, no. 1 (Winter), 8-9.

"Sentimental and Shallow Religion." CS, 9, no. 2 (Spring), 7-8.

["Slavery and Freedom." Review of Nicholas Berdyaev's Slavery and Freedom.] CS, 9, no. 3 (Summer), 40-41.

"Small Nations vs. Big Powers." A radio discussion by Reinhold Niebuhr, Antonin Bosch and Sir Bernard Pares. "The University of Chicago Roundtable," No. 351 (December 10).

1944

"Sovereignty and Peace." N, 159, no. 21 (November 18), 623.
    Review of Hans Kelsen's Peace Through Law.

"Stones From Glass Houses." CC, 4, no. 17 (October 16), 1-2.

"Survival and Religion." Contemporary Jewish Record, 7, no. 3
    (June), 239-246.
    A discussion of Waldo Frank's The Jew in Our Day.

"The Threat of Reaction." CS, 9, no. 4 (Fall), 8-9.

"Three Elements in Papal Leadership." CS, 9, no. 3 (Summer), 7-8.
    Reprinted in Essays in Applied Christianity.

["The Time for Decision." Review of Sumner Welles's The Time for
    Decision.] CC, 4, no. 15 (September 18), 2.

["Time Must Have a Stop." Review of Aldous Huxley's Time Must Have a
    Stop.] CS, 9, no. 4 (Fall), 47.

"The Unity and Depth of Our Culture." The Sewanee Review, 52, no. 2
    (April-June), 193-198.

"Vansittart's Obsession." N, 158, no. 1 (January 1), 20-21.
    Review of Lord Vansittart's Lessons of My Life.

"World War III Ahead?" N, 158, no. 13 (March 25), 356-358.

1945

"Anglo-Saxon Tensions." The Spectator, 174, no. 6086 (February 16),
    142-143.

"Answer to 'I Told You So.'" CC, 5, no. 8 (May 14), 8.
    Answer to a letter from a pacifist clergyman.

["Are Men Equal?" Review of H. A. Myers's Are Men Equal?] CS, 10
    no. 3 (Summer), 40.

"The Atomic Bomb." CS, 10, no. 4 (Fall), 3-5.
    Reprinted in Love and Justice.

"The Atomic Bomb." CS, 11, no. 1 (Winter), 3-4.

"The Atomic Issue." CC, 5, no. 17 (October 15), 5-7.

"A Catholic View." N, 161, no. 25 (December 22), 695-696.
    Review of F. E. McMahon's A Catholic Looks at the World.

"Chaim Weizmann." N, 160, no. 2 (January 13), 50-51.
    Review of Chaim Wiezmann, Statesman and Scientist, edited by
    M. Weisgal.

"Changing and Abiding Elements in the Human Situation." Current
    Religious Thought, 5, no. 6 (June), 23-28.

"Christian Faith and the Race Problem." CS, 10, no. 2 (Spring), 21-24.
> Reprinted in <u>Love and Justice</u>.

"The Coming Domestic Battle." CS, 10, no. 2 (Spring), 8-9.

"Concerning the Devil." N, 160, no. 7 (February 17), 188-189.
> Review of Denis de Rougement's <u>The Devil's Share</u>.

"The Conference of the 'Big Three.'" CC, 5, no. 3 (March 5), 1-2.

"The Contribution of Religion to Cultural Unity." The Hazen Pamphlets, No. 13, 12 pp.

"Croce Nods." N, 160, no. 11 (March 17), 310-311.
> Review of Benedetto Croce's <u>Politics and Morals</u>.

"The Death of a Martyr." CC, 5, no. 11 (June 25), 6-7.
> The Nazi murder of Dietrich Bonhoeffer.

"The Death of the President." CC, 5, no. 7 (April 30), 4-6.

"Dr. Merriam Sums Up." N, 161, no. 15 (October 13), 379-380.
> Review of C. E. Merriam's <u>Systematic Politics</u>.

"Editorial Notes." CC, 4, no. 23 (January 8), 2.
> Notes on Mr. Churchill and Greece; the reason for failure of international controls on aviation; and the tragedy in continued German resistance.

"Editorial Notes." CC, 5, no. 2 (February 19), 2.
> Notes on critical and uncritical loyalty to the nation; and pride of victors in war.

"Editorial Notes." CC, 5, no. 8 (May 14), 2.
> Note on the nonfraternization order of the American Army in Germany.

"Editorial Notes." CC, 5, no. 11 (June 25), 2.
> Note on deterioration of our relations with Russia and the causes for it.

"Editorial Notes." CS, 10, no. 4 (Fall), 9-11.
> Notes on Lend-Lease; the Murray-Wagner "full employment" bill; the Soviet-China pact; and the Potsdam agreements on the occupation of Germany.

"Editorial Notes." CC, 5, no. 19 (November 12), 2.
> Notes on vindictive passion among victorious peoples; trials and punishment of Nazis and/or Germans; and the French elections.

"Editorial Notes." CC, 5, no. 20 (November 26), 2.
> Note on the good and bad reasons for opposing the President's proposed new conscription act.

1945

"The End of the War." CS, 10, no. 4 (Fall), 5-7.

"The Epidemic of Strikes." CS, 11, no. 1 (Winter), 8-9.

["Fighting Liberal." Review of George W. Norris's Fighting Liberal.]
    CS, 10, no. 3 (Summer), 39.

"The Forms of Liberalism." N, 161, no. 21 (November 24), 553-554,
    556.
        Also in CS, 11, no. 1 (Winter), 42-43.

["Human Nature, The Marxian View." Review of Vernon Venable's Human
    Nature, The Marxian View.] CS, 10, no. 3 (Summer), 39.

"I Was Hungry." CC, 5, no. 5 (April 2), 6.

"If Thine Enemy Hunger Feed Him." CC, 5, no. 22 (December 24), 2.

"Introduction," to Christianity and the Cultural Crisis. By
    Charles D. Kean. New York: Association Press.

"Is This 'Peace in Our Time?'" N, 160, no. 14 (April 7), 382-384.

"The Jewish Case." N, 160, no. 25 (June 23), 701.
        Review of Ernst Frankenstein's Justice For My People.

"A Lecture to Liberals." N, 161, no. 19 (November 10), 491-493.

"Letter." The New York Times (June 10), p. 8.
        Letter on the denunciation of all Germans.

"A Living Process." N, 161, no. 20 (November 17), 526-527.
        Review of Carl L. Becker's Freedom and Responsibility in the
    American Way of Life. Also in CS, 11, no. 1 (Winter), 42-43.

"The Nonchalance of Faith." CS, 11, no. 1 (Winter), 9.

"Our Relations to Japan." CC, 5, no. 15 (September 17), 5-7.

"Our War With Japan." CS, 10, no. 3 (Summer), 9-10.

"The Outlines of Peace." CS, 10, no. 2 (Spring), 3-4.

["Philosophical Understanding and Religious Truth." Review of
    J. Frank's Philosophical Understanding and Religious Truth.]
    CS, 10, no. 2 (Spring), 37-38.

"The Plight of Germany." CS, 10, no. 2 (Spring), 6-8.

"Polemic Against Fatalism." N, 161, no. 2 (July 14), 40-41.
        Review of Jerome Frank's Fate and Freedom, a Philosophy for
    Free Americans.

1945

"Post-War Unemployment." CS, 10, no. 3 (Summer), 8.

["Re-Educating Germany." Review of Werner Richter's Re-Educating
   Germany.] The Union Review, 6, no. 2 (March), 25.
      Also in CS, 10, no. 2 (Spring), 36-37.

"Religious Faith and Historical Hope." CS, 10, no. 2 (Spring), 4-6.

["Religious Liberty." Review of M. Searle Bates's Religious Liberty,
   an Inquiry.] CS, 10, no. 4 (Fall), 36.
      Also in The Union Seminary Quarterly Review, 1, no. 1
   (November), 45.

"Roots of Our Thought." The New York Times Book Review (January 7),
   p. 4.
      Review of Ralph B. Perry's Puritanism and Democracy.

"Russia and Peace." Social Progress, 35, no. 5 (January), 8-9, 22-23.

"Russia and the West." CS, 10, no. 3 (Summer), 5-6.

"The Russian Enigma." CS, 11, no. 1 (Winter), 4-6.

"The San Francisco Conference." CS, 10, no. 3 (Summer), 3-5.
      Reprinted in Love and Justice.

"Soberness in Victory." CC, 5, no. 9 (May 28), 1-2.

"The Socialist Movement in Europe." CS, 11, no. 1 (Winter), 7-8.

"Spiritual Mobilization." CS, 10, no. 2 (Spring), 9-10.
      Reprinted in Love and Justice.

"The Spiritual Problem of the Coming Decades." CS, 10, no. 3
   (Summer), 7.

"Technics and the Generals." CS, 10, no. 3 (Summer), 9.
      Divorce of technics and morals by the German generals.

"Theologian and Church Statesman," in This Ministry, The Contribution
   of Henry S. Coffin. Edited by Reinhold Niebuhr. New York:
   Scribner's, pp. 117-128.

"Unfinished Debate." N, 160, no. 10 (March 10), 280.
      Review of Knight and Merriam's The Economic Order and Religion.

"The Vengeance of Victors." CC, 5, no. 20 (November 26), 1-2.

"The Victory of British Labor." CS, 10, no. 4 (Fall), 7-9.

"We're in to Stay." N, 160, no. 2 (January 13), 32-33.

"Which Question Comes First for the Church?" CC, 5, no. 19
   (November 12), 1-2.

"The Widow's Mite." CC, 5, no. 1 (February 5), 1-2.

"Will America Back Out?" N, 160, no. 2 (January 13), 42-43.

1945

"Will Civilization Survive Technics?" <u>Commentary</u>, 1, no. 2 (December), 2-8.
   First article in a series on "The Crisis of the Individual."

["World Order." Review of F. E. Johnson's <u>World Order</u>, along with MacIver's <u>Civilization and Group Relations</u>.] CS, 11, no. 1 (Winter), 43-44.

<u>1946</u>

["The Age of Jackson." Review of Arthur Schlesinger, Jr.'s <u>The Age of Jackson</u>.] CS, 11, no. 2 (Spring), 38-39.

"American Conservatism and European Politics." (RNS) M, 11, no. 25 (December 10), 6.

"The American Future." CS, 12, no. 1 (Winter), 5-6.

"The American Labor Movement." CS, 12, no. 1 (Winter), 6-8.

"American Liberals and British Labor." N, 162, no. 23 (June 8), 682-684.

"As Others See Us." CC, 6, no. 21 (December 9), 4-6.

"Berlin Impressions." (RNS) M, 11, no. 20 (October 1), 6.

"Catholic Politics in Europe." (RNS) M, 11, no. 18 (September 3), 7.

["Christian Ethics and Social Policy." Review of John Bennett's <u>Christian Ethics and Social Policy</u>.] CS, 12, no. 1 (Winter), 41.

["The Christian Significance of Karl Marx." Review of Alexander Miller's <u>The Christian Significance of Karl Marx</u>.] CS, 11, no. 2 (Spring), 39-40.

"The Church and the Kingdom." CS, 11, no. 2 (Spring), 3-4.
   A note on the "unusual identification of Christ and the church so familiar in Catholic thought."

"The Conflict Between Nations and Nations and Between Nations and God." CC, 6, no. 14 (August 5), 2-4.
   Reprinted in <u>Love and Justice</u>.

"The Crisis of Our Time." <u>The Listener</u>, 36, no. 921 (September 5), 299-300.

"Dietrich Bonhoeffer." <u>Union Seminary Quarterly Review</u>, 1, no. 3 (March), 3.

"The Ecumenical Issue in the United States." <u>Theology Today</u>, 2, no. 4 (January), 525-536.
   Reprinted in <u>Essays in Applied Christianity</u>.

1946

"Editorial Notes." CC, 6, no. 1 (February 4), 2.
Note on the British loan agreement.

"Editorial Notes." CC, 6, no. 3 (March 4), 2.
Notes on the food situation in Germany; the encouraging first
meeting of the U. N. Assembly; and on denouncing the use of the
atom bomb.

"Editorial Notes." CC, 6, no. 4 (March 18), 2.
Notes on the meeting of the provisional committee of the
World Council of Churches in Geneva; and the contrast of the
meeting of the Papal Consistory in Rome. The church, "whether
Catholic or Protestant, does not find it easy to validate the
principle that 'whosoever loseth his life for my sake shall find
it.'"

"Editorial Notes." CC, 6, no. 5 (April 1), 2.
Notes on our dealing with the starving world; the growing
tension between Russia and the West; civilian or military control of atomic energy; and the Federal Council Committee report
on the Christian attitude toward the atom bomb.

"Editorial Notes." CC, 6, no. 6 (April 15), 2.
Note on the Roman church and anti-Russian sentiment in this
country.

"Editorial Notes." CC, 6, no. 7 (April 29), 2.
Notes on the need for rationing; State Department proposal for
handling atomic energy; the Security Council and the disposal of
the Iranian issue; and the question of military conscription.

"Editorial Notes." CC, 6, no. 8 (May 13), 2.
Note on feeding hungry people and the need for food rationing
at home.

"Editorial Notes." CC, 6, no. 9 (May 27), 2.
Notes on tension among the nations; appeal of a national committee to President Truman to double food shipments to hungry
peoples; report of joint British-American Commission on Palestine;
and the election in France.

"Editorial Notes." CC, 6, no. 10 (June 10), 2.
Notes on Allied Coordinating Council's announcement on the
destruction of symbols of German militarism; reunification of
Germany; and the recovery of Europe retarded by the failure of
Russia and the West to agree on peace treaties.

"Editorial Notes." CC, 6, no. 11 (June 24), 2.
Notes on action of Presbyterian General Assembly and of U. S.
Senate on President's proposal to draft strikers in essential
industries; the railroad strike; individual initiative and the
necessities of feeding a hungry world; and "Christian Democratic"
parties in Holland, France and Italy.

1946

"Editorial Notes." CC, 6, no. 12 (July 8), 2.
   Notes on the Baruch Committee proposal; Bevan speech on
   Palestine criticizing American position; and the housing situa-
   tion in Germany.

"Editorial Notes." CC, 6, no. 15 (September 16), 2-3.
   Note on the conference on international relations of the World
   Council of Churches.

"Editorial Notes." CC, 6, no. 16 (September 30), 2-3.
   Notes on "random impressions" from Germany; reports of church
   conflict in Germany; and the "eschatological" meaning of the
   Christian faith in Germany.

"Editorial Notes." CC, 6, no. 17 (October 14), 1.
   Notes on Germany continued: the relief situation in Germany.

"Editorial Notes." CC, 6, no. 22 (December 23), 2.
   Note on British journal's criticism of American food policy--
   the justice and injustice of the criticism.

"Europe, Russia and America." N, 163, no. 11 (September 14), 288-289.

["Eyes of Faith." Review of Paul S. Minear's Eyes of Faith.] CS,
   12, no. 1 (Winter), 40-41.

"The Fight for Germany." Life, 21, no. 17 (October 21), 65-72.

"Germans Who Are Not Nazis." (RNS) M, 11, no. 21 (October 15), 6.

["God and the Atom." Review of Ronald Knox's God and the Atom.]
   CS, 11, no. 2 (Spring), 42-43.

"The Guilt of the Enemy." (RNS) M, 11, no. 26 (December 24), 10.

"I Was An Hungered and ye Gave Me No Meat!" CC, 5, no. 23
   (January 7), 5-6.

"Ideals and Hazards." N, 162, no. 1 (January 5), 21-22.
   Review of David Bryn-Jones's Toward a Democratic Order.

"The Ideological Factors in the World Situation." CS, 11, no. 3
   (Summer), 4-6.

"Ideology in the Social Struggle." CS, 11, no. 2 (Spring), 8-9.
   On N. A. M. propaganda about post-war industry. Reprinted in
   Love and Justice.

"The International Situation." CS, 11, no. 3 (Summer), 3-4.

"Is World Government Possible?" (RNS) M, 11, no. 16 (August 6), 6.

"Isolation of a Culture." (RNS) M, 11, no. 24 (November 26), 6.

["Justice and the Social Order." Review of Emil Brunner's Justice
   and the Social Order.] CS, 11, no. 3 (Summer), 41-42.

"Lessons From the Railroad Strike." (RNS) M, 11, no. 13 (June 25), 6.

"Letter." N, 162, no. 16 (April 20), 491-492.
     Reply to Clarence Streit's criticism of a statement by Niebuhr in his article "The Myth of World Government" (March 16).

"The Limits of Human Power." CS, 11, no. 2 (Spring), 3.

"Man's Defiance of God." Current Religious Thought, 6, no. 3 (March), 5-8.

"The Middle Way." CS, 12, no. 1 (Winter), 4-5.
     For Europe between conservatism and Communism.

"The Mistakes of Labor." CS, 11, no. 2 (Spring), 9-10.

"Mr. Wallace's Errors." CC, 6, no. 18 (October 28), 1-2.

"The Morals of an Occupation Army." CS, 12, no. 1 (Winter), 9-10.

"The Myth of World Government." N, 162, no. 11 (March 16), 312-314.

"The Nation is in Peril." CC, 6, no. 13 (July 22), 1.

"Neither War Nor Peace." (RNS) Basic, 1, no. 1 (December), 27.

"A New View of Palestine." The Spectator, 177, no. 6164 (August 16), 162-163.

"Our Constitutional Difficulties." CS, 12, no. 1 (Winter), 8-9.

"Our Proposals for Atomic Control." (RNS) M, 11, no. 15 (July 23), 7.

"Our Relations With Russia," in Toward a Better World. Edited by Bishop Will Scarlet. Philadelphia: John C. Winston Co., pp. 123-132.

"Palestine: British-American Dilemma." N, 163, no. 9 (August 31), 238-239.

"The Palestine Problem." (RNS) M, 11, no. 17 (August 20), 6.

"The Peril of America." CS, 11, no. 3 (Summer), 7-8.

"Positive Defense." CC, 6, no. 7 (April 29), 1-2.

"The Problem of Evangelical Christianity." CC, 6, no. 8 (May 13), 5-6.
     Reprinted in Essays in Applied Christianity.

"The Prospects for America." (RNS) M, 11, no. 23 (November 12), 6.

"Providence and Historical Confusion." CS, 11, no. 3 (Summer), 9-10.

"The Race Issue." CS, 11, no. 3 (Summer), 6-7.

"Rationing and the Food Crisis." (RNS) M, 11, no. 14 (July 9), 6.

1946

"Reinhold Niebuhr Insists." N, 162, no. 16 (April 20), 491-492.
     A letter critical of Clarence Streit's article "World Govern-
ment and Russia" and the "Union Now" movement, as being anti-
Russian and possibly leading to World War III.

"The Religious Level of the World Crisis." CC, 5, no. 24
     (January 21), 4-7.
     Originally published in The Christian News-Letter. Supplement
No. 246 (October 31), 5-11.

"A Report From Germany." CC, 6, no. 17 (October 14), 6-7.

"A Report on Great Britain." CS, 11, no. 4 (Fall), 5-6.

"The Russian and American Race." CS, 11, no. 2 (Spring), 6-7.

"Russia and the West." (RNS) M, 11, no. 19 (September 17), 7.

"The Russian Revolution." N, 162, no. 20 (May 18), 602-603.
     Review of Nicholas Timasheff's The Great Retreat, along with
Kravchenko's I Chose Freedom and Casey's Religion in Russia.
Timasheff is also reviewed in CS, 11, no. 3 (Summer), 43.

"Scientists and International Order." (RNS) M, 11, no. 22
     (October 29), 6.

"Technics, Logic and Salvation." CS, 11, no. 2 (Spring), 4-6.

"Unitarian Polemics." CS, 11, no. 3 (Summer), 10-11.

"The United Nations." CS, 12, no. 1 (Winter), 3-4.

"Victors' Justice: The War Crimes Trials." Common Sense, 15, no. 1
     (January), 6-9.

"We Face Inflation." CS, 11, no. 4 (Fall), 3-5.

"Will Germany Go Communist?" N, 163, no. 14 (October 5), 371-373.

"World Community and World Government." CC, 6, no. 3 (March 4), 5-6.

"The World Situation." CS, 11, no. 4 (Fall), 3.

1947

"American Power and European Health." CC, 7, no. 10 (June 9), 1-2.

"American Scene." The Spectator, 178, no. 6086 (February 14), 198.

"American Tolerance." (RNS) Basic, 1, no. 8 (July), 27, 32.

"American Wealth and the World's Poverty." CS, 12, no. 4 (Autumn),
     3-4.

"America's Precarious Eminence." The Virginia Quarterly Review, 23,
     no. 4 (Autumn), 481-490.

["Bridge or Battleground." Review of James P. Warburg's Bridge or
  Battleground.] CS, 12, no. 4 (Autumn), 27–28.

"Britain and Zionism." (RNS) Basic, 1, no. 7 (June), 31–32.

"British and American Ideologies." CS, 12, no. 4 (Autumn), 4–5.

"The Character of Ideology." CS, 12, no. 3 (Summer), 4–5.

"Children Pay for Unstable Homes." (RNS) M, 12, no. 12 (June 10), 6.

"Christianity as a Basis for Democracy." The Listener, 37
  (January 9), 64–65, 68–69.

"The Churches and the International Situation." CS, 12, no. 3
  (Summer), 7–8.

"The Church's Self-Degradation." (RNS) M, 12, no. 20 (September 30),
  7.

"The Clock Does Not Stop." (RNS), M, 12, no. 25 (December 9), 6.

"Democracy as a Religion." CC, 7, no. 14 (August 4), 1–2.

"The Difficult Role of America." (RNS) M, 12, no. 9 (April 29), 7.

"The Dilemma of Modern Man." N, 164, no. 8 (February 22), 205–209.

"Dishonest Praise." Basic, 1, no. 5 (April), 27–28.

"Editorial Correspondence." CC, 7, no. 3 (March 3), 6.
  Notes on moral and spiritual comparisons between Britain and
  America; fear of American economic failure; and what we may learn
  on the art of worship from the Scottish church.

"Editorial Correspondence." CC, 7, no. 5 (March 31), 6–7.
  Notes on the difficulties of understanding between Britain and
  America; prospective debate on British governmental decision on
  India; and Britain and Palestine.

"Editorial Correspondence (from Amsterdam)." CC, 7, no. 6
  (April 14), 6.
  Notes on the religious situation in Holland and Holland's rela-
  tion to the international situation.

"Editorial Correspondence." CC, 7, no. 6 (April 28), 6.
  Notes on the Ecumenical Institute.

"Editorial Correspondence (from Britain)." CS, 12, no. 2 (Spring),
  3–4.

"Editorial Notes." CC, 12, no. 1 (February 3), 2.
  Notes on developments in the Atomic Energy Commission; the
  luxury tax; and continued hunger in Germany.

"Editorial Notes." CC, 7, no. 2 (February 17), 2.
  Notes on the press campaign against Pastor Niemoeller.

1947

"Editorial Notes." CC, 7, no. 9 (May 26), 2.
Notes on the difficulties of international understanding; and
journalistic encouragement of the view that we are engulfed by
hysterical hatred of Russia.

"Editorial Notes." CC, 7, no. 12 (July 7), 2.
Notes on the encouraging developments in India and the
Communist regime in Hungary.

"Editorial Notes." CC, 7, no. 13 (July 21), 2.
Notes on the failure of the foreign ministers to agree on the
Marshall plan and Protestant excitement over Roman Catholic chil-
dren riding in state-owned buses.

"Editorial Notes." CC, 7, no. 14 (August 4), 2.
Notes on the Marshall Plan and our position on German
rehabilitation.

"Editorial Notes." CC, 7, no. 22 (December 22), 6.
Notes taking exception to Dr. Alec Vidler's criticism (in this
issue) of American religious pluralism.

"European Impressions." CC, 7, no. 8 (May 12), 2-4.

"Facts of Life." L, 30, no. 4 (October 22), 21.
Reasons why the Marshall Plan will be approved.

"Faith and Optimism." (RNS) M, 12, no. 23 (November 11), 7.

"Faith and the Future." (RNS) M, 12, no. 2 (January 21), 8.
Also in Basic, 1, no. 3 (February), 19.

"The Food Problem in Germany." (RNS) M, 12, no. 13 (June 24), 6.

"Freedom and Justice." (RNS) M, 12, no. 7 (April 1), 7.

"The German Tragedy." N, 165, no. 3 (July 19), 76.
Review of W. L. White's Report on the Germans.

"Great Britain's Opportunity." The Listener, 37, no. 950 (April 10),
527-528, 551.

"Honesty and Logic in Public Affairs." (RNS) M, 12, no. 1
(January 7), 8.
Also in Basic, 1, no. 2 (January), 21.

"Labor Coalition in Holland." N, 164, no. 16 (April 19), 447-448.

"Letter." The New York Times (June 16), p. 2.
Letter to President Truman urging the U. S. to change its
policy in Germany.

"Letter." The New York Times (October 10), p. 24.
On a reported accord between the Pastor Niemoeller faction and
the German Social Democratic Party.

Other Writings by Reinhold Niebuhr

"Letter." The New York Times (November 26), p. 22.
Backing Palestine partition.

"Looking at America From Sweden." L, 29, no. 34 (May 21), 12.

"Lynn Harold Hough in Detroit." The Drew Gateway, 18, no. 3 (Spring), 37.

"Man: The Creature and the Master of Fate." (RNS) Basic, 1, no. 4 (March), 23-24.

"The Marshall Plan." CC, 7, no. 17 (October 13), 2.

["Modern Nationalism and Religion." Review of Salo Baron's Modern Nationalism and Religion.] CS, 12, no. 4 (Autumn), 30-31.

"The Morals of Occupation Armies." L, 29, no. 25 (March 19), 20.
Also in M, 12, no. 11 (May 27), 8.

"Moslems and Hindus." CS, 12, no. 4 (Autumn), 7-8.

"The National Manufacturers Association and the Clergy." CS, 12, no. 4 (Autumn), 5-6.

"The New Flow of Exiles." (RNS) M, 12, no. 5 (March 4), 6.

"Niemoeller--Not a Nazi." N, 164, no. 14 (April 5), 407.
A letter to the Editor.

"The Organization of the Liberal Movement." CS, 12, no. 2 (Spring), 8-10.

"Orientation of the Social Sciences to Citizenship." Addresses at the Installation of Paul H. Appleby as Dean. Syracuse University: The Maxwell Graduate School of Citizenship and Public Affairs, May 11, pp. 7-19, 31-32.

"Our Chances for Peace." CC, 7, no. 2 (February 17), 1-2.

"Our Immigration Policy." (RNS) M, 12, no. 6 (March 18), 6.

"Our Niggardly Giving." (RNS) M, 12, no. 24 (November 25), 6.

"Our Relations With Catholicism." CC, 7, no. 15 (September 15), 5-7.
Reprinted in Essays in Applied Christianity.

"The Plight of Europe." (RNS) M, 12, no. 10 (May 13), 6.

"Preaching the Gospel in Our Age." CS, 12, no. 3 (Summer), 3-4.

"Race and the United Nations." (RNS) M, 12, no. 3 (February 4), 6.

"The Race Issue in Parochial Schools." (RNS) M, 12, no. 21 (October 14), 7.

"The Republicans and Labor." CS, 12, no. 3 (Summer), 8.

"The Resources of the Nations." CS, 12, no. 3 (Summer), 5-7.

1947

"The Reunion of the Church Through the Renewal of the Churches."
    CC, 7, no. 20 (November 24), 5-7.
        Reprinted in Essays in Applied Christianity.

["Scientific Man Versus Power Politics." Review of Hans J.
    Morgenthau's Scientific Man Versus Power Politics.] CS, 12,
    no. 2 (Spring), 33-34.

"Separation of Church and State." (RNS) M, 12, no. 16 (August 5), 21.

"The Situation in Germany." (RNS) M, 12, no. 8 (April 15), 6.

"Specialists Without Conscience." (RNS) M, 12, no. 22 (October 28),
    6.

"The Spiritual Problem of Youth." (RNS) M, 12, no. 18 (September 2),
    6.

"The Struggle of the Churches." (RNS) M, 12, no. 19 (September 16),
    7.

"The Tension Between Marxism and Christianity on the Continent."
    CS, 12, no. 3 (Summer), 9-11.

"They All Fear America." CCY, 64, no. 34 (August 16), 993-994.

"The Third Party." CS, 12, no. 4 (Autumn), 8.

"The Triumph of India." (RNS) M, 12, no. 14 (July 8), 6.

"Two Forms of Utopianism." CS, 12, no. 4 (Autumn), 6-7.
        About the liberal and Communist creeds.

"Two Ways With the Vanquished." (RNS) M, 12, no. 17 (August 19), 6.

"Unfair to Niemoeller." (RNS) M, 12, no. 4 (February 18), 6.

"The Virtues and Weaknesses of Our Nation." (RNS) M, 12, no. 15
    (July 22), 9.

"What's Behind the Price of Meat?" L, 29, no. 41 (July 9), 15-16.

1948

"American Pride and Power." The American Scholar, 17, no. 4
    (Autumn), 393-394.

"Americanism in Hollywood." CS, 13, no. 1 (Winter), 4-5.

"America's Eminence." CS, 13, no. 3 (Summer), 3-4.

"Amid Encircling Gloom." CC, 8, no. 6 (April 12), 41-42.

"The Amsterdam Achievements." L, 30, no. 53 (September 29), 12.
        Also in M, 13, no. 21 (October 12), 4.

"The Army and Race." (RNS) M, 13, no. 4 (February 17), 6.

1948

"Babel and Pentecost." CC, 8, no. 16 (October 4), 121-122.

"The Battle of Berlin." CS, 13, no. 4 (Autumn), 5-6.

"Can the Church Give a Moral Lead?" CC, 8, no. 14 (August 2), 105-106.
    Reprinted in Essays in Applied Christianity.

"Can we Avoid Catastrophe?" CCY, 65, no. 21 (May 26), 504-506.

"Churches and Society." The New Statesman and Nation, 36, no. 915 (September 18), 232-233.
    Essentially the same as "Protestantism in a Disordered World." N (September 18). See below.

"Churchill's Hour." N, 166, no. 26 (June 26), 720-721.
    Review of Winston Churchill's The Gathering Storm.

"Communism and Socialism in Europe." CS, 13, no. 1 (Winter), 5-6.

"Dangerous Decisions." L, 30, no. 43 (July 21), 19.

"Dark Light on Human Nature." L, 30, no. 24 (March 10), 20.
    Also in M, 13, no. 9 (April 27), 7.

"Editorial Notes." CC, 7, no. 24 (January 19), 2.
    Notes on difficulties in carrying out Economic Recovery Program; relation between domestic and foreign policy; and Wallace's announcement of candidacy for the Presidency.

"Editorial Notes." CC, 8, no. 2 (February 16), 10.
    Notes on pacifist opposition to E. R. P. and hopeful signs in Europe.

"Editorial Notes." CC, 8, no. 3 (March 1), 2.
    Notes on the inadequacy of the "de-Nazification" procedure.

"Editorial Notes." CC, 8, no. 5 (March 29), 34.
    Notes on Supreme Court Decision in Champaign, Illinois, case.

"Editorial Notes." CC, 8, no. 6 (April 12), 42.
    Notes on Masaryk's suicide and dangers in the Palestine situation.

"Editorial Notes." CC, 8, no. 9 (May 24), 66.
    Notes on Hromadka and the Christian stand against Communist maneuvers in East Germany.

"Editorial Notes." CC, 8, no. 19 (November 15), 146.
    Notes on the question of guilt in the German trials and The Christian Century's accusation that Israel is a "Godless" state.

"The Electoral Campaign." (RNS) M, 13, no. 20 (September 28), 15.

"Evading the Issue." CS, 13, no. 4 (Autumn), 6.
    Note on the Republican campaign strategy.

1948

"The Federation of Western Europe." CC, 8, no. 3 (March 1), 17-18.

"For Peace, We Must Risk War." Life, 25, no. 12 (September 20), 38-39.

"Foreword," to The University and the Modern World. By A. N. Nash. New York: Macmillan Co., pp. xii-xiii.

"The Forgotten Human Being." N, 166, no. 9 (June 26), 246-247.
     Review of V. Gollancz's Our Threatened Values.

"Frontier Fellowship." CS, 13, no. 4 (Autumn), 3.

"The Future of Israel." (RNS) M, 13, no. 12 (June 8), 6.

"The German Tragedy." N, 167, no. 2 (July 10), 50-51.
     Review of G. Barraclough's The Origin of Modern Germany, along with Karl Jaspers's The Question of German Guilt.

"The Glories of Free Enterprise." CS, 13, no. 2 (Spring), 6-7.

"The Godly and the Godless." CC, 8, no. 21 (December 13), 161-162.
     Reprinted in Essays in Applied Christianity.

"God's Design and the Present Disorder of Civilisation," introductory paper in The Church and the Disorder of Society. Volume III of the Amsterdam Studies. New York: Harper and Brothers, pp. 13-28.

"Gratitude Among Men and Nations." L, 30, no. 46 (August 11), 50.

"Het Christelijk getuigenis," in Wereld-conferentie, Amsterdam, pp. 91-102.
     Niebuhr's Amsterdam address.

"Housewife on Strike." L, 30, no. 20 (February 11), 22.

"The Impact of Protestantism Today." Atlantic, 181, no. 2 (February), 57-62.

"The Individual and the Modern World." (RNS) M, 13, no. 15 (July 20), 6.

"International Relations and the Personal Touch." (RNS) M, 13, no. 10 (May 11), 6.

"The Italian Elections." CS, 13, no. 3 (Summer), 7-8.

"The Kinsey Report." CS, 13, no. 4 (Autumn), 6-7.

["Man for Himself." Review of Erich Fromm's Man for Himself.]
     CS, 13, no. 2 (Spring), 26-27.

"Meditation on the Election." (RNS) M, 13, no. 24 (November 23), 7.

"Military and Moral Defense." (RNS) M, 13, no. 11 (May 25), 8.

["The Misinterpretation of Man." Review of Paul Roubizek's The Misinterpretation of Man.] CS, 13, no. 1 (Winter), 29.

1948

"Moral Responsibility in a Technical Society." L, 30, no. 45 (August 4), 16.

"The Morality of Nations." CS, 13, no. 2 (Spring), 7-8.

"The Morality of Nations." (RNS) M, 13, no. 16 (August 3), 6.

"Morals and Politics." CS, 13, no. 3 (Summer), 5.

"No Time for Hysteria." (RNS) M, 13, no. 8 (April 13), 6.
    Also in L, 30, no. 31 (April 28), 14-15.

"One World or None." CC, 8, no. 2 (February 16), 9-10.

"Our Free Society." (RNS) M, 13, no. 6 (March 16), 6.

"Our Spiritual Pilgrimage From a Century of Hope to a Century of Perplexity." Current Religious Thought, 8, no. 9 (November), 20-27.

"Palestine." CS, 13, no. 2 (Spring), 5-6.

"The Partition of Palestine." CS, 13, no. 1 (Winter), 3-4.

"Prayers," in To Will One Thing. St. Louis: Diocese of Missouri, pp. 3, 40, 92.

"The Presidential Campaign." CC, 8, no. 18 (November 1), 137-138.

"The Pride of a Righteous Nation." (RNS) M, 13, no. 26 (December 21), 7.
    Also in L, 31, no. 31 (May 4, 1949), 17.

"Progress Toward Maturity." CS, 13, no. 1 (Winter), 7-9.

"Prospects for 1948." (RNS) M, 13, no. 2 (January 20), 7.

"Protestantism in a Disordered World." A Report on the first meeting of the World Council of Churches." N, 167, no. 12 (September 18), 311-313.
    Reprinted in Essays in Applied Christianity.

"Protestants, Catholics and Secularists." CS, 13, no. 2 (Spring), 4-5.

["The Reconstruction of Humanity." Review of P. A. Sorokin's The Reconstruction of Humanity.] CS, 13, no. 3 (Summer), 29.

"Religion and Free Speech." L, 31, no. 5 (November 3), 50.

"Religion and Tolerance." (RNS) M, 13, no. 13 (June 22), 6.
    Also in L, 30, no. 39 (June 23), 18.

"Religion in the State of Israel." (RNS) M, 13, no. 25 (December 7), 6.

"Revision of the United Nations Charter." CS, 13, no. 3 (Summer), 8.

1948

["Russia's Europe." Review of Hal Ehram's Russia's Europe.] CS, 13, no. 1 (Winter), 27.

"Secularism and Christianity." (RNS) M, 13, no. 1 (January 6), 7.

"Sex Standards in America." CC, 8, no. 9 (May 24), 65-66.

"Should Churches be Optimistic?" L, 30, no. 23 (March 3), 15-16.

"The Sickness of American Culture." N, 166, no. 9 (March 6), 267-270.

"The Sin of Racial Prejudice." (RNS) M, 13, no. 3 (February), 6.

"The Situation in the U.S.A.," in The Church and the Disorder of Society. Volume III, Amsterdam Series. New York: Harper and Brothers, Chapter 6, pp. 80-82.

"Socialism and Christianity in Europe." CS, 13, no. 1 (Winter), 6-7.

"Spiritual Mobilization." CS, 13, no. 2 (Spring), 8-9.

"Success of a Mission." N, 166, no. 1 (January 3), 22-23.
    Review of J. G. Winant's Letter From Grosvenor Square.

"The 'Third Force' in Europe." (RNS) M, 13, no. 5 (March 2), 6.
    Also in CS, 12, no. 2 (Spring), 3-4.

"Two Forms of Tyranny." CC, 8, no. 1 (February 2), 3-5.

"The Unitary Man." N, 166, no. 12 (March 20), 328-329.
    Review of L. L. Whyte's The Next Development of Man.

"The United and Divided Church." (RNS) M, 13, no. 22 (October 26), 8.

["Unknown Germany." Review of Hanna Hofkesbrink's Unknown Germany.] CS, 13, no. 3 (Summer), 28-29.

"Wallace and War." (RNS) M, 13, no. 7 (March 30), 7.

"We are Men and Not God." CCY, 65, no. 43 (October 27), 1138-1140.
    Also in The Christian News-Letter, no. 323 (October 27), 11-16.
    Reprinted in Essays in Applied Christianity.

"What is Necessary is Not Always Possible." L, 31, no. 10 (December 8), 14-15.
    Difficulties in establishing a world government.

"What Shall We Do?" CS, 13, no. 3 (Summer), 5-7.

"What to Expect at Amsterdam." L, 30, no. 49 (September 1), 13.

"Women in the Church." (RNS) M, 13, no. 23 (November 9), 6.
    The discussion at Amsterdam.

"The World Council at Amsterdam." CC, 8, no. 15 (September 20), 114-116.
    Also printed in Union Seminary Quarterly Review, 4, no. 1 (November), 11-14. Reprinted in Essays in Applied Christianity.

1949

"The World Council at Amsterdam." The Pastor, 12, no. 4 (December),
    4-5.

"The World Council of Churches." (RNS) M, 13, no. 17 (August 24), 7.

"The World Council of Churches." CS, 13, no. 4 (Autumn), 3-5.
    Reprinted in Essays in Applied Christianity.

"The World State: Illusions and Realities." N, 166, no. 21
    (May 22), 578.
    Review of Crane Brinton's From Many One.

1949

"The American Scene." CS, 14, no. 1 (Winter), 3-4.

"Amsterdamer Fragen und Antworten," in Theologische Existenz Heute.
    By Barth, Danielou and Niebuhr. Munich: Chr. Kaiser Verlag,
    NS No. 15.

"An Answer to Karl Barth." CCY, 66, no. 8 (February 23), 234-236.
        Also in The Christian News-Letter, no. 332(March 2), 11-16. Re-
    printed in Essays in Applied Christianity.

"At Our Wit's End." M, 14, no. 23 (December 6), 9.

"The Attitude of Europeans to Americans." M, 14, no. 6 (March 15), 7.

"Backwoods Genius." N, 169, no. 27 (December 31), 648.
    Review of Perry Miller's Jonathan Edwards.

"Blind Leaders." CS, 14, no. 2 (Spring), 5-6.

"British Socialism." CS, 14, no. 2 (Spring), 7-8.

"The Christian Witness in the Social and National Order." The Con-
    gregational Quarterly, 27, no. 1 (January), 18-24.
        Address delivered at the First Assembly of the World Council
    of Churches, Amsterdam. Reprinted as Chapter 8 of Christian
    Realism and Political Problems from S.C.M. Press publication.

"Christians and the State of Israel." CS, 14, no. 3 (Summer), 3-5.

"Communism and Christianity in Asia." CS, 14, no. 3 (Summer), 7-8.

"The Crisis Between Britain and America." M, 14, no. 17
    (September 13), 7.

"The Cult of Freedom in America." CC, 9, no. 1 (February 7), 4-7.

"The Dilemma in China." M, 14, no. 1 (January 4), 7.

"Editorial Notes." CC, 8, no. 23 (January 10), 178-179.
        Notes on prosecutor Kempner and the Nuremberg Trials, and the
    debate in New York on divorce laws as illustrating the difficul-
    ties in Protestant-Catholic relations.

1949

"Editorial Notes." CC, 9, no. 2 (February 12), 10.
Notes on Cardinal Mindszenty's trial and the problem of break-
ing the vicious circle of mistrust between Russia and ourselves.

"Editorial Notes." CC, 9, no. 3 (March 7), 18.
Notes on the Roman church claim never to act from worldly
motives and the Soviet claim always to base diplomacy on "the
scientific analysis of objective reality."

"Editorial Notes." CC, 9, no. 9 (May 30), 66–67.
Notes on the Weizsaeker case as illustrating the grave perils
of "victors' justice."

"Editorial Notes." CC, 9, no. 18 (October 31), 138.
Notes on the Episcopal convention's refusal to seat women
delegates and the Russian formation of the "Free German Republic."

"Freedom as a Luxury." CS, 14, no. 4 (Autumn), 8–9.
Reprinted in Love and Justice.

"The French Dilemma." CS, 14, no. 1 (Winter), 6–7.

"Germany: Vengeance or Justice." N, 169, no. 4 (July 23), 90–92.
Review of Freda Utley's The High Cost of Vengeance, along with
Warburg's Last Call for Common Sense.

"Hazards and Resources." The Virginia Quarterly Review, 25, no. 2
(Spring), 194–204.

"The Heart of the Argument." N, 168, no. 17 (April 25), 480.
Review of Francis Biddle's The World's Best Hope.

"The Illusion of World Government." Foreign Affairs, 27, no. 3
(April), 379–388.
Reprinted by the Graphics Group, Whitestone, N. Y., 30 pp.
Reprinted as Chapter 2 of Christian Realism and Political Prob-
lems, and in The World Crisis and American Responsibility.

"The Middle Class in the Coming Decade." CS, 14, no. 1 (Winter),
4–5.

"The Miscalculation of Modern Man." M, 14, no. 4 (February 15), 6.

"The Nation and the International Community." M, 14, no. 19
(October 11), 11.

"The Nemesis of Nations." M, 14, no. 9 (April 26), 6.

"The New 'Fair Deal.'" CS, 14, no. 2 (Spring), 6–7.

"The North Atlantic Pact." CC, 9, no. 9 (May 30), 65–66.

"Our Uneasy Peace." CS, 14, no. 1 (Winter), 7–8.

"Peace Through Cultural Cooperation." CC, 9, no. 17 (October 17),
131–133.

Reprinted in part as "The Limits of Cultural Cooperation," and in The World Crisis and American Responsibility.

"The Plight of China." CS, 14, no. 1 (Winter), 5-6.

"Plutocracy and World Responsibilities." CS, 14, no. 4 (Autumn), 6-8.

"Politics in the Church." L, 31, no. 50 (September 14), 19.

"Preface," to The Cost of Discipleship. By Dietrich Bonhoeffer. New York: Macmillan.

"The Pride of a Righteous Nation." L, 31, no. 31 (May 4), 17.

"Providence and Human Decisions." CC, 8, no. 24 (January 24), 185-186.

"The Real Enemy." M, 16, no. 17 (August 23), 17.
    Not listed for the most part as RNS (Religious News Service); last RNS release was December 25, 1948, but several articles were published in journals formerly receiving RNS releases.

"Religion and Modern Knowledge," in Man's Destiny in Eternity. Edited by A. H. Compton. Boston: The Beacon Press, pp. 117-135.

"The Rising Catholic-Protestant Tension." CC, 9, no. 14 (August 8), 106-108.
    Reprinted in Essays in Applied Christianity.

["The Russian Idea." Review of N. Berdyaev's The Russian Idea.] Religion in Life, 18, no. 2 (Spring), 239-242.

"Socialized Medicine in Britain." CS, 14, no. 4 (Autumn), 5-6.
    Reprinted in Love and Justice.

"The Spirit and Mechanism of Partnership." CC, 9, no. 16 (October 3), 121-122.
    Partnership between Britain and the U. S.

"The Spiritual Dimension." M, 14, no. 2 (January 18), 6.

"The Spiritual Weakness of the Third Force." CS, 14, no. 3 (Summer), 5-7.

"Sports and the Race Issue." M, 14, no. 3 (February 1), 6.

"Streaks of Dawn in the Night." CC, 9, no. 21 (December 12), 162-164.
    Signs of better international situation.

"The Validation of the Christian View of Life and History." Theology Today, 6, no. 1 (April), 31-48.
    Reprinted as Chapter 10 of Faith and History.

"We Have This Treasure in Earthen Vessels." CS, 14, no. 4 (Autumn), 3-5.
    Fragmentariness of life evident too in international affairs.

1949

"What is a 'Spiritual Crisis?'" L, 31, no. 14 (January 5), 18.

"What is Justice?" CS, 14, no. 1 (Winter), 8.

"The Wisdom of the World." CS, 14, no. 2 (Spring), 3-5.

1950

"Big and Little Decision." L, 32, no. 24 (March 15), 19.

"The British Elections." CS, 12, no. 2 (Spring), 7-8.

"Can They Be Organized?" N, 171, no. 20 (November 11), 447.
    A letter answering A. Z. Carr's criticism of Niebuhr's review
of Carr's book, Truman, Stalin and Peace. Niebuhr questions the
possibility of a "third force" in Asia.

"Can We Legalize Mercy Killings?" Quick (March 6), 22-28.
    "Yes" by Dr. C. F. Potter; "No" by Niebuhr.

"The Captive Churches." CC, 10, no. 19 (November 13), 145-146.

"The Christian Conscience and Atomic War." CC, 10, no. 21
(December 11), 161.

"The Christmas Story." The Louisville Courier-Journal (Associated
Press release) (December 24).

"Communism in China." CS, 15, no. 1 (Winter), 6-7.

"The Conditions of Our Survival." The Virginia Quarterly Review, 26,
no. 4 (Autumn), 481-491.

"The Dignity of Man." M, 15, no. 22 (November 21), 5.
    Also in L, 33, no. 8 (November 22), 22-23.

"Editorial Notes." CC, 9, no. 23 (January 9), 178.
    Notes on the U. N. and the problem of Israel, particularly the
plan to internationalize Jerusalem.

"Editorial Notes." CC, 10, no. 1 (February 6), 2.
    Notes on the perplexities associated with the possible decision
to make the H bomb.

"Editorial Notes." CC, 10, no. 2 (February 20), 10.
    Notes on the eleven scientists' proposal on the H bomb.

"Editorial Notes." CC, 10, no. 17 (October 16), 130.
    Notes on Korea.

"Editorial Notes." CC, 10, no. 20 (November 27), 154.
    Notes on the Communist issue in the election and the relation
of Roman Catholicism to McCarthyism.

"Editorial Notes." CC, 10, no. 22 (December 25), 170.
   Notes on the military disaster in Korea and the division among the nation's leaders over the concentration of interest in Europe as against Asia.

"Fair Employment Practices Act." CS, 15, no. 3 (Summer), 3-5.
   Reprinted in Love and Justice.

"The False Defense of Christianity." CC, 10, no. 10 (June 12), 73-74.

"The False God of Freedom." M, 15, no. 14 (July 18), 8.
   Also in L, 32, no. 42 (July 19), 22-23.

"The Fifty-Fifty Split in Modern Culture." CS, 15, no. 3 (Summer), 5.

["The Gentleman and the Jew." Review of M. Samuel's The Gentleman and the Jew.] N, 171, no. 14 (September 30), 292.

"Grace and Self-Acceptance." L, 32, no. 29 (April 19), 25.
   Also in M, 15, no. 9 (April 25), 6.

"The Grace of Christ." M, 15, no. 7 (March 28), 6.

"Halfway to What?" N, 170, no. 2 (January 14), 26-28.
   An answer to the critics of the "Welfare State."

"Has the Church any Authority?" CC, 10, no. 5 (April 3), 35-36.
   Reprinted in Essays in Applied Christianity.

"The Hydrogen Bomb." CS, 15, no. 2 (Spring), 5-7.
   Reprinted in Love and Justice.

"The Hydrogen Bomb." M, 15, no. 5 (February 28), 7.

"The Idolatry of America." CS, 15, no. 2 (Spring), 3-5.
   Reprinted in Love and Justice.

"The Increasing Isolation of the Catholic Church." CC, 10, no. 15 (September 18), 113-114.
   Reprinted in Essays in Applied Christianity.

"Is There a Revival of Religion?" The New York Times Magazine (November 19), pp. 13, 60, 62-63.

"Justice and Love." CS, 15, no. 4 (Fall), 6-8.
   Reprinted in Love and Justice.

"Land Reform in Italy." CS, 15, no. 1 (Winter), 7, 33.

"Law and Grace." L, 32, no. 37 (June 14), 20.
   Also in M, 15, no. 13 (June 20), 5.

["The Life of Mahatma Gandhi." Review of Louis Fischer's The Life of Mahatma Gandhi.] NL, 33, no. 37 (September 16), 20-21.

1950

"The Long Cold War." N, 171, no. 17 (October 21), 368-369.
    Review of A. Z. Carr's <u>Truman, Stalin, and Peace</u>.

"Messianic Men." N, 171, no. 10 (September 2), 212.
    Review of Walter Schubart's <u>Russia and Western Man</u>.

"The National Study Conference on the Church and Economic Life."
    CC, 10, no. 3 (March 6), 22-23.

"New Light on the Old Struggle." CS, 15, no. 4 (Fall), 3-4.
    Differences between Nazi and Communist aggression.

"No Man is Good." L, 32, no. 26 (March 29), 18-19.

"Our Position in Asia." CS, 15, no. 3 (Summer), 6-7.

"Our Resources for the Struggle." CS, 15, no. 4 (Fall), 4-5.

"The Peril of Hysteria." CS, 15, no. 4 (Fall), 5-6.

"The Pope's Domesticated God." CCY, 67, no. 3 (January 18), 74-75.
    Reprinted in <u>Essays in Applied Christianity</u>.

"Preventive War is Immoral." M, 15, no. 19 (October 10), 5.
    Also in L, 33, no. 2 (October 11), 18-19.

"The Problem of Our Prosperity." M, 15, no. 17 (September 12), 7.
    Also in L, 32, no. 51 (September 20), 24-25.

"A Protest Against a Dilemma's Two Horns." <u>World Politics</u>, 2, no. 3
    (April), 338-344.
    Dilemma: idealists' world government and inevitable war.

"The Quaker Way." CS, 15, no. 1 (Winter), 4-6.
    Reprinted in <u>Love and Justice</u>.

"Redemption by Negation." N, 171, no. 23 (December 2), 511-512.
    Review of A. W. Watts's <u>The Supreme Identity</u>.

"The Relevance of Reformation Doctrine in Our Day," in <u>The Heritage</u>
    <u>of the Reformation</u>. Edited by E. J. F. Arndt. New York:
    R. R. Smith, pp. 249-264.

"The Role of the Newspaper in America's Function as the Greatest
    World Power." Minneapolis, May 26, 9 pp.
    The Fourth Annual Memorial Lecture, The Twin Cities Chapter of
    the American Newspaper Guild and the School of Journalism, the
    University of Minnesota.

"Search for Hope." N, 170, no. 10 (March 11), 232-233.
    Review of H. S. Hughes's <u>An Essay for Our Times</u>.

"The Second Focus of the Fellowship." CS, 15, no. 1 (Winter), 21-22.
    Discussion, with Paul Tillich and Eduard Heimann, of the mean-
    ing of eliminating the word "Socialist" from "The Fellowship of
    Socialist Christians" and the change to the name "The Frontier
    Fellowship."

1951

"The Second Half of the Century." M, 15, no. 2 (January 17), 9.
     Considers hazards not subject to reason or technics.

"Should We Be Consistent?" CC, 10, no. 1 (February 6), 1-2.

"The Simplified Goal." CS, 15, no. 3 (Summer), 7-9.
     Is it possible to achieve the motive power of Nazis and
Communists?

"The Soviet Reality." N, 171, no. 13 (September 23), 270-271.
     Review of Barrington Moore's <u>Soviet Politics: The Dilemma of</u>
<u>Power</u>.

"The Spirit of Justice." CS, 15, no. 3 (Summer), 5-6.
     Reprinted in <u>Love and Justice</u>.

"The Theory and Practice of UNESCO." <u>International Organization</u>, 4,
     no. 1 (February), 3-11.

"To Moscow and Back." N, 170, no. 4 (January 28), 88-90.
     Review of <u>The God That Failed</u>, edited by Crossman.

"Utilitarian Christianity and the World Crisis." CC, 10, no. 9
     (May 29), 66-69.
     Reprinted in <u>Essays in Applied Christianity</u>.

"We Are Responsible." M, 15, no. 11 (May 23), 6.
     Man's choice remains meaningful. Also in L, 32, no. 33
     (May 17), 27.

"What Can We Do?" CS, 15, no. 1 (Winter), 3-4.
     Schemes of the voluntarists and determinists in international
relations.

"The World Council and the Peace Issue." CC, 10, no. 14 (August 7),
     107-108.
     Reprinted in <u>Essays in Applied Christianity</u>.

"The World Council of Churches." M, 15, no. 15 (August 8), 7.
     Also in L, 32, no. 45 (August 9), 21.

1951

"American Conservatism and the World Crisis, A Study in Vacillation."
     <u>The Yale Review</u>, 40, no. 3 (March), 385-399.

"The American Power." CS, 16, no. 4 (Autumn), 6-8.

"The Christian Faith and the Crisis." M, 16, no. 2 (January 16), 7.
     Also in L, 33, no. 16 (January 17), 15-16.

"Christian Idealism." CS, 16, no. 3 (Summer), 5-6.

"Christians Have Hope for Today." L, 33, no. 52 (September 26), 27.

1951

"Coherence, Incoherence, and Christian Faith." The Journal of
    Religion, 31, no. 3 (July), 155-168.
        Also in Union Seminary Quarterly Review, 7, no. 2 (January),
    11-24. Reprinted as Chapter 11 of Christian Realism and Polit-
    ical Problems.

"Creating a New World Order." L, 34, no. 8 (November 21), 10.

"Distribution of Income in the U.S.A." CS, 16, no. 3 (Summer), 8.

"Editorial Notes." CC, 11, no. 4 (March 19), 26.
        Notes on a document entitled "Credo of Hope--1951."

"Editorial Notes." CC, 11, no. 18 (October 29), 138-139.
        Notes on the dangers of preoccupation with fear of Communism
    and those suspected of softness toward Communism and on Phillip
    Jessup's need for self-justification.

"Editorial Notes." CC, 11, no. 21 (December 10), 162.
        Notes on the mistrust of our policy by Europeans and Asians.

"The Embarrassment of Victors." CS, 16, no. 2 (Spring), 7-8.

"Food for India--Self-Interest or Generosity?" M, 16, no. 13
    (June 19), 7.

"Germany and Western Civilization," in Germany and the Future of
    Europe. Edited by Hans Morgenthau. Chicago: The University of
    Chicago Press, pp. 1-11.

"Honesty in America." L, 33, no. 43 (July 25), 18.
        Also in M, 16, no. 15 (July 31), 7.

"Hybris." CS, 16, no. 2 (Spring), 4-6.

"Idealism and Christian Charity." M, 16, no. 7 (March 27), 6.

"Idealism is Not Enough." L, 33, no. 25 (March 21), 15-16.

"If We Say We Have No Sin--" M, 16, no. 9 (April 24), 7.

"Inflation and Group Selfishness." CS, 16, no. 2 (Spring), 3-4.
        Reprinted in Love and Justice.

"The Japanese Peace Treaty." CS, 16, no. 4 (Autumn), 3-4.

"Let Anyone Who Thinks That He Stands--." M, 16, no. 24
    (December 18), 7.

"The Little and the Big Hope of Christians." M, 16, no. 18
    (September 25), 7.

"The MacArthur Episode." CS, 16, no. 3 (Summer), 3-4.

["Man and the State." Review of Eivind Berggrav's Man and the State.]
    CS, 16, no. 3 (Summer), 28.

"Man as Creature and Creator." M, 16, no. 22 (November 20), 6.

"The Mastery of History." CS, 16, no. 2 (Spring), 6-7.

"Nations are Selfish." L, 33, no. 38 (June 20), 24.

"A New Fellowship." CS, 16, no. 3 (Summer), 4-5.

"The New Venture." CS, 16, no. 4 (Autumn), 5-6.
About the new organization "Christian Action," devoted to Christian Social Action, and the discontinuance of "Frontier Fellowship."

"A Prayer for Thanksgiving." Advance, 143, no. 19 (November 26), 5.

"Our Relation to Asia." M, 16, no. 20 (October 23), 7.

"Our Relation to Oriental Lands." L, 34, no. 3 (October 17), 21.

"The Peril of War and the Prospects of Peace." CC, 11, no. 17 (October 15), 129-130.

"The Perils of Power." L, 33, no. 32 (May 9), 26.
Also published as "The Perils of American Power," M, 16, no. 11 (May 22), 6.

["The Pillar of Fire." Review of Anton Stern's The Pillar of Fire.] CS, 16, no. 2 (Spring), 28-29.

"The Poverty of Asia and Communism." CS, 16, no. 1 (Winter, 1950-51), 6-8.

"The Problems of a World Church." L, 33, no. 46 (August 15), 19-20.
Also in M, 16, no. 16 (August 21), 6. Reprinted in Essays in Applied Christianity.

"Religious Politics." CS, 16, no. 4 (Autumn), 4-5.
American economic conservatism.

"Remedy for Neurosis." L, 33, no. 29 (April 18), 29.

"The Saturation Point." CS, 16, no. 1 (Winter), 6.
Public reaction to advertising.

"Social Christianity." CS, 16, no. 1 (Winter), 3-5.

"Ten Fateful Years." CC, 11, no. 1 (February 5), 1-4.

"To Be Abased And to Abound." M, 16, no. 4 (February 13), 7.
We can learn patience, serenity and our limitations.

"Transatlantic Tension." The Reporter, 5, no. 6 (September 18), 14-16.

"The Two Dimensions of the Struggle." CC, 11, no. 9 (May 28), 65-66.
Struggle with Communism is military and also moral-political.

"Unconditional Surrender." CS, 16, no. 1 (Winter), 5-6.
Note on the fourth volume of Churchill's memoirs.

"We Aren't Used to Being in Trouble." L, 33, no. 18 (January 31), 16.

1951

"We Need an Edmund Burke." CS, 16, no. 3 (Summer), 6-8.

"The Weakness of Common Worship in American Protestantism." CC, 11, no. 9 (May 28), 68-70.
    Reprinted in Essays in Applied Christianity.

"Without Morals, The Alleys are Blind." The New York Times Book Review (February 11), p. 3.
    Review of Gerald Heard's Morals Since 1900.

1952

"Alternatives to the Christian Faith." M, 17, no. 12 (June 3), 6.

"The American Position in the World." CS, 17, no. 1 (Winter), 5-6.

"The Anomaly of European Socialism." The Yale Review, 42, no. 2 (December), 161-167.

"Biblical Thought and Ontological Speculation in Tillich's Theology," in The Theology of Paul Tillich. Edited by Kegley and Bretall. New York: Macmillan Co., pp. 216-227.

"The Campaign: The Issues are Drawn." CS, 17, no. 4 (Autumn), 3-4.

"Catholics and Politics: Some Misconceptions." The Reporter, 6, no. 2 (January 22), 9-11.
    Also in CC, 12, no. 11 (June 23), 83-85; and Perspectives, no. 6 (Winter 1954), pp. 24-29. Reprinted in Essays in Applied Christianity.

"Chastisements of God Apply to Nations." EC, 120, no. 51 (December 28), 8.

"Christian Action and the Layman." CS, 17, no. 1 (Winter), 3-4.

"Christian Faith and Political Controversy." CC, 12, no. 13 (July 21), 87-98.
    Reprinted in Love and Justice.

"Christian Religion in South Africa." EC, 118, no. 20 (May 25), 21.

"Christianity and Humanism." M, 17, no. 17 (September 9), 7.

"Christianity, Humanism Have Common Front Against Cynical, Nihilistic Creeds." EC, 120, no. 40 (October 12), 14.

"Christianity is a Religion of Grace." L, 35, no. 2 (October 8), 19-20.

"Despite Science There is a Fringe of Obscurantism in the World." EC, 118, no. 16 (April 27), 17.

"Divine Discipline." M, 17, no. 21 (November 4), 6.

1952

"Dutch Calvinism in South Africa." CS, 17, no. 3 (Summer), 7.

"Editorial Notes." CC, 11, no. 24 (January 21), 186.
    Notes on Korea and the European economic deterioration.

"Editorial Notes." CC, 12, no. 7 (April 28), 56.
    Notes on Sugrue's A Catholic Speaks His Mind and corruption
    in government.

"Editorial Notes." CC, 12, no. 9 (May 26), 66.
    Notes on Catholic reviewers' attack upon Thomas Sugrue's A
    Catholic Speaks His Mind and on problems of unifying Germany into
    the Western European community.

"Editorial Notes." CC, 12, no. 11 (June 23), 83.
    Notes on Chambers's The Witness.

"Editorial Notes." CC, 12, no. 22 (December 22), 170.
    Notes on testing the H bomb in the Pacific; anti-American
    sentiment in France; and Dennis Brogan's article "The Illusion
    of American Omnipotence."

"Faith, Poetry and Obscurantism." M, 17, no. 9 (April 22), 6.

"The Future Can't Be Controlled." L, 34, no. 17 (January 23), 11.

"Humanism and Religion." L, 34, no. 48 (August 27), 10-11.

"The Importance of the Religious Dimension." Christian Action, 2,
    no. 4 (May), 1.

"The Innocent Nation in an Innocent World." Religion in Life, 21,
    no. 2 (Spring), 207-222.
    Reprinted as Chapter 2 of The Irony of American History.

"Intellectuals Have Lost Confidence in Alternatives to Christian
    Faith." EC, 118, no. 25 (June 29), 15.

"Letter." The Reporter, 6, no. 11 (May 27), 3.
    About religion and politics, especially "spiritual mobilization."

"The Limits of American Power." CS, 17, no. 4 (Autumn), 5.

"Love and Law in Protestantism and Catholicism." The Journal of
    Religious Thought, 9, no. 2 (Spring-Summer), 95-111.
    Reprinted as Chapter 10 of Christian Realism and Political
    Problems.

"Means of Grace Can be Corrupted." L, 34, no. 31 (April 30), 11.

"Modern Intellectuals Discover Failure." L, 34, no. 40 (July 2), 18.

"Modern Man and the Unknown Future." M, 17, no. 2 (January 15), 6.

"The Moral Implications of Loyalty to the United Nations." The
    Hazen Pamphlets, no. 29, 9 pp.

1952

"Niemoeller's Hazardous Political Views." EC, 118, no. 30
(August 3), 13.

"Notes on Current Events." CS, 17, no. 1 (Winter), 6-8.
    Notes on Catholic political power; inflation; political can-
    didates; Churchill's election; and corruption in office.

"Our Country and Our Culture." Partisan Review, 19, no. 3
(May-June), 301-303.

"Our Faith and Concrete Political Decisions." CS, 17, no. 3
(Summer), 3-4.
    Reprinted in Love and Justice.

"Prayer and Politics." CC, 12, no. 18 (October 27), 138-139.
    Reprinted in Essays in Applied Christianity.

"Prayer and Religious Observances." L, 34, no. 45 (August 6), 12.

"Prayer at Conventions." M, 17, no. 15 (July 29), 6.

"Prayers at Two National Conventions." EC, 120, no. 34 (August 31),
    5.

"The Protestant Clergy and U. S. Politics." The Reporter, 6, no. 4
(February 19), 24-27.
    Reprinted in Perspectives, no. 6 (Winter), 16-24; also in
    Essays in Applied Christianity.

"Pure Idealism is a Loveless Thing." EC, 120, no. 44 (November 9),
    6.

"The Relation of Religious to Political Convictions." M, 17, no. 14
(July 8), 7.

"Religion in American Life." L, 34, no. 21 (February 20), 11.

"A Religion of Mercy." M, 17, no. 19 (October 7), 6.

"Religious Knowledge and Experience." L, 34, no. 29 (April 16), 12.

"The Republican Split on Foreign Policy." NL, 35, no. 19 (May 12),
    16-17.

"The Republican Victory." CC, 12, no. 20 (November 24), 153-154.

"South African Religious Racism." M, 17, no. 10 (May 6), 7.

"The Spectrum of Religion in America." M, 17, no. 5 (February 26),
    7.
        Also in EC, 118, no. 7 (February 24), 23.

"The 'Super Theologians' Meet." Union Seminary Quarterly Review, 7,
    no. 2 (January), 26-27.
        Discussion by Henry P. Van Dusen and Reinhold Niebuhr.

"Superfluous Advice." CS, 17, no. 1 (Winter), 4-5.

1953

"Teach us to Number Our Days." M, 17, no. 25 (December 30), 6.
    Keeping proper balance between man as creator and creature.

"Theology and Politics." L, 34, no. 41 (July 9), 9-10.

"Today is the Judgment Day." L, 35, no. 11 (December 10), 12.

"The Uncertain Future." EC, 118, no. 3 (January 27), 19.

"U. S. Protestantism and Free Enterprise." The Reporter, 6, no. 4
    (February 19), 24-27.

"War in Korea." L, 35, no. 7 (November 12), 13.

1953

"Adenauer and Catholic Policy." L, 36, no. 4 (October 28), 25.

"America: Pragmatism, Not Dogmatism." NL, 36, no. 25 (June 22), 15.
    Review of Daniel Boorstin's The Genius of American Politics.

"Can We Organize the World?" CC, 13, no. 1 (February 2), 1.

"The Case For Humility." M, 18, no. 16 (September 8), 4.

"Catholicism and Democracy." M, 18, no. 18 (October 6), 7.

"Change in Soviet Leadership." L, 35, no. 34 (May 20), 12.

"Channels of Grace." M, 18, no. 14 (July 28), 7.

"Christian Faith and Social Action," in Christian Faith and Social
    Action. Edited by John Hutchison. New York: Scribner's,
    pp. 225-242.
    Reprinted in Faith and Politics.

"The Christian Faith and the Economic Life of Liberal Society," in
    Goals of Economic Life. Edited by A. Dudley Ward. New York:
    Harper and Brothers, pp. 433-459.
    Reprinted in Faith and Politics.

"The Christian Witness in a Secular Age." CCY, 70, no. 29 (July 22),
    840-843.

"Christianity and Social Justice." L, 35, no. 23 (March 11), 19-20.

"Christianity and the Moral Law." CCY, 70, no. 48 (December 2),
    1386-1388.

"Christianity Doesn't Need Favorable Environment." L, 35, no. 44
    (July 29), 23.

"The Church and Political Decisions." CS, 18, no. 4 (Autumn), 6.

"Church Loyalties, Politics Vie in Germany." EC, 119, no. 28
    (July 19), 4.

1953

"The Church Speaks to the Nation." CC, 13, no. 20 (November 30), 153-154.
    Also in M, 18, no. 23 (December 15), 7. Reprinted in Essays in Applied Christianity.

"The Churches and the United Nations." CS, 18, no. 1 (Winter), 3-4.

"Coercion, Self-Interest, and Love," in The Organizational Revolution. Edited by Kenneth E. Boulding. New York: Harper and Brothers, pp. 228-244.

"Communism and the Clergy." CCY, 70, no. 33 (August 19), 936-937.
    Reprinted in Essays in Applied Christianity.

"Coronation Afterthoughts." CCY, 70, no. 26 (July 1), 771-772.

"Democracy, Secularism and Christianity." CC, 13, no. 3 (March 2), 19-20, 24.

"Editorial Notes." CC, 12, no. 23 (January 5), 178.
    Notes on segregation in the schools and the limits of the law.

"Editorial Notes." CC, 13, no. 1 (February 2), 2.
    Notes on approaches to the school issue and Protestant-Catholic tensions in education.

"Editorial Notes." CC, 13, no. 4 (March 16), 26.
    Notes on the Rosenberg case.

"Editorial Notes." CC, 13, no. 7 (April 27), 50-51.
    Notes on changes in Russia since Stalin's death and the continued Communist threat.

"Editorial Notes." CC, 13, no. 12 (July 6), 90.
    Notes on Eisenhower's failure effectively to oppose McCarthyism and the continued opposition to commutation of the Rosenberg death sentence.

"Editorial Notes." CC, 13, no. 13 (July 30), 98.
    Notes on the inner struggle for power in post-Stalin Russia; our failing reputation abroad because of McCarthyism; and the status of American opposition to McCarthyism.

"Editorial Notes." CC, 13, no. 21 (December 14), 162-163.
    Notes on the publication of Churchill's sixth volume of the history of the war, Triumph and Tragedy, and the unpredictability of history.

"Editorial Notes." CC, 13, no. 22 (December 28), 170.
    Notes on Eisenhower's address to the U. N.; his proposal for world pooling of fissionable material; and signs of the President's willingness to fight McCarthyism.

"Eisenhower's Problem on Taxes." CS, 18, no. 4 (Autumn), 5.

1953

"The Errors of Christian Individualism." EC, 119, no. 14
(April 12), 7.

"The Evidence is Clear." EC, 119, no. 41 (November 22), 12.
Religion makes a difference in sexual habits, as shown by the
Kinsey Report.

"The Evil of the Communist Idea." NL, 36, no. 23 (June 8), 16-18.
Published as Chapter 3 of Christian Realism and Political
Problems. Also reprinted in The World Crisis and American Responsibility, edited by Ernest Lefever. Both republications use
the title: "Why is Communism So Evil?"

"Faith and Political Decision." M, 18, no. 11 (June 2), 5-6.

"Faith Grows in Crisis." L, 35, no. 1 (July 8), 13.

"Faith Influences Attitudes on Sex." M, 18, no. 20 (November 3), 6.
Parallels listing above, "The Evidence is Clear."

"Faith, Morals and Kinsey." L, 36, no. 5 (November 4), 21.
About the same as pieces listed above in EC and M.

"'Favorable' Environment." M, 18, no. 5 (August 18), 6.
Historical context for faith and democracy.

"God Known by Reason is Less Than God." EC, 119, no. 5 (February 8),
5.

"The God of History." M, 18, no. 3 (February 10), 6-7.

"The Hazards and the Difficulties of the Christian Ministry."
Address for the Conference on the Ministry, Union Theological
Seminary, New York, March 29.
Published in Justice and Mercy.

"Historic Inevitability." EC, 119, no. 1 (September 27), 10.

"Hope Needs Faith and Love." The Ecumenical Review, 5, no. 4
(July), 358-363.
Reprinted in Essays in Applied Christianity.

"How Tolerant Should We Be?" M, 18, no. 7 (April 7), 6.

"Incident in Lucknow." L, 35, no. 29 (April 15), 12.

"Ironic Facts of the Christian Life." EC, 119, no. 31 (August 9), 5.

"Jaspers on History." NL, 36, no. 34 (August 24), 17.
Review of Karl Jaspers's The Origin and Goal of History.

"The Korean Peace." CS, 18, no. 4 (Autumn), 3-4.

"Lesson on Illusion of Omnipotence." EC, 119, no. 9 (March 8), 8.
American power and its limits.

"Letter." CC, 13, no. 8 (May 11), 71-72.
To Mrs. Vernon Skewes-Cox Ross, reaffirming earlier position
about the Russians and world government.

1953

"Liberals and the Marxist Heresy." NR, 129, no. 11 (October 12), 13-15.

"Man's Greatest Modern Evil: Thinking Either Too Well or Too Ill of Himself." EC, 119, no. 2 (January 18), 8.

"Masterful and Wise." NR, 128, no. 3 (July 27), 20.
      Review of Henry B. Parkes's <u>United States of America: A History</u>.

"The Meaning of the Shift in Soviet Policy." CS, 18, no. 1 (Winter), 5-6.

"Mr. Vogt's World of Progress." CCY, 70, no. 37 (September 16), 1051-1052.

"The Moral Implications of Loyalty to the United Nations." The Hazen Pamphlets, no. 29.
      Address at the National Conference on UNESCO, January. Reprinted in <u>Motive</u>, 16, no. 1 (January 1955), 17-20.

"The New Administration at Home and Abroad." CS, 18, no. 2 (Spring), 3-4.

"No Christian Peace in Korea?" CCY, 70, no. 5 (February 4), 127.
      Dr. Niebuhr's letter, published with two others under this editorial caption, in answer to the question: "What Can Christians Contribute to Peace in Korea?"

"Norman Thomas." CS, 18, no. 2 (Spring), 4-6.
      On change in Thomas's social and economic thought seen in recent book.

"Not a Responsible Conservatism." CS, 18, no. 3 (Summer), 3.

"Our Concord With Spain." CS, 18, no. 4 (Autumn), 4-5.

"The Peace Offensive." M, 18, no. 9 (May 5), 6.

"People Before an Atomic War." CS, 18, no. 4 (Autumn), 3.

"Piety and Politics." CS, 18, no. 3 (Summer), 3-4.

"Protestant Individualism." M, 18, no. 6 (March 24), 6.

"A Protestant Looks at Catholics." <u>The Commonweal</u>, 58, no. 5 (May 8), 117-120.

"The Puritan Conscience." NR, 129, no. 5 (August 31), 18.
      Review of Perry Miller's <u>The New England Mind: From Colony to Province</u>.

"The Reach for One World." NR, 129, no. 17 (November 23), 16-17.
      Review of G. A. Borgese's <u>World Republic</u>.

"Religion of Intellectuals." L, 35, no. 19 (February 11), 12.

"Responsibility and the Church." L, 36, no. 11 (December 16), 18.

"Rosenzweig's Message." Commentary, 15, no. 3 (March), 310-312.
Review of N. N. Glatzer's Franz Rosenzweig: His Life and Thought.

"Sex and Religion in the Kinsey Report." CC, 13, no. 18 (November 2), 138-141.
Reprinted in An Analysis of the Kinsey Reports on Sexual Behavior in the Human Male and Female, edited by Donald P. Geddes. New York: E. P. Dutton Co., pp. 62-70.

"The Significance of Dr. Fosdick in American Religious Thought." Union Seminary Quarterly Review, 8, no. 4 (May), 3-6.
Reprinted in CCY, 70, no. 22 (June 3), 657-658.

"Sorrow and Joy According to the Christian Faith." Current Religious Thought, 13, no. 1 (January-February), 7-11.
From an address to the Chicago Sunday Evening Club. Almost the same sermon published from a typescript in Advance, 145, no. 14 (July 13), 5-7, 27. Reprinted in Great Preaching Today, edited by Alton M. Matter. New York: Harper and Brothers, pp. 121-129.

"A Spiritual and Political Pilgrim." The New York Times Book Review (June 21), p. 17.
Review of William C. Kernan's My Road to Certainty.

"The Task of American Liberalism." A D A World, 8, no. 5 (May), 1M.

"Temper Power With Patience." L, 35, no. 15 (January 14), 15.

"Temptations of Power." M, 18, no. 2 (January 27), 7.

"To Suspect Innocent Ones of Guilt Does Not Make Guilty Men Innocent." Look, 17, no. 23 (November 17), 37.
Niebuhr's statement on "Communism and the Protestant Clergy," along with statements by Bishop Oxnam and J. B. Matthews.

"We Stand Alone." CC, 13, no. 15 (September 21), 113-114.
American nationalistic arrogance drives allies away.

"Where Man's Power Fails." L, 35, no. 51 (September 16), 28.

["Who Speaks for Man?" Review of Norman Cousins's Who Speaks for Man?] The United Nations World, 7, no. 3 (March), 61-62.

"Will We Resist Injustice?" CC, 13, no. 6 (April 13), 41-42.
About McCarthyism.

"World's Ultimate Perils Remain." EC, 119, no. 22 (June 7), 12.

1954

"Alternatives to the H-Bomb." NL, 37, no. 31 (August 2), 12-14.

"America and the Asians." N, 37, no. 22 (May 31), 3-4.

"American Attitudes on World Organization: Comment." Public Affairs
    Quarterly, 17, no. 4 (Winter), 435-438.

"American Leadership in the Cold War." CC, 14, no. 17 (October 18),
    129-130.

"Analysis of Evanston Assembly Theme." L, 36, no. 44 (August 4),
    15-16.

"Beria and McCarthy." NL, 37, no. 1 (January 4), 3-4.

"Britain and America in World Leadership." CS, 19, no. 3 (Autumn),
    5-6.

"The Case for Coexistence." NL, 37, no. 40 (October 4), 5-6.

"The Catholic Hierarchy's Analysis of the Ills of Our Day." CC, 14,
    no. 22 (December 27), 171-173.
        Also in British Weekly, 135, no. 3561 (February 10, 1955), 5.
    Reprinted in Essays in Applied Christianity.

"A Century of Cold War." NL, 37, no. 31 (August 2), 12-14.

"Christ and the Meaning of Our Existence." EC, 119, no. 24
    (November 28), 8.
        On Evanston meeting of World Council of Churches.

"Christ, the Hope of the World." M, 19, no. 15 (August 10), 9.

"Christ the Hope of the World--What Has History to Say?" Religion
    in Life, 23, no. 3 (Summer), 334-340.
        Niebuhr's comment on statement by K. S. Latourette in same
    issue. The article is also published in CC, 14, no. 14
    (August 9), 108-111, under the title "The Theme of Evanston."
    Reprinted in Essays in Applied Christianity.

"Christ vs. Socrates." The Saturday Review, 37, no. 51 (December 18),
    7-8, 37-39.

"The Church Gives Advice to the Nation." EC, 120, no. 2
    (January 24), 9.
        Cleveland Conference of the National Council of Churches.

"Clergymen Speak Their Minds." The Saturday Evening Post, 226,
    no. 44 (May 1), 24.

"Co-existence or Total War." CCY, 71, no. 33 (August 18), 971-973.

"Cold War and Hot Peace." M, 19, no. 3 (February 9), 6.
        Also in EC, 119, no. 9 (May 2), 8. [Volume numbered
    incorrectly.]

"Comment." <u>Public Opinion Quarterly</u>, 17, no. 4 (Winter), 435–438.
Comment on Elmo Roper's lead article, "American Attitudes on World Organization."

"The Commitment of the Self and the Freedom of the Mind," in <u>Religion and Freedom of Thought</u>. New York: Doubleday and Company, pp. 55–64.
The volume includes articles by Perry Miller, Robert L. Calhoun, Nathan M. Pusey and Reinhold Niebuhr.

"Communism and Historical Destiny." L, 36, no. 49 (September 8), 12.

"Concern for the People." CS, 19, no. 3 (Autumn), 30.
Review of Emmett McLoughlin's <u>Peoples' Padre</u>.

"Conference on International Politics." Rockefeller Foundation Summary Report (May 7–8). Mimeographed.

"The Conflict With Communism in Indo-China." CS, 19, no. 2 (Spring), 4.

"The Cultural Crisis of Our Age." <u>Harvard Business Review</u>, 32, no. 1 (January–February), 33–38.
Reprinted in <u>Pastoral Psychology</u>, 15, no. 149 (December, 1964), 13–20.

"The Decision on Separation." L, 36, no. 41 (July 14), 13–14.

"Democracy and the Party Spirit." NL, 37, no. 11 (March 15), 3–5.

"The Developments in Indo-China." CS, 19, no. 4 (Special Issue), 4.

"Dr. Henry Sloane Coffin." CC, 14, no. 21 (December 13), 163.

"Editorial Notes." CC, 13, no. 24 (January 25), 186.
Notes on Eisenhower's State of the Union message.

"Editorial Notes." CC, 14, no. 2 (February 22), 10–11.
Notes on Foreign Ministers' Conference in Berlin; the failure of unification plan for Germany; and reasons for the Russian position.

"Editorial Notes." CC, 14, no. 4 (March 22), 26.
Notes on President Eisenhower's failure to take a strong stand against McCarthy and his fight with the Army.

"Editorial Notes." CC, 14, no. 6 (April 19), 42–43.
Notes on explosion of the first hydrogen bomb and on the injustice of the Velde Committee in their accusations of Professor John Hutchison.

"Editorial Notes." CC, 14, no. 7 (May 3), 50.
Notes on denial of Dr. Oppenheimer's further access to atomic secrets, a result of McCarthyism.

1954

"Editorial Notes." CC, 14, no. 9 (May 31), 66.
Notes on the fall of Dienbienphu and its lessons about the inadequacy of threats of "massive retaliation."

"Editorial Notes." CC, 14, no. 10 (June 14), 74-75.
Notes on foreign policy differences with the British, especially over the organization of a defense community.

"Editorial Notes." CC, 14, no. 11 (June 28), 83.
Notes on Frederic Wertham's Seduction of the Innocent and his indictment of comic books.

"Editorial Notes." CC, 14, no. 13 (July 26), 98-99.
Notes on the Churchill-Eden visit to U. S., further revelations of our differences with Britain; and admission of Red China to the U. N.

"Editorial Notes." CC, 14, no. 15 (September 20), 114.
Notes on France's defeat of the European Defense Community.

"Editorial Notes." CC, 14, no. 19 (November 15), 146.
Notes on London agreements as a sign of progress toward unity among free nations.

"Editorial Notes." CC, 14, no. 21 (December 13), 162-164.
Notes on Eisenhower's moderate approach to Russia; Emmett McLoughlin's book, The Peoples' Padre; and the tragedy of William Remington's murder in Lewisburg prison.

"Einstein and the World Situation." M, 19, no. 23 (December 14), 6.
About Einstein's statement that he would be a plumber if he had to start his life again. Also in L, 37, no. 11 (December 15), 12; and EC, 119, no. 7 (December 26), 20.

"The Ethics of Loyalty, A Summary." Confluence, 3, no. 4 (December), 480-489.

"European Integration." CS, 19, no. 3 (Autumn), 3.

"Faith and Dogma." NR, 130, no. 7 (February 15), 20.
Review of Charles E. Raven's Natural Religion and Christian Theology.

"Faith in Christ and Christian Hope." M, 19, no. 18 (October 5), 5.

"A Farewell to Andre Vishinsky." CS, 19, no. 4 (Special Issue), 5.

"Foreword," to Harvest of Hate, The Nazi Program for the Destruction of Jews in Europe. By Leon Poliakov. Syracuse, N. Y.: Syracuse University Press, pp. vii-viii.

"The French Do Not Like Us." CS, 19, no. 1 (Winter), 9-12.

"Frustrations of American Power." NL, 37, no. 48 (November 29), 7-8.

"The Future Prospect." M, 19, no. 1 (January 12), 6.

1954

"The God That Failed." NR, 131, no. 17 (October 25), 19.
  Review of Arthur Koestler's The Invisible Writing.

"The Growing Tension Between Nationalists and Internationalists."
  CS, 19, no. 4 (Special Issue), 3-4.

"Healing Witness." CS, 19, no. 1 (Winter), 31.
  Review of James Pike's Beyond Anxiety.

"The Hydrogen Bomb and Moral Responsibility." M, 19, no. 9 (May 4),
  5.

"Ideals and Basic Law." NL, 37, no. 44 (November 1), 11.

"Ike's First Year." NL, 37, no. 6 (February 8), 3-5.

"Introduction," to Church in a Communist Society: A Study in J. L.
  Hromadka's Theological Politics. By Matthew Spinka. Hartford,
  Conn.: Hartford Seminary Press.

"Is History Predictable?" Atlantic Monthly, 194, no. 1 (July), 69-72.

"Is Tyranny Changing in Russia?" CS, 19, no. 3 (Autumn), 6.

"Jesus Christ, the Only Hope of the World." EC, 119, no. 16
  (August 8), 12.

"Law and Custom." M, 19, no. 13 (June 29), 7.

"Learning From History." NL, 37, no. 19 (May 10), 3-4.

"Letter." The New York Times (July 19), p. 18.
  Attacks American blocking of China's entry to U. N.

"Looking Ahead: Complacency and Hysteria." L, 36, no. 15
  (January 13), 12.

"Meaning of Faith in Life: Reflections on the Evanston Assembly
  Debate." L, 37, no. 3 (October 20), 13.

"Military Power and Moral Authority." L, 36, no. 37 (June 16), 20.

"Mind's Supremacy." NR, 130, no. 13 (March 29), 19-20.
  Review of Gilbert Highet's Man's Unconquerable Mind.

"The Moral and Spiritual Content of the Atlantic Community," in Five
  Years of the North Atlantic Alliance: A Symposium. New York:
  American Council on NATO, Inc., pp. 25-30.

"Moral Issues and the H-Bomb." L, 36, no. 34 (May 26), 12.

"More on Kinsey." CC, 13, no. 23 (January 11), 182-183.

"More on McCarthy." NR, 131, no. 9 (August 30), 19-20.
  Review of J. Rorty and M. Decter's McCarthy and the Communists.

"National Pride vs. the Church." L, 37, no. 6 (November 10), 12-13.

1954

"Our Dependence is on God." CCY, 71, no. 35 (September 1), 1034-1037.
    Address written for the Evanston Assembly of the World Council
    of Churches. Also in British Weekly, 135, no. 3545 (October 21),
    7-8. Published as "Unsere Abhängigkeit von Gott," in Evanston
    Dokumente. Witten: Luther Verlag, pp. 317-324. Also in
    Congregational Quarterly, 33, no. 1 (January), 29-36; and
    reprinted in Essays in Applied Christianity.

"Our Relations to Asia." M, 19, no. 11 (June 1), 7.
    Also in EC, 119, no. 14 (July 11), 11.

"Patience and the Cold War." L, 36, no. 20 (February 17), 12.

"The Peril of Complacency in the Nation." CC, 14, no. 1 (February 8),
    1-2.

"The Peril of Sophistication." CS, 19, no. 3 (Autumn), 29.
    Review of Karl Barth's Against the Stream.

"A Plea for Humility." M, 19, no. 21 (November 16), 7.

"The Poet and Society." NR, 130, no. 5 (February 1), 18.
    Review of Peter Viereck's Dream and Responsibility.

"The Predicament of American Power." CS, 19, no. 1 (Winter), 3.

"Private and Public Power." CS, 19, no. 4 (Special Issue), 5.

"The Problem of Germany and France." CS, 19, no. 4 (Special Issue),
    4-5.

"The Providence of God." Advance, 146, no. 12 (June 14), 5-6, 20.

"Question About the Concept of Equality." EC, 119, no. 15 (July 25),
    7.

"The Question of Secularism." M, 19, no. 7 (April 6), 7.
    Also in EC, 119, no. 11 (May 30), 8.

"Religion and Politics." Perspectives, no. 6 (Winter), pp. 16-19.

"Religious Insight Versus Political Discrimination." M, 19, no. 5
    (March 9), 6.

"Right and Left." L, 36, no. 28 (April 14), 11.

"Sex and Religion in the Kinsey Report." Union Seminary Quarterly
    Review, 9, no. 2 (January), 3-9.

"The Significance of the Growth of 'Christian Action.'" CC, 14,
    no. 4 (March 22), 30-32.

"The Spread of Infection." CS, 19, no. 2 (Spring), 5-6.
    McCarthyism among the people and in Washington officialdom.

"The Supreme Court on Segregation in the Schools." CC, 14, no. 10
    (June 14), 75-77.

1955

"The Theme of Evanston." CC, 14, no. 14 (August 9), 108–111.
     Reprinted from Religion in Life, 23, no. 3 (Summer), 334–340.

"This is Prejudice," in "This is Prejudice." By Weldon Wallace.
     The Baltimore Sun (October 11 and November 1), pp. 13–15.
          Reprinted as a pamphlet.

"Tolstoy and History." NL, 37, no. 12 (March 22), 24.
     Review of Isaiah Berlin's The Hedgehog and the Fox.

"Toward a Responsible Conservatism." CS, 19, no. 1 (Winter), 6.

"The Tyranny of Science." Theology Today, 10, no. 4 (January),
     464–473.

"Why They Dislike America." NL, 37, no. 15 (April 12), 3–5.

1955

"About Christian Apologetics." EC, 120, no. 8 (April 17), 13.

"The Abundance of Things a Man Possesses." M, 20, no. 15 (August 16),
     7.
          Also in EC, 120, no. 17 (August 21), 18.

"America's Spiritual Resources for International Cooperation." A
     working paper prepared for the Fifth National Conference of the
     U. S. National Commission for UNESCO. Cincinnati, November 3–5.
          Second part of the paper reprinted in The World Crisis and
     American Responsibility.

"The Anatomy of American Nationalism." NL, 38, no. 9 (February 28),
     16–17.
          Reprinted in The World Crisis and American Responsibility.

"Approach to Unbelievers." L, 37, no. 29 (April 20), 12–13.

"Billy Graham's Christianity and the World Crisis." CS, 20, no. 2
     (Spring), 3–4.

"Britain, the USA, and China." CS, 20, no. 2 (Spring), 4.

"Buchmanism Under Scrutiny." CC, 15, no. 8 (May 16), 62, 64.
          Reprinted from The Observer (February 23). Review of the
     Church of England report on Moral Rearmament.

"The Change in Russia." NL, 38, no. 39 (October 3), 18–19.

"Christian Action." CS, 20, no. 4 (Autumn), 5–6.

"Christian Faith—A Live Option." EC, 120, no. 10 (May 15), 11.

"Christians in Two Dimensions." L, 38, no. 5 (November 2), 25.

"The CIO-AFL Merger and the Labor Movement." CS, 20, no. 2 (Spring),
     5–6.

1955

"Conversation: On the International Affairs Report From the Evanston Assembly of the World Council of Churches" (Niebuhr and R. M. Fagley). CS, 20, no. 2 (Spring), 7-8.

"Critic of the Religious Scene." L, 37, no. 50 (September 14), 12.
Notes on Will Herberg's Protestant, Catholic, and Jew.

"Determinism in History." NL, 38, no. 46 (November 21), 23-24.
Review of Isaiah Berlin's Historical Inevitability.

"Does Religion Make Conformists of Us?" L, 37, no. 41 (July 13), 12.

"Eden's Victory." CS, 20, no. 3 (Summer), 5.

"Editorial Notes." CC, 14, no. 23 (January 10), 178-179.
Notes on worsened situation in South Africa, and the books and "wisdom" which have come out of the Policy Planning Staff of the State Department.

"Editorial Notes." CC, 15, no. 3 (March 7), 18.
Notes on policy on Formosa and China, and the dangers of Khrushchev's rise to power.

"Editorial Notes." CC, 15, no. 5 (April 4), 34-35.
Notes on the Yalta papers and on E. O. Reischauer's Wanted: An Asian Policy.

"Editorial Notes." CC, 15, no. 6 (April 18), 42.
Notes on conflict between Christian and Communist loyalty for the young in East Germany, and on Lutheran and Catholic bishops in opposition.

"Editorial Notes." CC, 15, no. 7 (May 2), 50-51.
Notes on the Supreme Court desegregation order, and the Bandung conference of Asian and African countries.

"Editorial Notes." CC, 15, no. 10 (June 13), 74.
Notes on the probability of a Big Four meeting and what this may mean.

"Editorial Notes." CC, 15, no. 13 (July 25), 98.
Notes on the possibility of a "summit" meeting as a sign of weakened McCarthyism.

"Editorial Notes." CC, 15, no. 15 (September 19), 114.
Notes on Geneva Conference, the question of Russian flexibility, and the "Atoms for Peace" conference.

"Editorial Notes." CC, 15, no. 17 (October 17), 130.
Notes on the possible far-reaching consequences of Eisenhower's illness.

"Editorial Notes." CC, 15, no. 19 (November 14), 146.
Notes on the Episcopal Bishops and the Pastoral Letter on East and West, and on Western democracy's losses to Communism in Asia and Africa.

"Editorial Notes." CC, 15, no. 21 (December 12), 162, 168.
Notes on heresy trials of three young Lutheran pastors; the
failure of the second Geneva conference; and on Communist gains
in the Islamic world.

"Eisenhower and the Democrats." CS, 20, no. 4 (Autumn), 3.

"Emphasis on Fellowship." L, 37, no. 19 (February 9), 12.
Also in EC, 120, no. 4 (February 20), 15; and M, 20, no. 4
(February 22), 6.

"False Prophets of Revival." L, 37, no. 15 (January 12), 12.

"The Fate of European Socialism." NL, 38, no. 25 (June 20), 6-8.

"France's 'Liberal' Colonialism: Old Evils, New Slogans." NL, 38,
no. 42 (October 24), 16-17.

"A Glimpse into the Future." CS, 20, no. 4 (Autumn), 4-5.

"God Wills Both Justice and Peace" (with Angus Dun). CC, 15, no. 10
(June 13), 75-78.

"Grace and Sin in Human Nature." L, 37, no. 24 (March 16), 12.
Also in EC, 120, no. 6 (March 20), 9.

"The Heresy Trials." CC, 15, no. 22 (December 26), 171-172.

"Ike Committed to New Dealism." Time, 65, no. 18 (May 2), 25.
Reprint of selective parts of "Why Ike is Popular." NL, 38,
no. 17 (April 25), 14-15.

"The Illusion of World Government." Japan Christian Quarterly, 21,
no. 4 (October), 316-318.
Condensation of material in Chapter 2 of Christian Realism and
Political Problems.

"The Individual and the Social Dimension of Our Existence." EC, 120,
no. 21 (October 16), 9.

"Introduction," to Eighty Adventurous Years: An Autobiography. By
Sherwood Eddy. New York: Harper and Brothers, pp. 9-11.

"Is There Another Way?" The Progressive, 19, no. 10 (October), 13-14.
Comment on a Quaker publication, "Speak Truth to Power."
Reprinted in Love and Justice.

"Jewish Socialist Analyzes Religious Scene in U.S.A." L, 37, no. 50
(September 14), 12.
Herberg's Protestant, Catholic, and Jew.

"Law and Grace in Christianity and Secularism." CC, 15, no. 11
(June 27), 81-82.

"Letter." NR, 132, no. 11 (March 14), 31.
More on Blanshard and religion.

1955

"Liberalism and Conservatism." CS, 20, no. 1 (Winter), 3-4.

"Liberalism: Illusions and Realities." NR, 133, no. 27 (July 4), 11-13.

"Limitations of the Scientific Method: An Answer to Pierre Auger." Bulletin of the Atomic Scientists, 11, no. 3 (March), 87.

"The Limits of Military Power." NL, 38, no. 22 (May 30), 16-17. Reprinted in The World Crisis and American Responsibility.

"Material Luxuries and the Spiritual Life." L, 37, no. 47 (August 24), 12.

"The Meaning of Labor Unity." NL, 38, no. 13 (March 28), 8-9.

"Minute on the Death of Dr. Coffin." Union Seminary Quarterly Review, 10, no. 2 (January), 5-7.

"Moral and Religious Problems in an Economy of Abundance" (with Leland Gordon), in Your Christian Conscience and American Abundance. Theme of the Third National Study Conference on the Church and Economic Life. New York: The National Council of Churches, pp. 34-41.

"Moral Problems of Desegregation." EC, 120, no. 24 (November 27), 10.

"Morals and Percentages." CS, 20, no. 4 (Autumn), 3-4.

"The National Interest and International Responsibility." Social Action, 21, no. 6 (February), 25-29.

"The Nationalism of Cyprus." CS, 20, no. 4 (Autumn), 4.

"The New Interest in Religion." L, 37, no. 34 (May 25), 12.

"Nobody Predicted Today." NL, 38, no. 1 (January 3), 9-10. Contingencies of history make prediction hazardous.

"Old Evils, New Slogans." NL, 38, no. 42 (October 24), 16-17. French "liberalism" and British "conservatism."

"Our Fifteenth Birthday." CC, 15, no. 1 (February 7), 1-3.

"Our Security is in God." M, 20, no. 11 (June 1), 4-5.

"A Plea for More Humility." M, 20, no. 7 (April 5), 6-7.

"Politics and Morality." L, 37, no. 37 (June 15), 12.

"Portents of Japan." CS, 20, no. 1 (Winter), 5.

"Principles in School Segregation." L, 38, no. 8 (November 23), 18.

"Problems of Desegregation." M, 20, no. 20 (November 15), 5.

"Protestant, Catholic and Jew in America." EC, 120, no. 19 (September 18), 19.

1955

"The Race Problem in America." CC, 15, no. 22 (December 26), 169-170.

"Reason and Religious Ultimates." NR, 133, no. 11 (September 12), 17-18.
    Review of Karl Jaspers's Reason and Existenz.

"Reasons Why." Newsweek, 46, no. 26 (December 26), 44-45.
    State of the new religious revival.

"Religiosity and the Christian Faith." CC, 14, no. 24 (January 24), 185-186.
    Reprinted in What The Christian Hopes for in Society. Edited by Wayne H. Cowan. New York: Association Press, 1957, pp. 121-125. Also reprinted in Essays in Applied Christianity.

"Religiosity Versus the Christian Gospel." M, 20, no. 1 (January 11), 7.
    Also in EC, 120, no. 2 (January 23), 12.

"Religious Faith and Conformity." M, 20, no. 13 (July 5), 6-7.
    Also in EC, 120, no. 12 (July 24), 10.

"Religious People and...Public Opinion." L, 37, no. 41 (July 13), 12.

"The Role of Religion." M, 20, no. 16 (September 6), 7.
    Review of Will Herberg's Protestant, Catholic and Jew.

"The Second Geneva." NL, 38, no. 47 (November 28), 7-8.

"The Semantics of Coexistence," in Alternatives to the H-Bomb.
    Edited by Anatole Shub. Boston: Beacon Press, pp. 30-36.

"Sin and Grace." M, 20, no. 5 (March 8), 5-6.

"The Social Dimension of Our Existence." M, 20, no. 18 (October 4), 6.

"Some Predictions." CS, 20, no. 3 (Summer), 4.

"The Sources of American Prestige." NL, 38, no. 5 (January 31), 6-8.

"The South African Tragedy." CS, 20, no. 2 (Spring), 4-5.

"Speak Truth to Power." The Progressive, 19, no. 10 (October), 13-14.
    In a symposium on Robert Pickus's Speak Truth to Power.

"The State of the Union." CS, 20, no. 1 (Winter), 4.

"The Tide of Religious Faith." M, 20, no. 9 (May 3), 7.

"Unpredictable History." CS, 20, no. 3 (Summer), 3-4.

"The Validity of Religious Symbolism." L, 38, no. 12 (December 21), 18.

"Varieties of Religious Revival." NR, 132, no. 23 (June 6), 13-16.

1955

"What is Heresy?" M, 20, no. 23 (December 13), 7.
    Also in EC, 120, no. 26 (December 25), 30-31.

"Why Ike is Popular." NL, 38, no. 17 (April 25), 14-15.

"Winston Churchill and Great Britain." CC, 15, no. 7 (May 2), 51-52.

"Your Christian Conscience and American Abundance" (with Leland
    Gordon). New York: Department of the Church and Economic Life,
    The National Council of Churches, 46 pp.
    Questions suggested for study and discussion in the churches
    on the theme of the Third National Study on the Church and Eco-
    nomic Life, 1956.

1956

"Answer to a Letter." CC, 16, no. 1 (February 6), 7.
    Answer to a letter by the Reverend M. V. Oggel, on the ques-
    tion of physical resurrection.

"The Antichrist." M, 21, no. 9 (May 1), 5.
    New Testament symbols of evil seen applying to recent purge of
    Stalin myths by Communists. Also in L, 38, no. 33 (May 16), 19;
    and EC, 121, no. 12 (June 10), 26.

"Die Aufgabe einer selbständigen christlichen Ethik," in Glaube und
    Handeln: Grundprobleme evangelischer Ethik. Bremen:
    C. Schünemann, pp. 6-11.
    Selections from An Interpretation of Christian Ethics, 1935,
    pp. 20-21, 30-34.

"Be Ye Therefore Perfect." EC, 121, no. 15 (July 22), 22.
    Perfectionism may lead to social irresponsibility.

"Biblical Religion and Ontological Speculation in Tillich's Theology,"
    in The Theology of Paul Tillich. Edited by C. W. Kegley and
    R. W. Bretall. New York: Macmillan Co., pp. 216-227.

["Biblical Religion and the Search for Ultimate Reality." Review of
    Paul Tillich's Biblical Religion and the Search for Ultimate
    Reality.] Union Seminary Quarterly Review, 11, no. 2 (January),
    59-60.

"The British and the Island of Cyprus." CS, 21, no. 2 (Spring), 22.

"British Experience and American Power." CC, 16, no. 8 (May 14),
    57-58.

"The Cause and Cure of the American Psychosis." The American Scholar,
    21, no. 1 (Winter), 11-20.

"The Christian Faith and the Christian Church." EC, 121, no. 20
    (September 30), 27.

"The Christian Faith and the Presidential Campaign." M, 21, no. 19 (October 9), 17-18.
>   Also in EC, 121, no. 22 (October 28), 30.

"The Christian Life and An Economy of Abundance." <u>Union Seminary Quarterly Review</u>, 11, no. 2 (January), 25-31.
>   Briefer version in <u>New Christian Advocate</u>, 1, no. 1 (October), 13-16.

"Christian Resources and Integration." L, 38, no. 28 (April 11), 23-24.

"Christian Witness." EC, 121, no. 7 (April 1), 20.

"Christianity and the Satellites' Revolt." EC, 121, no. 26 (December 23), 24.

"The Christians and Politics." L, 39, no. 2 (October 10), 23-24.

"Christians Must Be Perfect." L, 38, no. 41 (July 11), 19-20.

"Clericalism in Europe." NL, 39, no. 1 (January 2), 17-18.

"Complexity of Race Issue." M, 21, no. 15 (August 7), 5.

"Conscience and Community." M, 21, no. 1 (January 10), 6-7.
>   The church and race relations in the South. Also in EC, 121, no. 2 (January 22), 31.

"The Crisis in the Suez Canal." CC, 16, no. 15 (September 17), 113-114.

"The Desegregation Issue." CS, 21, no. 2 (Spring), 3-4.

"Editorial Notes." CC, 15, no. 23 (January 9), 178, 183-184.
>   Notes on Hugh Gaitskell's election to leadership of the Labour Party as a reflection of pragmatic policies in Western democracies; Communism's advantage over democracies in Asia and Africa struggles; and foreign aid winning out in Eisenhower's case as against a balanced budget.

"Editorial Notes." CC, 16, no. 1 (February 6), 2-3.
>   Notes on National Council of Churches sponsoring a television program, "Theology of the Dance"; on a higher level, though not totally satisfying, was Tillich's talk on the same day on religious art.

"Editorial Notes." CC, 16, no. 3 (March 5), 18-19.
>   Notes on Billy Graham's coming to New York City and the irrelevancies of it.

"Editorial Notes." CC, 16, no. 5 (April 2), 34-35.
>   Notes on official religiosity of Eisenhower's higher government officers, and the precarious situation in the Middle East.

Other Writings by Reinhold Niebuhr

1956

"Ethics and the Gospel." M, 21, no. 17 (September 11), 5.

"The Ethics of Loyalty (A Summary)." Confluence, 3, no. 4 (December), 480-489.

"Faith and Repentance." L, 39, no. 8 (November 21), 21.

"Farewell...." CS, 21, no. 3 (Summer), 3-4.
    Last issue of Christianity and Society.

"Foreword," to Dying We Live. Edited by H. Gollwitzer, Käthe Kuhn, and R. Schneider. New York: Pantheon Books, pp. xiii-xix.

"The Formidable Foe." CS, 21, no. 2 (Spring), 5-6.
    Post-Stalin Communism.

"From Diagnosis to Cure." Advance, 9, no. 9 (May 2), 4-5.
    From recognition of guilt to acceptance of forgiveness.

"Fruits Versus Talk." L, 38, no. 25 (March 21), 25.

"German Reunification." CC, 16, no. 11 (June 25), 83.

"The God Who Has Become the Devil." CS, 21, no. 2 (Spring), 4-5.
    Attack upon Stalin by the Russian oligarchy.

"How Can Christians Be Perfect?" L, 38, no. 41 (July 11), 19-20.

"If Races 'Mix,' Won't There be Intermarriage?" L, 38, no. 45 (August 8), 17-18.

"Ike is no Sure Thing." NL, 39, no. 11 (March 12), 3-4.

"The Indeterminate Possibilities for Good and Evil," in Sermons From an Ecumenical Pulpit. Edited by Max Daskam. Boston: Starr King Press, pp. 15-26.

"Intellectual Autobiography," in Reinhold Niebuhr: His Religious, Social and Political Thought. Edited by Kegley and Bretall. New York: Macmillan Co., pp. 2-23.

"Is There A Right and Wrong Way to Pray?" McCalls, 83, no. 12 (September), 29.
    Also printed by Good Reading Rack Service, 1957.

"Is This the Collapse of Tyranny?" CS, 21, no. 3 (Summer), 4-6.
    Speculation about possible Russian internal collapse.

"Judgment by Evildoers." NL, 39, no. 8 (February 20), 8-9.
    Why do we explode when Communists accuse us of colonialism or race bias?

"Justice as an Instrument of Love." L, 38, no. 37 (June 13), 19.

"Ku Klux Klan in Refined Version Rides Again." L, 38, no. 15 (January 11), 28.

"Literalism, Individualism and Billy Graham." CCY, 73, no. 21
    (May 23), 640-642.
        Reprinted in Essays in Applied Christianity.

"Love and Justice." M, 21, no. 12 (June 12), 5.
        Also in EC, 121, no. 13 (June 24), 28.

"Love and Law." The Pulpit, 27, no. 1 (January), 19-23.
        From sermons honoring Charles Clayton Morrison.

"The Middle East and Hungary." NL, 39, no. 48 (November 26), 7-8.

"Mideast Impasse: Is There a Way Out?" NL, 39, no. 23 (June 4),
    9-10.

"The Mysteries of Faith." The Saturday Review of Literature, 39,
    no. 16 (April 21), 18.
        Review of Abraham Heschel's God in Search of Man.

"The National Council Delegation to the Russian Church." CC, 16,
    no. 7 (April 30), 49-50.
        Reprinted in Essays in Applied Christianity.

"The New Face of the Communist Conspiracy." CS, 21, no. 1 (Winter),
    3-4.

"New Hopes for Peace in the Middle East." CC, 16, no. 9 (May 28),
    65-66.

"The New International Situation." CC, 16, no. 19 (November 12),
    150-151.

"Nikita Krushchev's Meditation on Josef Stalin." CC, 16, no. 12
    (July 9), 89-90.

"Not Argument But Witness is Required." M, 21, no. 5 (March 6), 7.

"Nullification." NL, 39, no. 10 (March 5), 3-4.
        Southern rebellion against Supreme Court desegregation decision.

"Our Involvement in Collective Evil." EC, 121, no. 18 (September 2),
    23.
        Comment on two letters about the race issue.

"Our Moral and Spiritual Resources for International Cooperation."
    Social Action, 22, no. 6 (February), 5-24.

"Polish and Hungarian Revolts." M, 21, no. 23 (December 4), 5.

"The Political Situation in America." CS, 21, no. 1 (Winter), 4-6.

"The Power of Love and the Will to Justice." Advance, 148, no. 18
    (October 5), 8-9, 24.

"Preface," to Adventurous Preaching. By James H. Robinson. Great
    Neck, N. Y.: Channel Press.

1956

"Proposal to Billy Graham." CCY, 73, no. 32 (August 8), 921–922.

"A Qualified Faith." NR, 134, no. 7 (February 13), 14–15.

"Race and Christian Conscience." CC, 16, no. 13 (July 23), 99.

"Repentance and Faith." M, 21, no. 21 (November 6), 4–5.
    Also in EC, 121, no. 24 (November 25), 28.

"Reply to Interpretation and Criticism," in <u>Reinhold Niebuhr: His
    Religious, Social, and Political Thought</u>. Edited by Kegley and
    Bretall. New York: Macmillan Co., pp. 431–451.

"School, Church, and the Ordeals of Integration." CC, 16, no. 16
    (October 1), 121–122.

"The Sense of Duty and our Duty." L, 38, no. 19 (February 8), 31.
    Also in EC, 121, no. 4 (February 19), 10.

"Seven Great Errors in U. S. Foreign Policy." NL, 39, no. 52
    (December 24–31), 3–5.

"Sermon on the Mount." L, 38, no. 51 (September 19), 16–17.

"The Significance of Suez." CC, 16, no. 16 (October 1), 123.

"Stalin--Deity or Demon." CC, 16, no. 6 (April 16), 42–43.

"Stevenson, the Democrats and Civil Rights." NL, 39, no. 28
    (July 9), 11.

"The Struggle in Hungary." CC, 16, no. 22 (December 24), 174.

"A Superb Portrait of F. D. R." NL, 39, no. 50 (December 10), 11–12.
    Review of James M. Burns's <u>Roosevelt: The Lion and the Fox</u>.

"A Theologian's Comments on the Negro in America." <u>The Reporter</u>, 15,
    no. 9 (November 29), 24–25.

"There is no Peace." CC, 16, no. 16 (November 26), 121–122.

"A Thorn in the Flesh." NR, 134, no. 22 (May 28), 20–21.
    Review of Trevor Huddleston's <u>Naught for Your Comfort</u>.

"Trials of Conscience." M, 21, no. 3 (February 7), 5–6.
    Duty and inclination.

"The Tyrant as Symbol of Community." NL, 39, no. 21 (May 21), 13–14.

"The Way of Non-Violent Resistance." CS, 21, no. 2 (Spring), 3.

"What Resources Can the Christian Church Offer to Meet Crisis in Race
    Relations?" M, 21, no. 7 (April 3), 9.
        Also in L, 38, no. 28 (April 11), 23–24; and EC, 121, no. 9
    (April 29), 24. Reprinted in <u>Love and Justice</u>.

"Why I am For Stevenson." NR, 135, no. 18 (October 29), 11.

"Why Ike is in Trouble." NL, 39, no. 39 (September 24), 3–5.

"World News Notes, Catholics and Communism." L, 39, no. 9
(November 28), 9-10.

"Yesterday's Anticipations and Today's Realities." CC, 16, no. 11
(June 25), 81-82.

"You...Must Be Perfect." M, 21, no. 14 (July 17), 9.
Perfectionism may lead to social irresponsibility.

1957

"About Historical Symbols." M, 22, no. 3 (January 29), 5.

"After Comment, the Deluge." CCY, 74, no. 36 (September 4), 10
1034-1035.
Attacks by correspondents on Life article on Billy Graham.

"And Now There is One." CC, 17, no. 20 (November 25), 155.
Khrushchev becomes "boss"; Zhukov out.

"The Anglo-Saxon Alliance." CC, 17, no. 8 (May 13), 58-59.

"Bad Days at Little Rock." CC, 17, no. 17 (October 14), 131.

"Barth on Hungary--An Exchange." CCY, 74, no. 15 (April 10),
454-455.
Reprinted in Essays in Applied Christianity.

"The Billy Graham Campaign." M, 22, no. 12 (June 4), 5.
Also in Advance, 149, no. 12 (June 14), 6; and EC, 122, no. 12
(June 23), 26.

"Bread, Freedom and Marxist Orthodoxy." CC, 17, no. 11 (June 24),
82.

"The British Nuclear Arms Proposals." CC, 17, no. 9 (May 27), 66.

"The Cardinal and the Commissar." NL, 40, no. 42 (October 21), 5-6.
"The curious alliance which has developed between the church
and the Communist State."

"Changes in the Kremlin." CC, 17, no. 14 (August 5), 107.

"China and the United Nations." Journal of International Affairs, 11,
no. 2 (1957), 187-189.

"The Christian and the Truth." EC, 122, no. 6 (March 17), 32.
Also in Advance, 149, no. 6 (March 22), 6.

"Church and State in South Africa." Advance, 149, no. 16
(September 6), 6.

"Civil Rights and Democracy." CC, 17, no. 12 (July 8), 89.

"The Civil Rights Bill." NL, 40, no. 37 (September 16), 9-11.

1957

"Comment." CC, 16, no. 23 (January 7), 186.
     A comment on K. W. Thompson's article "Europe's Crisis and
America's Dilemma."

"Commentary." Social Action, 23, no. 5 (January), 12-14.
     By Niebuhr and others on Eduard Heimann's "The Economy of
Abundance: An Ethical Problem." Reprinted as a pamphlet.
Westport, Conn.: C. K. Kazanijian Economics Foundation, 1957.

"Common Sense is Not Contrary to Truth." L, 39, no. 25 (March 20),
19.

"The Conquest of Space." NL, 40, no. 47 (November 25), 7-8.

"The Decline of Britain and France." CC, 17, no. 2 (February 18),
10-11.

"Democracy and Foreign Policy." NL, 40, no. 14 (April 8), 9-11.

"Democracy and the Trade Unions." CC, 17, no. 8 (May 13), 57-58.

"Differing Views on Billy Graham" (with J. S. Bonnell). Life, 43,
no. 1 (July 1), 92.
     Niebuhr's title: "Theologian says evangelist is over-
simplifying the issues of life."

"Djilas Dissects Communism." NL, 40, no. 36 (September 9), 17-19.
     Review of Milovan Djilas's The New Class: An Analysis of the
Communist System.

"Dilemma in a Nuclear Age." M, 22, no. 14 (July 2), 5.

"The Disarmament Debate." CC, 17, no. 11 (June 24), 82.

"The Dismal Prospects for Disarmament." CC, 17, no. 15 (September 16),
113-114.

"The Double Effect of Law." M, 22, no. 10 (May 7), 5.
     Also in Advance, 149, no. 10 (May 17), 6; and EC, 122, no. 11
(May 26), 23.

"Draft ADA Statement of Principles." ADA World, 12, no. 1 (January),
3M.
     Niebuhr the dominant voice in the draft statement.

"The Effect of the Supreme Court Decision." CC, 17, no. 1
(February 4), 3.
     Outlawing segregated schools.

"The Eisenhower Doctrine." NL, 40, no. 5 (February 4), 8-10.

"Eisenhower's Theory of Power and Morals." NL, 40, no. 10 (March 11),
3-4.

"Faith and Fanaticism." M, 22, no. 16 (August 13), 5.

"Filling the Middle East Vacuum." CC, 16, no. 24 (January 21),
189-190.

"Foreword," to <u>Journey into Mission</u>. By Philip Williams. New York: Friendship Press, pp. ix-x.

"Foreword," to <u>What the Christian Hopes for in Society</u>. Edited by Wayne H. Cowan. New York: Association Press.

"God's Mercy is the Answer." L, 39, no. 29 (April 17), 22.

"Greek Orthodoxy and the Ecumenical Movement." M, 22, no. 19 (October 8), 5.
  Also in <u>Advance</u>, 149, no. 19 (October 18), 6. Reprinted in <u>Essays in Applied Christianity</u>.

"The Heresy of Mao Tse-Tung." CC, 17, no. 11 (June 24), 82-83.

"Higher Education in America." <u>Confluence</u>, 6, no. 1 (Spring), 3-14.

"Hoffa and the Teamsters." CC, 17, no. 18 (October 28), 137-138.

"Human Creativity and Self-Concern in Freud's Thought," in <u>Freud and the 20th Century</u>. Edited by Benjamin N. Nelson. New York: Meridian Books, pp. 259-276.

"The Individual and the Community." <u>Advance</u>, 149, no. 23 (December 13), 6.

"Introduction," to <u>Social Responsibility in Mass Communication</u>. By Wilbur Schramm. New York: Harper and Brothers, pp. xi-xxiii.

"Is Israel a Mistake?" NR, 136, no. 9 (March 4), 23.
  Letter answering William E. Potter's criticism of Niebuhr's February 4 article.

"Justice and the Death Penalty." NR, 137, no. 9-10 (August 26), 18-19.
  Review of Arthur Koestler's <u>Reflections on Hanging</u>.

"Kashmir and Nehru." CC, 17, no. 3 (March 4), 18.

"A Landmark in American Religious History." M, 22, no. 13 (June 18), 11-13.
  Uniting of the Evangelical and Reformed Church with the Congregational Christian Churches.

"Law Without Grace." L, 39, no. 32 (May 8), 15.

"Liberty and Equality." <u>The Yale Review</u>, 47, no. 1 (September), 1-14.
  Reprinted in <u>Faith and Politics</u>.

"Limited Warfare." CC, 17, no. 19 (November 11), 146-147.
  Review of Henry Kissinger's <u>Nuclear Weapons and Foreign Policy</u>.

"Man Under the Machine." NL, 40, no. 4 (January 28), 23-24.
  Review of Daniel Bell's <u>Work and Its Discontents</u>.

"Mao Tse-Tung: Heir or Heretic?" CC, 17, no. 13 (July 22), 97.

Other Writings by Reinhold Niebuhr

1957

"The Moral Dilemma in a Nuclear Age." EC, 122, no. 13 (July 21), 34.
    Also in Advance, 149, no. 21 (November 15), 6.

"Morality and Politics." L, 39, no. 15 (January 9), 18.

"Morals and International Politics." Advance, 149, no. 2 (January 25), 6.
    Also in EC, 122, no. 3 (February 3), 28.

"The Mystery of Conscience." CC, 17, no. 21 (December 9), 162–163.
    Review of Annedore Leber's The Revolt of Conscience.

"Neither Adam Smith Nor Karl Marx." NL, 40, no. 51 (December 23), 8–9.

"The New British Strategy." CC, 17, no. 7 (April 29), 50–51.

"On Freedom, Virtue and Faith," in This is My Philosophy. Edited by Whit Burnett. New York: Harper and Brothers, pp. 262–286.
    Also published in London by Allen and Unwin, 1959, with paging the same. Taken from Faith and History.

"Our Human Predicament." M, 22, no. 23 (December 3), 5.

"Our Moral Dilemma." M, 22, no. 21 (November 5), 5.

"Our Stake is in the State of Israel." NR, 136, no. 5 (February 4), 9–12.

"The Past Affects the Present and Future." L, 39, no. 21 (February 20), 22–23.

"Pauline Doctrine." M, 22, no. 8 (April 9), 4–5.
    Also in Advance, 149, no. 8 (April 19), 6; and EC, 122, no. 9 (April 28), 32.

"Piety and Secularism in America." Atlantic Monthly, 200, no. 5 (November), 180–184.

"Politics and Morals." M, 22, no. 1 (January 1), 5.

"Power and Prestige in Empires and Alliances." NL, 40, no. 20 (May 20), 16–18.

"The President's Budget." CC, 17, no. 10 (June 10), 73–74.

"Protestant and Catholic." L, 40, no. 3 (October 16), 22.

"Religious Faith and Fanaticism." EC, 122, no. 14 (August 18), 40.

"Report on Hungary." CC, 17, no. 13 (July 22), 98.

"The 'Right to Work' Laws." CC, 17, no. 4 (March 18), 25–26.

"Salvation Isn't Only for Individuals." L, 40, no. 10 (December 4), 16–17.

Other Writings by Reinhold Niebuhr

"The Security and Hazard of the Christian Ministry." Union Seminary Quarterly Review, 13, no. 1 (November), 19-23.
    Address delivered at the 121st Union Theological Seminary Commencement, May 28. Reprinted in Essays in Applied Christianity.

"The Situation in the Middle East." CC, 17, no. 6 (April 15), 42-43.

"South African Race Struggle." L, 39, no. 47 (August 21), 23.

"Space Rocket Dilemma." L, 40, no. 6 (November 6), 16-17.

"The Supreme Court and the Rights of Individuals." CC, 17, no. 12 (July 8), 90.

"The Symbols of Freedom." EC, 122, no. 4 (February 17), 24.
    About a visit with the sister of Jan Masaryk.

"The Teamsters and Labor's Future." NL, 40, no. 34 (August 26), 3-5.

"Terrible Realities." M, 22, no. 25 (December 31), 5.
    Maintaining security with H-bomb threats.

"Theology and Political Thought in the Western World." The Ecumenical Review, 9, no. 3 (April), 253-262.
    Reprinted in Faith and Politics.

"Those 'Right to Work' Laws." American Federationist, 64, no. 2 (February), 14.

"Tragedy in South Africa." M, 22, no. 17 (September 3), 5.

"Triumph of a 'Backward' Technology." CC, 17, no. 20 (November 25), 153-154.

"The Truth in Christ." M, 22, no. 6 (March 12), 5.

"The Truth in Myths," in Evolution and Religion. Edited by Gail Kennedy. Boston: Heath, pp. 88-97.
    This chapter has been printed and reprinted numbers of times since 1937. Check 1937 listing for the original and other printings.

"The Two Sources of Western Culture," in The Christian Idea of Education. Edited by Edmund Fuller. New Haven: Yale University Press, pp. 237-254.

"The Ultimate Validity and the Ideological Distortions of Moral Concepts in International Politics." A paper prepared for the meeting of the American Political Science Association, September 6.

"The U. N. is Not a World Government." The Reporter, 16, no. 5 (March 7), 30-32.

"We Run the Risk." L, 39, no. 46 (August 14), 22.
    The dangers of fanaticism.

Other Writings by Reinhold Niebuhr

1957

"Why is Barth Silent on Hungary?" CCY, 74, no. 4 (January 23),
108-110.
Reprinted in Essays in Applied Christianity.

"World News Notes, The Dilemma of Disarmament." L, 39, no. 41
(July 10), 11.

1958

"After Sputnik and Explorer." CC, 18, no. 4 (March 17), 29-30.
Reprinted in The World Crisis and American Responsibility.

"An Awful Week." NL, 41, no. 22 (June 2), 7.
World troubles and more modest U. S. ambitions.

"Christianity and Darwin's Revolution," in A Book That Shook the
World. Anniversary Essays on Charles Darwin's Origin of Species.
Pittsburgh: The University of Pittsburgh Press, pp. 30-37.

"The Dialogue Between the Will and Conscience of the Self." Pastoral
Psychology, 9, no. 85 (June), 9-12, 14.
Excerpt from Chapter 3 of The Self and the Dramas of History.

"Disaster in United States Foreign Policy." CC, 18, no. 5
(September 15), 117-118.

"The Disaster of U. S. Policy." NL, 41, no. 30 (August 18-25), 8-9.

"Discriminate Justice in Technical Society." NL, 41, no. 3
(January 20), 13-14.

"Foreword," to Free Society and Moral Crisis. By Robert C. Angell.
Ann Arbor: University of Michigan Press, pp. vii-viii.

"France's Malady." NL, 41, no. 13 (March 31), 17-18.

"Freedom," in A Handbook of Christian Theology. Edited by Marvin
Halverson. New York: Meridian Books, Inc., pp. 139-141.
Reprinted in Faith and Politics.

"The General's Progress; DeGaulle Separates Algerian Army From
Colonial Diehards." NL, 41, no. 39 (October 27), 11.

"The Gospel in Future America." CCY, 75, no. 25 (June 18), 712-716.

"Humphrey for President?" NL, 41, no. 48 (December 29), 5.

"Implications for the Elections." CC, 18, no. 20 (November 24),
161-162.

"The Janus Face of American Diplomacy." NL, 41, no. 8 (February 24),
16-17.

"Man and Spirit." The Kiwanis Magazine (November), p. 15.

1958

"Martyrdom in East Germany." CC, 17, no. 24 (January 20), 186.

"Mike Wallace Interview With Reinhold Niebuhr." Santa Barbara: Center for the Study of Democratic Institutions, April 27.

"Mr. Eisenhower and the State of the Union." CC, 18, no. 1 (February 3), 2–3.

"Moral Dilemma of Nuclear Warfare." L, 40, no. 1 (January 15), 14–15.

"The Moral Insecurity of Our Security." CC, 17, no. 23 (January 6), 177–178.

"The Moral World of Foster Dulles." NR, 139, no. 22 (December 1), 8.

"Morals and the Cold War." NL, 41, no. 15 (April 14), 26, 28.
    Review of Ernest Lefever's The Ethics of U. S. Foreign Policy.

"The Next Twenty Years." Fortune, 57, no. 7 (January), 190.
    Niebuhr and others (fifty in all) were asked about projected economic problems of the next twenty years.

"A Note on Pluralism," in Religion in America. Edited by John Cogley. New York: Meridian Books, Inc., pp. 42–50.

"An Orthodox Christian Anthropology." NR, 139, no. 25 (December 22), 17.

"Personalities and Social Forces." NL, 41, no. 44 (December 1), 7–8.

"A Predicament We Share With Russia." NL, 41, no. 16 (April 21), 10–11.

"Reinhold Niebuhr Comments." M, 23, no. 1 (January 14), 5.

"The Relations of Christians and Jews." CCAR Journal [Central Conference of American Rabbis], no. 21 (April), pp. 18–32.
    Reprint of Chapter 7 of Pious and Secular America.

"A Rich Nation in a Poor World." CC, 18, no. 5 (March 31), 38–39.

"The 'Right' to Teach." CC, 18, no. 22 (December 22), 178.
    Comment on the Catholic Bishops' assertion of the right of the church to teach her doctrines. Niebuhr questions: 1. "Where do the Bishops get a 'right to a hearing?'...and 2. "Why did the Bishops believe, as I assume they did, that this statement would win many erring or confused souls back to pure doctrine?"

"Right to Work Laws." Ohio Christian News, 31, no. 4 (April), 16.

"The Self," in A Handbook of Christian Theology. Edited by Marvin Halverson. New York: Meridian Books, Inc., pp. 342–345.

"Sin," in A Handbook of Christian Theology. Edited by Marvin Halverson. New York: Meridian Books, Inc., pp. 348–351.

"The Situation in the Middle East." CC, 18, no. 14 (August 4), 109–110.

1958

"The States' Rights Crisis." NL, 41, no. 35 (September 29), 6-7.

"Survival and Freedom." A Mike Wallace Interview. American Broad-
casting Company, April 27. Printed by the Fund for the Republic,
11 pp.
    Listed above under "Mike Wallace Interview."

"Tactical and Strategic Weapons." Advance, 150, no. 1 (January 17),
6.

"Uneasy Peace or Catastrophe." CC, 18, no. 7 (April 28), 54-55.

"Walter Rauschenbusch in Historical Perspective." Religion in Life,
27, no. 4 (Autumn), 527-536.
    Reprinted in Essays in Applied Christianity.

"Why We Are Losing to the Russians." NL, 41, no. 2 (January 13), 6-7.

"Will DeGaulle Save France?" NL, 41, no. 26 (June 30), 6-7.

1959

"Abraham Lincoln and the Self-Image of America." The Berkshire Eagle,
67, no. 239 (February 12), 1, 25.
    Dr. Niebuhr submitted articles to the Eagle into 1963 and once
in 1969. Most of the articles were the same as the ones sent to
The New Leader and were sometimes published under different titles.

"The Art of Advancing From the Brink." The Berkshire Eagle, 68,
no. 106 (September 5), 1.

"The Art of the Possible." NL, 42, no. 34 (September 21), 3-4.

"'Balance of Terror': Credit and Debit." NL, 42, no. 29
(August 3-10), 4-5.

"Barth's East German Letter." CCY, 76, no. 6 (February 11), 167-168.

"Biblical Faith and Socialism: A Critical Appraisal," in Religion
and Culture: Essays in Honor of Paul Tillich. Edited by Walter
Liebrecht. New York: Harper and Brothers, pp. 44-57.

"The Church in the World." Theology Today, 15, no. 4 (January),
542-548.

"Civil Rights and the Filibuster." CC, 19, no. 1 (February 2), 2-3.

"Coexistence Under a Nuclear Stalemate." CC, 19, no. 15
(September 21), 121-122.

"The Cold War and Nuclear Dilemma." Cross Currents, 9, no. 3
(Summer), 212-224.

"Cold War and Nuclear Dilemma." NR, 141, no. 21 (November 23), 17-18.
    Review of W. E. Hocking's The Strength of Men and Nations.

"The Dangers of the Nuclear Test Bans." NL, 42, no. 23 (June 8), 11–12.

"A Decade of Dizzy and Rapid Change." CC, 19, no. 22 (December 28), 191–192.

"DeGaulle Balance Sheet." NL, 42, no. 14 (April 6), 6–7.

"The Democratic Elite and American Foreign Policy," in <u>Walter Lippmann and His Time</u>. Edited by Marquis W. Childs. New York: Harcourt, Brace and Co., pp. 168–188.

"Does God Reward the Righteous and Punish the Unrighteous?" <u>United Church Herald</u>, 2, no. 19 (October 15), 33–34.

"Education and the World Scene." <u>Daedalus</u>, 88, no. 1 (Winter), 107–120.
    Reprinted in <u>Education in the Age of Science</u>, edited by Brand Blanshard. New York: Basic Books, 117–129.

"Freiheit und Gleichheit." <u>Zeitschrift für evangelische Ethik</u>, 3, no. 1 (January), 37–47.

"From Progress to Perplexity," in <u>The Search for America</u>. Edited by Huston Smith. Englewood Cliffs, N. J.: Prentice-Hall, Inc., pp. 135–146.

"Geneva: Preface and Problems." CC, 19, no. 10 (June 8), 78–79.

"The Giants Change Weapons." <u>The Berkshire Eagle</u>, 68, no. 81 (August 7), 14.

"The Image of America." NL, 42, no. 8 (February 23), 8–10.
    Discussion of why Lincoln "achieved supremacy over all other heroes in the national pantheon."

"Introduction," to Benjamin Ginzberg's <u>Rededication to Freedom</u>. New York: Simon and Schuster, pp. vii–viii.

"The Irresistible Joneses." <u>The Berkshire Eagle</u>, 68, no. 60 (July 14), 14.

"Is DeGaulle's Honeymoon Over?" <u>The Berkshire Eagle</u>, 67, no. 270 (March 20), 18.

"A Khrushchev Visit to America?" CC, 19, no. 14 (August 3), 113–114.

"Letter." CC, 19, no. 16 (October 5), 141.
    An answer to a letter in the same issue by E. A. Gaede criticizing Niebuhr's June 22 article entitled "A New Look at the Sobell Case."

"The Long Haul of Co-existence." CC, 19, no. 20 (November 30), 172–173.

"The Long Ordeal of Co-existence." NR, 140, no. 13 (March 30), 10–12.

1959

"Lunik and Ike's Budget." NL, 42, no. 4 (January 26), 7.

"Macmillan and the Peace." NL, 42, no. 19 (May 11), 8-9.

"Macmillan: Second-Fiddle Virtuoso." The Berkshire Eagle, 67, no. 305 (April 30), 20.

"Man the Creator." Discussion by Lyman Bryson (Moderator), Reinhold Niebuhr, Milton Nahm and Louis Finkelstein. Mimeographed. [N.P.]

"Mr. Khrushchev and Post-Stalin Russia." CC, 19, no. 3 (March 2), 17-18.

"Modern Answers to An Enigma." Life, 46, no. 20 (May 18), 135, 137. Discussion of MacLeish's J. B.

"Moral and Political Judgments of Christians." CC, 19, no. 12 (July 6), 99-103.

"Morality," in The Search for America. Edited by Huston Smith. Englewood Cliffs, N. J.: Prentice-Hall, Inc., pp. 147-153.

"Negotiation in the Berlin Crisis." CC, 18, no. 23 (January 5), 185.

"A New Look at the Sobel Case." CC, 19, no. 11 (June 22), 91.

"The New Nations: Seeds, Buds and Flowers." CC, 19, no. 5 (March 30), 34-35.

"New Voice in the West." NL, 42, no. 45 (December 7), 12. DeGaulle has spurred a "reassertion of French prestige."

"Niebuhr on Gottwald." CCY, 76, no. 50 (December 16), 1477. Reply to Gottwald's letter (November 11) called "Niebuhr on Nuclear War."

"The Pope's Proposal." CC, 19, no. 2 (February 16), 11. Pope John's proposal for an ecumenical council.

"The Possible Peace of Stalemate." The Berkshire Eagle, 68, no. 14 (May 19), 14.

"Power and Ideology in National and International Affairs," in Theoretical Aspects of International Relations. Edited by W. T. R. Fox. Notre Dame: The University of Notre Dame Press, pp. 107-118. Reprinted in Faith and Politics.

"The Problem of a Protestant Social Ethic." Union Seminary Quarterly Review, 15, no. 1 (November), 1-11.

"The Problem of Justice and the Power of Love." The United Church Herald, 2, no. 1 (January 1), 34.

Other Writings by Reinhold Niebuhr

"Something Ventured, Nothing Gained." NL, 42, no. 38 (October 19),
9.
    Khrushchev's visit to the U. S. and the U. N.

"Steel Strike: Glory of an Open Society." CC, 19, no. 17
(October 19), 145-146.

"The Test of Christian Faith Today." CCY, 76, no. 43 (October 28),
1239-1243.

"A Visit With Reinhold Niebuhr" by Arthur Herzog. Think (December),
pp. 9-11.

1960

"The Aftermath of Imperialism." The Berkshire Eagle, 69, no. 174
(November 25), 22.

"Berlin, Disarmament and the Summit." CC, 20, no. 2 (February 22),
10-11.

"Catholics and the Presidency." NL, 43, no. 19 (May 9), 3-4.

"Catholics and the State." NR, 143, no. 17 (October 17), 13-15.

"The Changing United Nations." CC, 20, no. 16 (October 3), 133-134.

"The Christian Moral Witness and Some Disciplines of Modern Culture."
Pastoral Psychology, 11, no. 101 (February), 45-54.
    Also in Making the Ministry Relevant, edited by Hans Hoffmann.
New York: Scribner's, pp. 39-53.

"A Christian View of the Future." Interview by Henry Brandon.
Harper's Magazine, 221, no. 1327 (December), 71-77.

"The Church and the South African Tragedy." CC, 20, no. 7 (May 2),
53-54.

"The Church Issue in Retrospect." The Berkshire Eagle, 69, no. 179
(December 1), 22.

"Cold Comfort of a 'Mystic Unity.'" CC, 20, no. 8 (May 16), 65-66.
    The Dutch Reformed church of South Africa and its racial views.

"Disaster in American Policy." The Berkshire Eagle, 68, no. 169
(June 28), 1.

"The Eisenhower Era." NL, 43, no. 38 (October 3), 3-4.

"The Election and the Next President." CC, 20, no. 20 (November 28),
169-170.

"The Election--The Religious Issue." NL, 43, no. 48 (December 12),
3-4.

1960

"'End of an Era' for Organized Labor." NL, 43, no. 1 (January 4), 15-16.

"Failure at the Summit." CC, 20, no. 9 (May 30), 73.

"The Failure of U. S. Diplomacy." NL, 43, no. 31 (August 1-8), 6-7.

"First Steps Toward a New Diplomacy." NL, 43, no. 25 (June 20), 7-8.

"The Folly of Racial Arrogance." The Berkshire Eagle, 69, no. 202 (December 30), 14.

"Foreword," to Community of Fear. By H. S. Brown and James Real. Santa Barbara: Center for the Study of Democratic Institutions, pp. 4-6.

"Foreword," to The Self in Pilgrimage. By Earl A. Loomis. New York: Harper and Brothers, pp. ix-x.

"France's Fifth Republic and its General." NL, 43, no. 7 (February 15), 12-13.

"Have We Gone Soft?" [America--1960--A Symposium.] NR, 142, no. 7 (February 15), 15.

"Imperialism in Perspective." NL, 43, no. 44 (November 14), 7-8.

"Khrushchev and the United Nations." CC, 20, no. 18 (October 18), 155.

"Khrushchev's Rumanian Rhapsody." CC, 20, no. 12 (July 11), 98-99.

"National Goals and Purposes." CC, 20, no. 22 (December 26), 191-192.

"The Negro Dilemma." NL, 43, no. 15 (April 11), 13-14.

"Niebuhr Assails Pacifists' Theory." The New York Times (January 24), p. 29.

"The President's Triumphal Journey." CC, 19, no. 23 (January 11), 202-203.

"The Problem of a Protestant Political Ethic." CCY, 77, no. 38 (September 21), 1085-1087.

"Protestants in Politics." NR, 143, no. 19 (October 31), 31. A letter.

"The Public Interest is Paramount." CC, 19, no. 23 (January 11), 202.

"The Quality of our Lives." CCY, 77, no. 19 (May 11), 568-572. In the series "How My Mind Has Changed."

"Religion and Politics," in Religion and Politics. Edited by Peter H. Odegard. New York: Oceana Publications, pp. 107-112. Reprinted from Perspectives (Winter 1954).

"The Religious Issue." NL, 43, no. 48 (December 12), 3-4.

1961

"The Religious Traditions of Our Nation." The Saturday Evening Post, 233, no. 4 (July 23), 26-27, 45, 48.

"Stray Thoughts on the Political Scene." CC, 20, no. 14 (August 8), 124.

"The Tasks of Liberalism in America." Program of ADA (13th Annual Convention), Washington, D. C., May 6-8, 3 unnumbered pages.
    On the occasion of ADA honoring Dr. Niebuhr.

"A Third of a Century at Union." Union Seminary Tower, 7, no. 1 (May), 3.

"Two Questions and Two Answers." United Church Herald, 3, no. 5 (March 3), 14-15.
    Righteousness, guilt and forgiveness.

"Why Christianity and Crisis?" CC, 20, no. 1 (February 8), 1-2.

1961

"Berlin and Prestige in Europe." NR, 145, no. 12 (September 18), 17-19.

"The Catholic President and the Hierarchy." The Berkshire Eagle, 69, no. 268 (March 16), 12.

"Christianity and Darwin's Revolution," in A Book That Shook the World: Anniversary Essays on Charles Darwin's Origin of Species. Pittsburgh: The University of Pittsburgh Press, pp. 30-37.

"Communist Dogma and Latin America." NL, 44, no. 22 (May 29), 17-18.

"The Death Throes of a Way of Life." The Berkshire Eagle, 70, no. 34 (June 12), 16.
    Freedom riders in a changing South.

"Democracy's Foreign Policy Dilemma." NL, 44, no. 34 (October 2), 22-23.

"The Eichmann Trial." CC, 21, no. 5 (April 3), 47-48.

"The Eternal Church and the Modern World." CCY, 78, no. 38 (September 20), 1105-1108.
    Summary and excerpts in Time, 78, no. 13 (September 29), 61A-62.

"The Federal Shelter Program." CC, 21, no. 22 (December 25), 227.

"Foreign Policy and Democracy." The Berkshire Eagle, 70, no. 108 (September 8), 18.

"From Euphoria to Harsh Reality." The Berkshire Eagle, 70, no. 58 (July 11), 14.
    From the first summit meeting in 1955 to the "realism" of Geneva in 1961.

Other Writings by Reinhold Niebuhr

1961

"The Gravity of Our Contest With Communism." CC, 21, no. 13 (July 24), 129-130.

"How My Mind Has Changed," in How My Mind Has Changed. Edited by Harold E. Fey. New York: Meridian Books, pp. 116-132.

Hutchins, Robert M. Two Faces of Federalism: An Outline of an Argument About Pluralism, Unity, and Law. Discussion members: Harrison Brown, Scott Buchanan, Eugene Burdick, William O. Douglas, Eric F. Goldman, John Courtney Murray, Reinhold Niebuhr, and I. I. Rabbi. Santa Barbara: Center for the Study of Democratic Institutions. Niebuhr's comments appear on pages 27-28, 38, 52, 53, 60, 65, 66, 68, 70, 71, 75-76, 77-78, 79-80, 81, 83, 88, 89, 97-98, 99, 100, 103, 104, 110, 112, 113.

"Introduction," to The Varieties of Religious Experience. By William James. New York: Collier Books, pp. 5-8.

"Laos and Cuba: Problems for Review." CC, 20, no. 24 (January 23), 209-210.

"Living With Fear." NL, 44, no. 37 (November 13), 23.

"Mater et Magister." CC, 21, no. 14 (August 7), 142-143.
    Also in The Berkshire Eagle, 70, no. 91 (August 18), 20.

"Mistaken Venture." NL, 44, no. 18 (May 1), 3-4.
    Assessment of the Bay of Pigs.

"The Montgomery Savagery." CC, 21, no. 10 (June 12), 102-103.

"Morality at the Shelter Door." CC, 21, no. 19 (November 13), 197.

"The New Feudalism." NL, 44, no. 31 (August 28), 13-14.
    Hoffa's succession to Presidency of the Teamsters.

"Niebuhr's History, An Exchange." Columbia University Forum, 4, no. 4 (Fall), 81-82.
    A letter replying to critics of his article in the Summer issue of the Forum.

"The Nuclear Dilemma--A Discussion." CC, 21, no. 19 (November 13), 202.

"On Ambitious Politicians." NR, 144, no. 9 (February 27), 14-15.

"Persuasion, Politics and Power," in The Agreeable Autocracies: A Series of Conversations on American Institutions. Edited by Joseph P. Lyford. New York: Oceana Publications, pp. 128-141.

"Pluralism at the Inaugural." CC, 21, no. 2 (February 20), 15.

"Present Heritage of the Long Encounter Between Christian Faith and Western Civilization." The Harvard Divinity Bulletin, 26, no. 1 (October), 1-11.

Other Writings by Reinhold Niebuhr

"President Kennedy's Cuban Venture." CC, 21, no. 8 (May 15), 69-70.

"Prospects for the South." NL, 44, no. 25 (June 19), 3-4.

"Putting Hoffa in Perspective." The Berkshire Eagle, 70, no. 79
(August 4), 14.

"Reflections on Democracy as an Alternative to Communism." Columbia
University Forum, 4, no. 3 (Summer), 10-18.
Condensed version published in The Wall Street Journal
(August 8), p. 12, and (August 9), p. 101. Also Current, no. 17
(September), 63-68.

"Religion and Its Substitutes." NR, 144, no. 16 (April 17), 17-19.
Review of Gerhard Szczesny's The Future of Unbelief.

"The Resumption of Nuclear Testing." CC, 21, no. 16 (October 2),
161-162.

"Rising Hopes For Arms Control." CC, 21, no. 3 (March 6), 21-22.

"The Rising Tide of Color." NL, 44, no. 4 (January 23), 16-17.

"School Aid, the President and the Hierarchy." NL, 44, no. 12
(March 20), 8-9.

"A Study of American Character." Fund for the Republic Meeting,
Washington, D. C., June 1. Printed in The Congressional Record.
87th Congress, First Session, August 7.
Niebuhr's original presentation was done at the Fund "Conference on the American Character" and was considerably longer.

"Tractors for Freedom." CC, 21, no. 11 (June 26), 109-110.

"The Unintended Virtues of an Open Society." CC, 21, no. 13
(July 24), 132-138.

"The U. N.: An End to Illusions." NL, 44, no. 9 (February 27), 3-4.

"Well-Tempered Evangelism." NR, 144, no. 26 (June 26), 11-12.
Limitations of liberal democracy in much of the world.

1962

"Algeria: Political Heights and Depths." CC, 22, no. 12 (July 9),
117-118.

"The Alternatives to Communism." NR, 147, no. 14 (October 1), 15-16.

"American Hegemony and the Prospects for Peace." The Annals, 342
(July), 154-160.
Reprinted in Faith and Politics.

"Boulder in the Currents." The Spectator, 209, no. 7006 (October 5),
488, 490.

1962

Reference to General DeGaulle as "an impressive boulder which has survived the torrents when the ice age receded."

"Can Democracy Work?" NL, 45, no. 11 (May 28), 8-9.

"The Case for Congo Unity." NL, 45, no. 1 (January 8), 3-4.

"The Common Market Paradox." The Berkshire Eagle, 71, no. 89 (August 16), 20.

"The Concept of 'Order of Creation' in Emil Brunner's Social Ethic," in The Theology of Emil Brunner. Edited by C. W. Kegley. New York: Macmillan, pp. 265-271.

"Cuba: Avoiding the Holocaust." CC, 22, no. 20 (November 26), 204-205.

"The Cuban Crisis in Retrospect." NL, 45, no. 25 (December 10), 8-9.

"Despair Can be a Source of Danger." Vogue, 139, no. 1 (January 1), 70-71.

"A Dissenting Opinion." NL, 45, no. 14 (July 9), 3-4.
    On the Supreme Court's "Regents' Prayer" decision.

"Drama on the Cuban Stage." NL, 45, no. 5 (March 5), 11.

"Elections at Mid-Term." NL, 45 no. 22 (October 29), 19-20.

"History as Seen From the Radical Right." NL, 45, no. 8 (April 16), 24-25.
    Review of F. H. Johnson's No Substitute for Victory.

"Internationalism and DeGaulle's Nationalism." CC, 22, no. 10 (June 11), 98-99.

"The Intractability of Race Prejudice." CC, 22, no. 18 (October 29), 181.

"It's Very Late in Latin America." The Berkshire Eagle, 71, no. 68 (July 23), 16.

"Katanga and Primitive Anti-Communism." CC, 21, no. 24 (January 22), 245.

"Logical Consistency and the Nuclear Dilemma." CC, 22, no. 5 (April 2), 48.
    A letter.

"Nuclear Dilemma." Union Seminary Quarterly Review, 17, no. 3 (March), 239-242.
    Review of Nuclear Weapons and the Conflict of Conscience, edited by John C. Bennett.

"On Living in Two Worlds at Once." NR, 146, no. 20 (May 14), 32-33.
    Review of Louis J. Halle's Men and Nations.

1963

"One Year of the New Frontier." CC, 22, no. 1 (February 5), 1-2.

"Our Latin American Policy." CC, 22, no. 5 (April 2), 42-43.

"Our Stake in the Common Market." CC, 22, no. 2 (February 19), 13-14.

"A Plea for Tolerance." The Atlantic Monthly, 210, no. 2 (August), 72-77.
    Part of a symposium on "The Roman Catholic Church in America."

"Preface," to What Are Human Rights? By Maurice C. Cranston. New York: Basic Books, Inc., pp. v-viii.

"President Kennedy's Defeats and Victories." CC, 22, no. 14 (August 6), 133-134.

"The Problem of the Modern Church: Triviality." CC, 22, no. 21 (December 10), 223-226, 228.

["Reason and Faith in Modern Society." Review of Eduard Heimann's Reason and Faith in Modern Society.] Union Seminary Quarterly Review, 17, no. 4 (May), 374-376.

"The Regents' Prayer Decision." CC, 22, no. 13 (July 23), 125-126.

"Reinhold Niebuhr Replies." NL, 45, no. 16 (August 6), 27.
    Reply to critics of his article on "Regents' Prayer" decision in July 9 issue.

"School Prayer--An Interview." NR, 147, no. 2 (July 9), 4.
    From an interview with Religious News Service, June 26.

"U. S. Steel and the U.S.A." CC, 22, no. 8 (May 14), 69-70.

"Who is My Brother's Keeper?" (with Carl F. H. Henry). The Christian Herald, 85, no. 1 (January), 14-17, 57-58.
    The welfare system--strengths and weaknesses.

"Witness to an Ancient Truth." Time (April 20), p. 59.
    Comment on Karl Barth's visit to the U. S.

"Woe Unto Them That Spoil." CC, 22, no. 16 (October 1), 159-160.

1963

"Advent of Compulsory Arbitration." CC, 23, no. 16 (September 30), 166-167.

"America the Smug." The Saturday Evening Post, 236, no. 40 (November 16), 12, 17.

"The Christian and the Cold War." L, NS 1, no. 3 (January 30), 6-8.

"The Clay Committee Report." CC, 23, no. 7 (April 29), 65-67.

1963

"The Crisis in American Protestantism." CCY, 80, no. 49
(December 4), 1498-1501.

"The Development of a Social Ethic in the Ecumenical Movement," in
The Sufficiency of God, Essays on the Ecumenical Hope (In honor
of W. A. Visser't Hooft). Edited by Robert C. Mackie and
Charles C. West. Philadelphia: The Westminster Press,
pp. 111-128.
Published in London by the SCM Press. Reprinted in Faith and
Politics.

"Dilemma of U. S. Power." NL, 46, no. 24 (November 25), 11-12.

"Federal Aid to Education: A Call to Action." CC, 23, no. 18
(October 28), 189-191.
Writing with others on the same subject.

"For Our Inheritance: A Thanksgiving Prayer." United Church Herald,
6, no. 21 (November 15), 7.

"Foreword," to The Ideologies of the Developing Nations. By Paul E.
Sigmund, Jr. New York: Frederick A. Praeger, pp. v-vi.
Revised edition, 1967.

"History's Limitations in the Nuclear Age." NL, 46, no. 3
(February 4), 18-19.

"How Liberal is the Pope?" NL, 46, no. 15 (July 22), 10-11.

"John Fitzgerald Kennedy." CC, 23, no. 21 (December 9), 221.

"The Mounting Racial Crisis." CC, 23, no. 12 (July 8), 121-122.

"Pacem in Terris: Two Views" (with John Bennett). CC, 23, no. 8
(May 13), 81, 83.
Also in United Church Herald, 6, no. 11 (May 30), 6-7, 32.

"The Peril of a New Napoleon." CC, 23, no. 3 (March 4), 22-23.
DeGaulle's attempts to form a "united Europe" under French
hegemony.

"Pragmatic Economics." NL, 46, no. 8 (April 15), 7.

"The President's European Hegira." CC, 23, no. 13 (July 22), 133.

"The Problem of South Vietnam." CC, 23, no. 14 (August 5), 142-143.

"The Recession in Church-Going." The Berkshire Eagle, 71, no. 289
(April 12), 18.

"The Religious Situation in America," in Religion and Contemporary
Society. Edited by Harold Stahmer. New York: Macmillan,
pp. 145-155.

"Revolution in an Open Society." NL, 46, no. 11 (May 27), 7-8.

1964

"A Tentative Assessment." NL, 46, no. 25 (December 9), 7-8.
    In a series of four articles on Kennedy--"The Kennedy Legacy."

"The Test Ban Agreement." CC, 23, no. 15 (September 16), 155.

"Winter of Discontent." CC, 23, no. 4 (March 18), 35.
    Difficulties faced by President Kennedy.

1964

"After the Second Session." NL, 47, no. 2 (January 20), 11-12.
    The Vatican Council.

"The Ark and the Temple," in The Religious Experience. Edited by
    George Brantl. Vol. II. New York: Braziller, pp. 569-577.
    Chapter 3 of Beyond Tragedy.

"Christian Attitudes Toward Sex and Family." CC, 24, no. 7
    (April 27), 73-75.

"The Deputy." CC, 24, no. 4 (March 16), 32.
    Review of the drama on the Roman Catholic church and Nazi
    anti-Semitism.

"The Discontents of an Affluent Society." CC, 24, no. 15
    (September 21), 169.

"The End of an Era." CC, 24, no. 9 (May 25), 96-97.
    Unions and industrial automation.

"Foreword," to St. George's Church. By Elizabeth Moulton. New York:
    St. George's Church.

"Further Reactions to Vatican II." CC, 23, no. 24 (January 20),
    259-260.

"The Giant and the Dwarf." CC, 24, no. 1 (February 3), 1-2.
    Considers the issues separating the U. S. and Panama, on the
    occasion of the riots in Panama.

"Goldwater vs. History." NL, 47, no. 22 (October 26), 16-17.

"Introduction," to On Religion. By Karl Marx and Friedrich Engels.
    New York: Schocken Books, pp. vii-xiv.

"Johnson and the Myths of Democracy." NL, 47, no. 11 (May 25),
    18-20.
    Reprinted in Faith and Politics.

"Man, the Unregenerate Tribalist." CC, 24, no. 12 (July 6), 133-134.

"The New Trinity." NL, 47, no. 6 (March 16), 17-18.
    Protestant, Catholic and Jewish advisers on The Deputy.

"The Panama Crisis." NR, 150, no. 5 (February 1), 5-6.

1964

"The Politics of Nostalgia." NL, 47, no. 14 (July 20), 3-4.
    Senator Goldwater and the Republicans.

"Prayer and Justice in School and Nation." CC, 24, no. 9 (May 25),
    93, 95-97.

"Preface," to The Nature and Destiny of Man. Vol. 1. New York:
    Scribner's Library, pp. vii-ix. (paperbound)

"President Johnson's Foreign Policy." CC, 24, no. 4 (March 16),
    31-32.

"Prisoner of the South." NL, 47, no. 9 (April 27), 16-17.
    Senators Fulbright and Russell.

"Progress Toward Sanity." NL, 47, no. 1 (January 6), 26-27.
    Review of John P. Roche's The Quest for the Dream.

"Protestant Individualism and the Goldwater Movement." CC, 24,
    no. 21 (December 14), 248-250.

"The Struggle for Justice." NL, 47, no. 14 (July 6), 10-11.

"Triumph of Primitivism." NL, 47, no. 16 (August 17), 5-6.
    Implications of Republican nomination of Goldwater.

"The Two Themes of Evanston." NYHT (Main section) (March 29), p. 10.

1965

"Adlai Stevenson: 1900-1965." CC, 25, no. 14 (August 9), 169-170.

"Caribbean Blunder." CC, 25, no. 9 (May 31), 113-114.
    Johnson's ordering the Marines into the Dominican Republic.

"Civil Rights Climax in Alabama." CC, 25, no. 5 (April 5), 61.

"Consensus at the Price of Flexibility." NL, 48, no. 19
    (September 27), 18-20.
    Attacking Johnson's support of the Vietnam war "by consensus."

"A Diplomatic Rap on the Crosier." Book Week (July 4), p. 4.
    Review of Xavier Rynne's The Third Session, Vatican II.

"The Drama of the Vatican Council." CC, 24, no. 23 (January 11),
    275-276.

"The Fateful Triangle." NL, 48, no. 1 (January 4), 18-20.
    Russia, China and the U. S. will determine peace for a long
    time.

"Felix Frankfurter--In Memoriam." CC, 25, no. 5 (April 5), 69-70.

"For Emanuel Romero." The New York Post (March 16) (Magazine section),
    p. 4.
    Letter to the editor.

1966

"Foreword," to <u>Mississippi Black Paper</u>. New York: Random House, 2 unnumbered pages.

"Lessons of the Detroit Experience." CCY, 82, no. 16 (April 21), 487-490.

"Martin Buber: 1878-1965." CC, 25, no. 12 (July 12), 146-147.

"Martin Buber: In Memoriam." <u>The Saturday Review</u>, 48, no. 30 (July 24), 37.

"Norman Thomas: Incarnate Conscience." CC, 24, no. 23 (January 11), 271-272.
    On the occasion of his eightieth birthday.

"Paul Tillich in Memoriam." <u>Union Seminary Quarterly Review</u>, 21, no. 1 (November), 11.

"Pretense and Power." NL, 48, no. 5 (March 1), 6-7.

"Prospects of the Johnson Era." CC, 25, no. 2 (February 22), 13-14.

"The Religion of Abraham Lincoln." CCY, 82, no. 6 (February 10), 172-175.

"Roosevelt and Johnson: A Contrast in Foreign Policy." NL, 48, no. 15 (July 19), 5-8.

"Senator Fulbright's Achievement." CC, 25, no. 17 (October 18), 209-210.

"Some Things I Have Learned." <u>The Saturday Review</u>, 48, no. 45 (November 6), 63-64.

"Vietnam: An Insoluble Problem." CC, 25, no. 1 (February 8), 1-2.

"Winston Churchill and Great Britain." CC, 25, no. 1 (February 8), 8-10.

<u>1966</u>

"The Army in the New Nations." CC, 26, no. 7 (May 2), 83-84.

"A Christian Journal Confronts Mankind's Continuing Crisis." CC, 26, no. 2 (February 21), 11-13.
    <u>Christianity and Crisis</u>--past and future.

"The CIA: Tool or Policy-Maker?" CC, 26, no. 9 (May 30), 105-106.

"Faith as the Sense of Meaning in Human Existence." CC, 26, no. 10 (June 13), 127-131.
    Observations on the "death of God" theologians. Reprinted in <u>Faith and Politics</u>.

Other Writings by Reinhold Niebuhr

1966

"An Interview With Reinhold Niebuhr." By John Cogley. McCall's, 93, no. 5 (February), 90-91, 166-171.

"An Interview With Reinhold Niebuhr." By Patrick Granfield. Commonweal, 85, no. 11 (December 16), 315-321.

"The Peace Offensive" (with Ursula M. Niebuhr). CC, 25, no. 24 (January 24), 301-302.

"The President on 'The Arrogance of Power.'" CC, 26, no. 10 (June 13), 125-126.

"Reinhold Niebuhr Discusses the War in Vietnam." NR, 154, no. 5 (January 29), 15-16.
    Answers to questions posed by The New Republic.

"Some Things I Have Learned," in What I Have Learned, A Saturday Review Book. New York: Simon and Schuster, pp. 233-249.

"To America and Back," in I Knew Dietrich Bonhoeffer. Edited by Wolf-Dieter Zimmermann and G. Smith. New York: Harper and Row, p. 165.

"The Unresolved Religious Problem in Christian-Jewish Relations." CC, 26, no. 21 (December 12), 279-283.

"Vietnam and the Imperial Conflict." NL, 49, no. 12 (June 6), 15-18.

"Vietnam: The Tide Begins to Turn." CC, 26, no. 17 (October 17), 221-223.

1967

"Christian Revolutionary." The New York Times Book Review, 116 (April 16), p. 6.
    Review of The Essays of A. J. Muste, edited by Nat Hentoff.

"David and Goliath." CC, 27, no. 11 (June 26), 141-142.
    On the six-day war.

"Escalation Objective." The New York Times (March 14), p. 46.
    A letter to the Editor.

"The Ethics of War and Peace in the Nuclear Age" (with Hans Morgenthau). War/Peace Report, 7, no. 2 (February), 3-8.

"Foreign Policy in a New Context." NL, 50, no. 5 (February 27), 17-19.
    Reprinted in Faith and Politics.

"Foreword," to Dr. Martin Luther King, Jr., et al, Speak on the War in Vietnam. New York: Clergy and Laymen Concerned about Vietnam, p. 3.

"An Interview With Reinhold Niebuhr," in Theologians at Work. By
Patrick Granfield. New York: Macmillan Co., pp. 51-68.
Originally published in Commonweal (December 16, 1966).

"Letter." CC, 27, no. 1 (February 6), 14.
Reply to David M. Stowe's letter criticizing Niebuhr's position in his article of December 12, 1966: "The Unresolved Religious Problem in Christian-Jewish Relations."

"Our Schizoid Vietnam Policy." CC, 26, no. 24 (January 23), 313-314.

"Politics, Patriotism and Integrity." CC, 27, no. 4 (March 20),
45-46.

"Reischauer's War Stand." The New York Times (February 8), p. 30.
A letter to the Editor.

"The Social Myths of the 'Cold War.'" Journal of International
Affairs, 21, no. 1 (1967), 40-56.
Reprinted in Faith and Politics.

"The Vietnam Elections." CC, 27, no. 15 (September 18), 199-200.

"Vietnam: Study in Ironies." NR, 156, no. 25 (June 24), 11-12.

"Ways of Believing." Book Week (January 8), 4, 18-19.
Review of Frederick Herzog's Understanding God and Gabriel
Vahanian's No Other God.

"Without 'Advice and Consent.'" NL, 50, no. 17 (August 28), 5-6.
President Johnson and the Vietnam War.

"Words for the Memorial Service of Dr. Harry F. Ward." The Union
Seminary Tower, 14, no. 1 (Winter), 1.

1968

"Fighting an Intractable Dwarf." NL, 51, no. 15 (August 5), 12-13.
The U. S. against North Vietnam.

"Foreword," to The Religious Situation: 1968. Edited by Donald
Cutler. Boston: Beacon Press, pp. ix-xv.

"Ideology vs. Power." NL, 51, no. 22 (November 18), 16-17.

"Let Love be the Motive and Justice the Method." Katallagete
(Winter), p. 1.

"The Negro Minority and Its Fate in a Self-Righteous Nation." Social
Action, 35, no. 2 (October), 53-64. Alternate title: Social
Progress, 55, no. 1 (September/October).

"Preface," to Faith and Politics. By Ronald H. Stone. New York:
Braziller, pp. vii-viii.

Other Writings by Reinhold Niebuhr

1968

"A Question of Priorities." NL, 51, no. 2 (January 15), 9-11.
The civil rights movement and the Vietnam War. Reprinted in
Faith and Politics.

"A Threat to All Mankind." NL, 51, no. 7 (March 25), 11.
The continuing Vietnam War.

"A Time for Reassessment." CC, 28, no. 5 (April 1), 55-56.
On the Vietnam War.

1969

"An Interview With Reinhold Niebuhr." By Ronald H. Stone. CC, 29,
no. 4 (March 17), 48-52.

"The King's Chapel and the King's Court." CC, 29, no. 14 (August 4),
211-213.
Official worship at the White House.

"The Moon Landing" (with Conte). The Berkshire Eagle (July 21).

"The President's Error." CC, 29, no. 15 (September 15), 227-228.
President Johnson declared that a nation that could go to the
moon could gather all nations in peace, justice and concord.
Niebuhr says the President's error "Quite simply...is the error
of identifying the self with the mind."

"Toward Intra-Christian Endeavors." CCY, 86, no. 53 (December 31),
1662-1667.
In the series "How My Mind Has Changed."

1970

"Indicting Two Generations." NL, 53, no. 19 (October 5), 13-14.
The workers' discontent of the 1930's and student discontent
today.

"John Coleman Bennett: Theologian, Churchman, and Educator," in
Theology and Church in Times of Change. Essays in Honor of John
Coleman Bennett. Edited by E. L. Long and Robert T. Handy.
Philadelphia: The Westminster Press, pp. 233-236.

"The Presidency and the Irony of American History." CC, 30, no. 6
(April 13), 70-72.

"'Redeemer Nation' To Super Power." The New York Times (December 4),
p. 47.

"A Window into the Heart of a Giant." The New York Times Book Review
(May 10), pp. 6, 34.
Review of Paul Tillich's My Travel Diary: 1936.

1971

"Mission and Opportunity; Religion in a Pluralistic Culture," in
Social Responsibility in an Age of Revolution. Edited by Louis
Finkelstein. New York: Jewish Theological Seminary, pp. 177–211.

"Without Consensus There is no Consent." The Center Magazine, 4,
no. 4 (July/August), 2–9.

1972

The Reminiscences of Reinhold Niebuhr. New York: Columbia University Oral History Research Office.

1973

"Germany." Worldview, 16, no. 6 (June), 13–18.
Prepared for publication about 1962; now published for the
first time.

1974

"Britain." Worldview, 17, no. 7 (July), 30–33.
Published here for the first time.

Writings about Reinhold Niebuhr

1925

BRIGHTMAN, E. S. "Dr. Brightman Replies." CCY, 42, no. 45
    (November 5), 1382-1383.
        Reply to Niebuhr's review of Brightman's Religious Values.

1927

LASKER, BRUNO. "The Negro in Detroit." The Survey, 58, no. 2
    (April 15), 72-73.
        The Mayor's Committee on Race Relations in Detroit and
    Reinhold Niebuhr's contribution as Chairman of the Committee.

1928

ANON. "A Challenge to Complacency." CCY, 45, no. 6 (February 16),
    208-210.
        Review of Does Civilization Need Religion?

ANON. "Editorial." Journal of Religion, 8, no. 2 (April), 330.

ANON. Review of Does Civilization Need Religion? Times Literary
    Supplement (September), p. 671.

BELL, BERNARD I. Review of Does Civilization Need Religion?
    Saturday Review of Literature, 5, no. 10 (September 27), 164.

WARD, HARRY F. Review of Does Civilization Need Religion? WT, 11,
    no. 1 (January), 38-39.

1929

JONES, E. D. "Whole Wheat Bread and Tabasco Sauce." CCY, 46, no. 32
    (August 7), 990-991.
        Review of Leaves From the Notebook of a Tamed Cynic.

1929

LUCCOCK, HALFORD E. "Tamed--Or Untamed?" WT, 12, no. 8 (August),
344-345.
Review of Leaves From the Notebook of a Tamed Cynic.

1930

ANON. "The Week." NR, 65, no. 839 (November 31), 174-175.
Report of Niebuhr speaking to a meeting of the Foreign Policy
Association in New York about the drift of German youth to ex-
treme parties.

1931

HOMRIGHAUSEN, E. G. "Barthianism and the Kingdom." CCY, 48, no. 28
(July 15), 922.

KELLER, D. ADOLF. Der Weg der dialektischen Theologie durch die
kirchliche Welt, Eine kleine Kirchenjunde der Gegenwart. Munich:
Chr. Kaiser Verlag, pp. 124-135.

1932

THOMAS, NORMAN. Review of Moral Man and Immoral Society. WT, 15,
no. 22 (December 14), 565-567.

1933

ANON. "Niebuhr Questions Vitality of the Protestant Religion."
Newsweek, 1 (April 29), 28.

ANON. "Putting Just Enough Poison in the Baby's Porridge." The New
York Times Book Review (February 5), p. 4.
Review of Moral Man and Immoral Society.

ANON. Review of Moral Man and Immoral Society. Times Literary
Supplement (March 23), pp. 187-188.

ANON. Review of Moral Man and Immoral Society. The New Statesman
and Nation, 5, no. 3 (April 8), 456.

CASE, SHIRLEY J. "Religion and Social Morals." Journal of Religion,
13, no. 3 (July), 359-361.
Review of The Contribution of Religion to Social Work.

COE, GEORGE A. "Coe vs. Niebuhr." CCY, 50, no. 11 (March 15), 362-363.

ELLWOOD, CHARLES A. Review of Moral Man and Immoral Society. The American Journal of Sociology, 39, no. 2 (September), 271-272.

GOLDENWEISER, ALEXANDER. "The Way to Justice." The Saturday Review of Literature, 9, no. 42 (May 6), 575.
Review of Moral Man and Immoral Society.

HOMRIGHAUSEN, E. G. "Inspired by Niebuhr's Book." WT, 16, no. 5 (February 1), 118.
Review of Moral Man and Immoral Society.

HUME, THEODORE C. "Prophet of Disillusion." CCY, 50, no. 1 (January 4), 18-19.
Review of Moral Man and Immoral Society.

JOHNSON, F. ERNEST. "Religion and Social Work." WT, 16, no. 9 (March 1), 213.
Review of The Contribution of Religion to Social Work.

JONES, E. D. "Reinhold Niebuhr," in American Preachers of To-Day. An Intimate Appraisal of Thirty-Two Leaders. Indianapolis: Bobbs-Merrill Co., pp. 248-253.

KENDALL, MARGARET. "Ideas." The Commonweal, 17, no. 25 (April 19), 695-696.
Review of Moral Man and Immoral Society.

LOVETT, ROBERT M. "Ethics and Politics." NR, 73, no. 946 (January 18), 273.
Review of Moral Man and Immoral Society.

MURRY, J. MIDDLETON. Review of Moral Man and Immoral Society. WT, 16, no. 15 (April 12), 360.
Reprinted from the British New Leader.

PAPE, L. M. Review of Moral Man and Immoral Society. American Political Science Review, 27, no. 2 (April), 296-297.

SEARS, LAURENCE. Review of Moral Man and Immoral Society. The Journal of Philosophy, 30, no. 17 (August 17), 467-469.

SMITH, T. V. Review of Moral Man and Immoral Society. International Journal of Ethics, 43, no. 3 (April), 370-372.

1933

TODD, ARTHUR J. Review of The Contribution of Religion to Social
Work. The American Journal of Sociology, 39, no. 2 (September),
274.

WOOD, H. G. Review of Moral Man and Immoral Society. Spectator,
150, no. 5462 (March 3), 303.

1934

BARNES, HARRY E. Review of Reflections on the End of an Era. The
American Journal of Sociology, 40, no. 3 (November), 403-404.

DAVIS, ELMER. "A Herald of the New Barbarism." The Saturday Review
of Literature, 10, no. 34 (March 10), 533-535.
Review of Reflections on the End of an Era.

DEWEY, JOHN. "Intelligence and Power." NR, 78, no. 1012
(April 25), pp. 306-307.
Dewey's answer to Niebuhr's challenge to his views on the
status of intelligence.

GORDON, KING. "The Twilight of This Age." WT, 17, no. 5 (March 1),
115-117.
Review of Reflections on the End of an Era.

KNOWLES, CLIVE. "Reinhold Niebuhr's Philosophy of Social Reconstruction." M.A. thesis, University of Chicago.

LOVETT, ROBERT M. "The Christian Realist." NR, 78, no. 1011
(May 2), 288-289.
Review of Reflections on the End of an Era.

MATTHEWS, J. B. "Critique of Reinhold Niebuhr." WT, 17, no. 11
(May 24), 282.
Critique of Niebuhr's analysis of the "Appeal to the Members
of the Socialist Party."

MORRISON, C. C. "Good Wholesome Pessimism." CCY, 51, no. 10
(March 7), 323-324.
Review of Reflections on the End of an Era.

VOELKEL, E. E. "Study in Black and White." CCY, 51, no. 22
(May 30), 725-727.
Article aimed against Niebuhr's Reflections on the End of an
Era.

Writings about Reinhold Niebuhr

1938

WOOD, H. G. "The End of Our Time." Spectator, 152, no. 5519 (April 6), 548-549.

1935

ATKINS, GAIUS G. "Does Mr. Niebuhr Attack a Straw Man?" CCY, 52, no. 9 (February 27), 276.

MONAT, R. B. Review of Moral Man and Immoral Society. Hibbert Journal, 33 (April), 321-330.

1936

AUBREY, EDWIN E. "Reinhold Niebuhr's Social Gospel," in Present Theological Tendencies. New York: Harper and Brothers, pp. 103-112.

PAUCK, WILHELM. Review of An Interpretation of Christian Ethics. Ethics, 1, no. 2 (Winter), 33-36.

WHITCHURCH, I. G. "Transcendental Ethics." CCY, 53, no. 1 (January 1), 19-20.
    Review of An Interpretation of Christian Ethics.

1937

BENNETT, JOHN C. "The Contribution of Reinhold Niebuhr." Religion in Life, 6, no. 1 (Winter), 268-283.

ROBERTS, DAVID. "Theist and Socialist." RR, 3, no. 1 (Winter), 38-41.
    Review of Beyond Tragedy.

WYCKOFF, ALBERT C. "Choice of Religions." The Saturday Review of Literature, 17, no. 19 (December 25), 20.

1938

BENNETT, JOHN C. Review of Beyond Tragedy. The Journal of Religion, 18, no. 3 (July), 335-337.

BUEHRER, EDWIN T. "The Mythology of Theology." CCY, 55, no. 9 (March 2), 277-278.
    Review of Beyond Tragedy.

Writings about Reinhold Niebuhr

1938

HORTON, W. M. "The New Orthodoxy." The American Scholar, 7, no. 1 (Winter), 3-11.
 Relates Niebuhr to the whole movement.

RICHARDSON, CYRIL C. Review of Beyond Tragedy. The Review of Religion, 2, no. 3 (March), 331-338.

1940

HAMMAR, GEORGE. "Reinhold Niebuhr's Way From Social Ethics to a Realistic Theology," in Christian Realism in Contemporary American Theology. Uppsala: A.-B. Lundequistaska Bokhandeln, pp. 167-253.

HAROUTUNIAN, JOSEPH. Review of Christianity and Power Politics. RR, 6, no. 1 (Winter), 37-38.

MACINTOSH, D. C. "Is Theology Reducible to Mythology?" Review of Religion, 4, no. 2 (January), 140-158.

_____. "A Rejoinder to Professor Niebuhr's Reply." Review of Religion, 4, no. 4 (May), 434-437.

ROBERTS, RICHARD. "An Open Letter to Niebuhr." CS, 5, no. 2 (Spring), 41-43.

1941

ANON. "Church Journal Upholding War Planned to Counter Pacifism." Newsweek, 17 (January 27), 58.

ANON. "Niebuhr's Essay on Man." Christendom, 6, no. 3 (Summer), 426-430.
 Review of The Nature and Destiny of Man, Vol. I.

AUDEN, W. H. "The Means of Grace." NR, 104, no. 22 (June 2), 765-766.
 Review of The Nature and Destiny of Man, Vol. I.

BAILLIE, JOHN. "Niebuhr's Gifford Lectures." The Union Review, 2, no. 3 (March), 7-8.

BIXLER, J. S. Review of The Nature and Destiny of Man, Vol. I. The Review of Religion, 6, no. 11 (November), 86-89.

BOSLEY, HAROLD. "Illusions of the Disillusioned." CCY, 58, no. 1
(January 1), 14-16.
   Review of Christianity and Power Politics.

CARPENTER, J. H. "Niebuhr Launches a New Journal." CCY, 58, no. 3
(January 22), 133.
   The beginning of Christianity and Crisis.

DE ROUGEMONT, DENIS. Review of The Nature and Destiny of Man, Vol. I.
N, 152, no. 12 (March 22), 328-329.

GIBSON, GEORGE M. "The Flight of Moral Leadership." CCY, 58, no. 26
(June 25), 829-830.
   Niebuhr discussed along with Barth and John Bennett.

GRAHAM, RUSSELL. "Macgregor vs. Niebuhr." The Union Review, 3,
no. 1 (December), 31-32, 36.

HARKNESS, GEORGIA, et al. "A Symposium on Reinhold Niebuhr's The
Nature and Destiny of Man, Vol. I." Christendom, 6, no. 4
(Autumn), 567-582.

HENEL, H. "A Modern Philosophy." Queen's Quarterly, 48 (May),
149-156.

HOOK, SIDNEY. "Social Change and Original Sin: Answer to Niebuhr."
NL, 24, no. 43 (November 11), 5, 7-8.

KEELY, MARY K. Review of The Nature and Destiny of Man, Vol. I.
Wisconsin Library Bulletin, 37, no. 7 (July), 133.

KNOX, JOHN. Review of Christianity and Power Politics. The Journal
of Religion, 21, no. 2 (April), 229-230.

LAM, ELIZABETH. "Reinhold Niebuhr: From Detroit to Edinburgh."
The Journal of Liberal Religion, 3, no. 1 (Summer), 23-36.

MACGREGOR, G. H. C. "The Relevance of an Impossible Ideal: A Reply
to Reinhold Niebuhr." London: The Fellowship of Reconciliation,
87 pp.
   Published originally in The Christian Pacifist, London.

MEYER, W. W. "When Did Adam Fall? Niebuhr's Dualism." CCY, 58,
no. 43 (October 22), 1308-1309.

MORRISON, C. C. "Strain on the Tie That Binds." CCY, 58, no. 27
(July 2), 853-855.
   Decrying Niebuhr's article in CC entitled "Pacifism and
America First."

1941

MORRISON, C. C. "Is Neutrality Immoral?" CCY, 58, no. 46
(November 12), 1399-1401.
Directed against Niebuhr's CC article favoring repeal of the
Neutrality Act.

ORR, W. I. Review of Christianity and Power Politics. Review of
Religion, 5, no. 3 (March), 326-330.

TAYLOR, W. R. "Man, Nature and Revelation." University of Toronto
Quarterly, 11, no. 1 (October), 111-115.
Review of The Nature and Destiny of Man, Vol. I.

TILLICH, PAUL. Review of The Nature and Destiny of Man, Vol. I.
CS, 6, no. 2 (Spring), 34-37.

VLASTOS, GREGORY. "Sin and Anxiety in Niebuhr's Religion." CCY, 58,
no. 40 (October 1), 1202-1204.

WOOLBERT, ROBERT G. Review of Christianity and Power Politics.
Foreign Affairs, 19, no. 3 (April), 674.

1942

BALDWIN, ROGER. "Liberty in War Time." N, 154, no. 6 (February 7),
175.
Criticism of Niebuhr's January 24th article, "The Limits of
Liberty."

KAGAN, GEORGE. "Post-War Germany." N, 154, no. 18 (May 2), 528.
Argues against Niebuhr's view that "German domination of a
federated Europe is not inevitable."

MILLER, BENJAMIN. "Mythological Naturalism." The Journal of Religion,
22, no. 3 (July), 270-287.

PRINZ, JOACHIM, et al. "Dr. Niebuhr on the Jews." N, 154, no. 12
(March 21), 351-352.
Letters expressing a variety of views on Niebuhr's article,
"The Jews After the War."

SCHUMAN, F. L. "The Federation of the Free." N, 154, no. 4
(January 24), 103.
Criticism of Niebuhr's review of book Schuman coauthored on
the Design for Power.

1943

ANON. Review of The Nature and Destiny of Man, Vol. I. Times Literary Supplement (August 7), p. 380.

COOMARASWAMY, A. K. "Caste and Vocation." N, 156, no. 5 (January 30), 179-180.
Criticism of Niebuhr's review of Shridharani's Warning to the West.

DE ROUGEMONT, DENIS. Review of The Nature and Destiny of Man, Vol. II. N, 156, no. 13 (March 27), 457-458.

GARNETT, CAMPBELL. "The Christian View of Man." CCY, 60, no. 44 (November 3), 1258-1260.
Review of The Nature and Destiny of Man.

GRAHAM, RUSSELL. "I Hate Because I Love." The Union Review, 4, no. 2 (March), 11-13, 26.
Niebuhr's position compared to Walter Bowie's on "hating the enemy."

HOOK, SIDNEY. "The New Failure of Nerve." Partisan Review, 10, no. 1 (January-February), 2-23.

LEHMANN, PAUL, et al. "Human Destiny--Reinhold Niebuhr." The Union Review, 4, no. 2 (March), 18-26.

MORRISON, C. C. "Dr. Niebuhr's Unorthodox Orthodoxy." CCY, 60, no. 11 (March 7), 322-325.
Review of The Nature and Destiny of Man.

MURPHY, ARTHUR E. Review of The Nature and Destiny of Man. The Journal of Philosophy, 40, no. 16 (April 5), 458-468.

1944

BENARD, E. D. "Reinhold Niebuhr and the Catholic Church." American Ecclesiastical Review, 111, no. 5 and 6 (November-December), 321-329, 401-418.

BOLMAN, F. deWOLF. "A Theology of the Non-Natural." Review of Religion, 8 (March), 254-267.

CALHOUN, R. L. Review of The Nature and Destiny of Man. The Journal of Religion, 24, no. 1 (January), 59-64.

1944

GARNETT, A. C. "Solid Ground for Democracy." CCY, 61, no. 49
(December 6), 1414.
Review of The Children of Light and the Children of Darkness.

GUERARD, ALBERT. "Good and Evil, Here and Now." N, 159, no. 24
(December 9), 720-722.
Review of The Children of Light and the Children of Darkness.

HEIMANN, EDUARD. Review of The Children of Light and the Children of
Darkness. CS, 10, no. 1 (Winter), 44-47.

JACOBSON, N. P. "Niebuhr's Philosophy of History." Harvard Theological Review, 37, no. 4 (October), 237-268.
Review of The Nature and Destiny of Man, Vol. II.

LEHMANN, PAUL. "A Watershed in American Theology." Theology Today,
1, no. 2 (July), 234.

MORRISON, C. C. "Dr. Niebuhr at Chicago." CCY, 61, no. 52
(December 27), 1494-1495.

TEAD, ORDWAY. Review of The Nature and Destiny of Man. Ethics, 54,
no. 2 (January), 150-152.

VOSS, CARL H. "Reinhold Niebuhr: 20th Century Prophet." Advance,
136, no. 7 (July), 9-12.

1945

AUBREY, EDWIN E. Review of The Children of Light and the Children of
Darkness. The Journal of Religion, 25, no. 4 (October), 287-288.

BENARD, E. D. "Reinhold Niebuhr and the Catholic Church." American
Ecclesiastical Review, 112, no. 2 (February), 81-94.

GREEN, MARVIN W. "Contemporary Theories of Evil. An Ethical View:
Reinhold Niebuhr; A Philosophical View: E. S. Brightman; A
Theological View: Edwin Lewis." Ph.D. dissertation, Drew
University.

ROLSTON, HOLMES. Review of The Children of Light and the Children
of Darkness. Theology Today, 2, no. 2 (July), 276-277.

STEINBERG, MILTON. "The Outlook of Reinhold Niebuhr--A Description
and Appraisal." The Reconstructionist, 11, no. 15 (December 14),
10-15.

THOMAS, GEORGE F. Review of The Children of Light and the Children of Darkness. The Review of Religion, 9, no. 4 (May), 407-410.

TRINKAUS, C. E. "Man and Faith in the 'Forties: A Review Article." The Review of Religion, 9, no. 4 (May), 366-379.
   Review of The Nature and Destiny of Man, along with Erich Kahler's Man the Measure and Lewis Mumford's The Condition of Man.

1946

ANON. "On Niebuhr's 'Myth.'" N, 162, no. 15 (April 13), 446-447.
   Eight letters about Niebuhr's article "The Myth of World Government."

ANON. "Reinhold Niebuhr, a Biographical Sketch." The Southern Churchman, 112, no. 46 (November 16), 8.

ANON. Review of Discerning the Signs of the Times. The Expository Times, 58, no. 7 (October), 1-2.

BOSLEY, HAROLD. "Niebuhr the Preacher." Christendom, 11, no. 4 (Autumn), 525-528.
   Review of Discerning the Signs of the Times.

GUERARD, ALBERT. "The World Come of Age." N, 162, no. 16 (April 20), 457-459.
   Discussion of Niebuhr's article "The Myth of World Government."

KNIGHT, MARCUS. "Niebuhr on Our Times." Spectator, 177, no. 6161 (July 26), 92.
   Review of Discerning the Signs of the Times.

McGREGOR, PATRICIA. "And A Vote For Niebuhr." N, 162, no. 21 (May 25), 638.
   A letter approving Niebuhr's position in "The Myth of World Government" as against Guerard's "The World Come of Age."

PATTERSON, CHARLES H. "Man's Pride and Inconsistency." CCY, 63, no. 27 (July 3), 839.
   Review of Discerning the Signs of the Times.

SCHLESINGER, ARTHUR, JR. "Niebuhr's Vision of Our Time." N, 162 no. 25 (June 22), 753-754.
   Review of Discerning the Signs of the Times.

1946

SCHROEDER, JOHN C. "Appeal to Religion." The Yale Review, 36,
no. 2 (December), 366-368.
Review of Discerning the Signs of the Times.

STREIT, CLARENCE. "Clarence Streit Protests." N, 162, no. 16
(April 20), 490-491.

SWANSON, HARVEY, et al. "What is Neo-Orthodoxy?" Boston: American
Unitarian Association.
A pamphlet.

THELAN, MARY F. Man as Sinner in Contemporary American Realistic
Theology. New York: King's Crown Press.
Deals with Niebuhr's theology and that of others.

1947

ANON. "The Challenge of Niebuhr." The Listener, 37, no. 945
(March 6), 332-333.

ANON. "Churchman With Teachers: Approval of Free Bus Transport."
Ave Maria, 66 (August 9), 162.

BAGBY, GROVER C. "Human Freedom and Responsibility in the Light of
the Writings of Reinhold Niebuhr." Ph.D. dissertation, Drew
University.

BRUNNER, HANS H. "Coercive Power." Th.D. dissertation, Union
Theological Seminary.

CHRISTIAN, WILLIAM. Review of Discerning the Signs of the Times.
Review of Religion, 11, no. 4 (May), 407-409.

HARTSHORNE, CHARLES. Review of Religious Liberals Reply. The
Christian Register, 126, no. 9 (October), 412-413.
A good portion of the review is given to Niebuhr.

HEINEMANN, F. A. Review of Discerning the Signs of the Times.
Hibbert Journal, 45, no. 2 (February), 189-190.

LEWIS, H. D. Morals and the New Theology. London: Victor Gollanz.
Published in the U. S. by Harper and Brothers.

WIEMAN, HENRY N., et al. Religious Liberals Reply. Boston: The
Beacon Press.

1948

ANON. "Compliment of Heresy: Dr. Niebuhr's Promotion of Heresy." Tablet, 192 (September 4), 147.

ANON. "Faith for a Lenten Age." Time, 51, no. 10 (March 8), 70-79. This issue of Time featured Niebuhr, including a cover picture.

BROWN, STUART M. "The Theology of Reinhold Niebuhr." The Review of Religion, 12, no. 3 (March), 262-276.

GILL, THEODORE A. Recent Protestant Political Theory. Zurich: The University of Zurich, pp. 143-167.

HUGHLEY, J. N. "Dialectical Theological Socialism," in Trends in Protestant Social Idealism. New York: King's Crown Press, Chapter 7.

SCHREY, HEINZ-HORST. "Sozialethische Literatur Des Auslandes." Theologische Rundschau Neue Folge, 11: 216-271.

STONE, JOSEPH L. "The Concept of Sin in the Writings of F. F. Tennant and Reinhold Niebuhr." B.D. Thesis, Duke University.

1949

ANON. Review of Faith and History. Current History, 17, no. 98 (October), 227.

ANON. Review of Faith and History. The New Yorker, 25, no. 15 (June 4), 94-95.

BARTH, KARL. "Continental vs. Anglo-Saxon Theology, A Preliminary Reply to Reinhold Niebuhr." CCY, 66, no. 7 (February 16), 201-204.
Also in Christian News-Letter no. 263 (December 8), 9-16.

BERNHARDT, WILLIAM H. Review of Faith and History. The Journal of Bible and Religion, 17, no. 4 (October), 251-252.

BOURNE, HOWARD A. "The Economic Concepts of Emil Brunner and Reinhold Niebuhr." Ph.D. dissertation, University of Chicago.

GOODENOUGH, ERWIN R. "Neo-Orthodoxy." The Yale Review, 39, no. 1 (September), 162-165.
Review of Faith and History.

1949

HICKMAN, R. A. "Niebuhr on Progress and Sin." Expository Times
(Edinburgh), 60, no. 1 (1948-1949), 4-7.

HOUGH, L. H. "Niebuhr on the Meaning of History." The Pastor, 12,
no. 11 (July), 2-3.
Review of Faith and History.

KERR, HUGH T. "The Barth-Niebuhr Colloquy." Theology Today, 6,
no. 2 (July), 235.

LÖWITH, KARL. Review of Faith and History. Theology Today, 6, no. 3
(October), 422-425.

MILLER, PERRY. "The Great Method." N, 169, no. 6 (August 6),
138-139.
Review of Faith and History.

MORRISON, C. C. Review of Faith and History. Religion in Life, 18,
no. 4 (Autumn), 607-609.

SCHLESINGER, ARTHUR, JR. Review of Faith and History. CS, 14, no. 3
(Summer), 26-27.

SPERRY, WILLARD L. "The Nature of Time." Saturday Review of Literature, 32, no. 24 (June 11), 17-18.
Review of Faith and History.

STEWART, DAVID A. "Neo-Orthodoxy of Niebuhr." University of Toronto
Quarterly, 18 (July), 347-357.

WHITE, MORTON. Social Thought in America: The Revolt Against Formal-
ism. New York: The Viking Press, pp. 247-280.
Reprinted by Oxford University Press, 1976.

1950

ANON. Review of Faith and History. Saturday Review of Literature,
33, no. 7 (February 18), 42-43.

BATTENHOUSE, PAUL F. "Theology in the Social Gospel: 1918-1946."
Ph.D. dissertation, Yale University.

CARNELL, EDWARD J. "The Concept of Dialectic in the Theology of
Reinhold Niebuhr." Ph.D. dissertation, Harvard University.

_____. The Theology of Reinhold Niebuhr. Grand Rapids: Eerdmans.

1951

COOK, MARVIN W. "Ethical Relativism in Reinhold Niebuhr." Ph.D. dissertation, Boston University.

FITCH, R. E. "Reinhold Niebuhr, Excubitor!" The Pacific Spectator, 4, no. 3 (Summer), 306-318.

HEPPENSTALL, RAYNER. "Redeeming the Time." New Statesman and Nation, 39, no. 985 (January 21), 72.
    Review of Faith and History.

HERBERG, WILL. "The Theology of Reinhold Niebuhr." An Outline. Mimeographed and distributed by the Frontier Fellowship.

JOSEFSON, RUBEN. "Grundproblemet i Reinhold Niebuhrs sociala etik." Svensk telologisk Kvartalskrift, 3-4 (January 26), 276-285.

KLAUSNER, NEAL W. Review of Faith and History. Journal of Religion, 30, no. 3 (July), 228-230.

LEWIS, H. D. "The Theology of Niebuhr." The Victoria Institute, Transactions, 82: 195-218.

LYON, HUGH. "The Modern Heresy." Spectator, 184, no. 6344 (January 27), 122-124.
    Review of Faith and History.

ROBINSON, N. H. G. Faith and Duty. New York: Harper and Brothers, pp. 56-83, 126.

WIGHT, MARTIN. "History, Judgment, Butterfield, Niebuhr and the Technical Historian." The Frontier, 1, no. 8 (August), 301-314.
    Review of Faith and History.

1951

ALLEN, E. L. Christianity and Society: A Guide to the Thought of Reinhold Niebuhr. New York: The Philosophical Library, 46 pp.

ANON. "Dr. Niebuhr Speaks Out on Church and State in the U. S." Ave Maria, 73 (May 12), 578.

DAVIS, HARRY R. "The Political Philosophy of Reinhold Niebuhr." Ph.D. dissertation, University of Chicago.

1951

MacKINNON, D. M. Review of Faith and History. Scottish Journal of Theology, 4, no. 4 (December), 415.

MARTIN, JAMES L., JR. "The Doctrine of Sin in the Theology of Emil Brunner and Reinhold Niebuhr." Ph.D. dissertation, Yale University.

NASH, ARNOLD S., ed. Protestant Thought in the Twentieth Century. New York: The Macmillan Company, pp. 131-141.

ROBINSON, N. H. G. "Dr. Niebuhr's Political and Religious Thought." Expository Times (Edinburgh), 62, no. 7 (July), 219-222.

SMALLEY, STIMSON R. "The Concept of Salvation in American Realistic Theology." Ph.D. dissertation, Drew University.

THOMSON, J. S. "Reinhold Niebuhr." Transactions of the Royal Society of Canada. Third Series. 45, section 11 (June), 91-98.

1952

AGAR, HERBERT. "America's Philosopher." Spectator, 189, no. 6494 (December 12), 819-820.
    Review of The Irony of American History.

ANON. "The Rich Orphan." Saturday Review of Literature, 35, no. 20 (May 17), 20.
    Review of The Irony of American History.

ANON. "The U. S. in the World Today." Atlantic Monthly, 189, no. 5 (May), 78-80.
    Review of The Irony of American History.

ANON. "A Voice in the Wilderness." Commonweal, 55, no. 18 (February 8), 437-438.

BURKHARDT, FRED. "The Liberal's Soft Heel." Saturday Review of Literature, 35, no. 14 (April 5), 11-12.
    Review of The Irony of American History.

DAVIDSON, ROBERT F. Philosophies Men Live By. New York: The Dryden Press, pp. 410-466.

EGBERT, D. D., and PERSONS, STOW, eds. "The Christian Socialist Philosophy of History of Reinhold Niebuhr," in Socialism in America. Princeton, N. J.: Princeton University Press, pp. 229-232.

1952

FITCH, ROBERT E.   "Reinhold Niebuhr as Prophet and as Philosopher
     of History." The Journal of Religion, 32, no. 1 (January), 31-46.

GARRISON, W. E.   "The Laughter of God." CCY, 69, no. 20 (May 14),
     590-591.
     Review of The Irony of American History.

HARTT, JULIAN N.   "Dialectic, Analysis, and Empirical Generalization
     in Theology." Crozer Quarterly, 29, no. 1 (January), 1-17.
     Hartt discusses Niebuhr's Nature and Destiny of Man as "an
     illustration of problems of synthesis of methods in systematic
     theology."

HUTCHINS, ROBERT M.   "Criticism of Niebuhr's Views on World Govern-
     ment," in Principles and Problems of International Politics.
     Edited by Morgenthau and Thompson. New York: Alfred A. Knopf,
     pp. 142-148.

LEUCHTENBURG, W. E.   "Niebuhr: The Theologian and the Liberal."
     NL, 35, no. 47 (November 24), 23-24.
     Review of The Irony of American History.

RAMSEY, PAUL.   Review of The Irony of American History. The Journal
     of Religion, 32, no. 3 (July), 226-227.

REVELEY, WALTER T.   "A Christian Critique of Modern Liberal Demo-
     cratic Theory as Reflected in the Writings of Jacques Maritain,
     A. D. Lindsay, and Reinhold Niebuhr." Ph.D. dissertation, Duke
     University.

ROBERTS, HENRY L.   Review of The Irony of American History. Foreign
     Affairs, 31, no. 1 (October), 157.

ROBSHAW, CHARLES P.   "The Paradox in American Neo-Orthodoxy." S.T.D.
     dissertation, Temple University.

SCHLESINGER, ARTHUR, JR.   Review of The Irony of American History.
     CS, 17, no. 4 (Autumn), 25-27.

WILLIAMS, DANIEL D.   What Present-Day Theologians are Thinking.
     New York: Harper and Row, pp. 100, 133-146.

WIMPEE, W. J.   "The Theology of Reinhold Niebuhr as Related to his
     Doctrine of Sanctification." Th.D. dissertation, Southwestern
     Baptist Seminary.

1953

1953

ANON. "Reinhold Niebuhr and a 'By-Product.'" NYHT (October 11), p. 8.

ANON. "Reinhold Niebuhr's Admission." Ave Maria, 78 (September 19), 5.

BOULDING, KENNETH. "In Reply to Professor Niebuhr," in The Organizational Revolution. Edited by Kenneth Boulding. New York: Harper and Brothers, 245-254.

DAHLBERG, BRUCE T. Correspondence to the Editor. CC, 13, no. 6 (April 13), 47-48.
    Critical of Niebuhr's March 16 editorial notes defending the death penalty for the Rosenbergs.

FITCH, ROBERT E. "The Philosophy of Dr. Niebuhr." NL, 36, no. 49 (December 7), 16-17.
    Review of Christian Realism and Political Problems.

HOWELL, R. F. "Political Philosophy on a Theological Foundation; An Expository Analysis of the Political Thought of Reinhold Niebuhr." Ethics, 63, no. 2 (January), 79-99.

McCREARY, EDWARD D., JR. "The Social Thought of Reinhold Niebuhr." The Journal of Religious Thought, 10, no. 1 (Autumn-Winter), 25-33.

MALLOCH, J. M. "Protestant Looks at Catholics; Reply." Commonweal, 58, no. 11 (June 19), 274-275.

OSGOOD, ROBERT E. Ideals and Self-Interest in America's Foreign Relations. Chicago: University of Chicago Press, pp. 381-383.

RIVETT, KENNETH. "An Agnostic's Reflections on Reinhold Niebuhr." Australian Quarterly, 25, no. 4 (1953), 79-87.

SOPER, D. W. Major Voices in American Theology. Six Contemporary Leaders, Vol. I. Philadelphia: The Westminster Press, pp. 37-69.

STORY, M. L. "Dewey and Niebuhr: A Brief Juxtaposition." Educational Theory, 3, no. 2 (April), 182-184.

VOGT, V. OGDEN. "The Secular Witness in a Christian Age." CCY, 70, no. 37 (September 16), 1049-1050.

1954

BARTLETT, DONALD E. "The Concept of the End of History in the Writings of Reinhold Niebuhr and Paul Tillich." Ph.D. dissertation, Yale University.

COFFIN, HENRY S. A Half Century of Union Seminary. New York: Scribner's, pp. 149-152.

DeWOLF, L. HAROLD. Review of Christian Realism and Political Problems. The Journal of Bible and Religion, 22, no. 2 (April), 125-126.

DUFF, EDWARD. The Social History of the World Council of Churches. New York: Association Press, pp. 156-158. Many references in Notes. See Index.

HILTNER, SEWARD. "Niebuhr on Kinsey." CC, 13, no. 23 (January 11), 179-182.

HOFMANN, HANS. "Die Theologie Reinhold Niebuhrs im Lichte seiner Lehre von der Sünde." Ph.D. dissertation, University of Zürich. Published: Zürich: Zwingli Verlag.

_____. Review of Christian Realism and Political Problems. Theology Today, 11, no. 3 (October), 405-406.

HUTCHINSON, PAUL. "The Grim Protestant Truth." Saturday Review of Literature, 36, no. 15 (April 10), 31. Review of Christian Realism and Political Problems.

KING, ALBION R. Review of Christian Realism and Political Problems. The Journal of Religion, 34, no. 4 (October), 298-299.

KING, RACHAEL H. The Ommission of the Holy Spirit From Reinhold Niebuhr's Theology. New York: Philosophical Library.

KOLBE, HENRY C. "Religion and Politics." CCY, 71, no. 18 (May 5), 551-552. Review of Christian Realism and Political Problems.

MACGREGOR, GEORGE H. C. The New Testament Basis of Pacifism and the Relevance of an Impossible Ideal. Nyack, N. Y.: Fellowship Publications.

MAIER, ANTON. "Das Menschenbild Reinhold Niebuhr, Der Mensch in Gemeinschaft und Geschichte." Ph.D. dissertation, Heidelberg.

1954

MANN, GOLO. <u>Vom Geist Amerikas</u>. Stuttgart: Urban Bücherei, pp. 110-116.

MILLER, FRANCIS P. "Man's Predicament." <u>Interpretation</u>, 8, no. 3 (July), 340-341.
Review of <u>Christian Realism and Political Problems</u>.

ROBERTS, HENRY L. Review of <u>Christian Realism and Political Problems</u>. <u>Foreign Affairs</u>, 32, no. 3 (April), 505.

RYRIE, C. E. Review of <u>Christian Realism and Political Problems</u>. <u>Bibliotheca Sacra</u>, 3, no. 441 (January), 88-89.

WEICHENHAN, OTTBRECHT. "Die Sozialethischen Voraussetzungen und Zielsetzungen der Theologie Reinhold Niebuhrs." Ph.D. dissertation, Göttingen.

WILLIAMS, JOHN R., JR. "The Doctrine of the <u>Imago Dei</u> in Contemporary Theology: A Study in Karl Barth, Emil Brunner, Reinhold Niebuhr, and Paul Tillich." Ph.D. dissertation, Columbia University.

1955

ADAMS, JAMES L. Review of <u>The Self and the Dramas of History</u>. CS, 20, no. 4 (Autumn), 23-24.

BIERSTEDT, ROBERT. "What is This I Who Am Me...?" <u>Saturday Review of Literature</u>, 38, no. 20 (May 14), 18.
Review of <u>The Self and the Dramas of History</u>.

CAREY, STEPHEN, and PINKUS, ROBERT. "Reply to Critics--Reinhold Niebuhr." <u>The Progressive</u>, 19, no. 19 (October), 19-20.
Reply to Niebuhr's "Is There Another Way?", a criticism of the Quaker "Speak Truth to Power."

ELLIOTT, ROBERT E. Review of <u>The Self and the Dramas of History</u>. <u>Perkins School of Theology Journal</u>, 9, no. 1 (Fall), 34-35.

HARDON, J. A. "Evanston and Rome." <u>American Ecclesiastical Review</u>, 132, no. 1-6 (January-June), 322-326.

HEARN, ARNOLD W. "Report on a Conversation: Niebuhr and dePury." CS, 20, no. 1 (Winter), 20-23, 29.

1956

HESS, M. W. "Reinhold Niebuhr Versus Socrates." The Catholic World, 182, no. 1 (October), 31-41.

HOFMANN, HANS. Review of The Self and the Dramas of History. Theology Today, 12, no. 3 (October), 414-415.

HORDERN, WILLIAM. "American Neo-Orthodoxy: Reinhold Niebuhr," in A Layman's Guide to Protestant Theology. New York: The Macmillan Co., pp. 145-164.

KEAN, CHARLES D. Review of The Self and the Dramas of History. The Journal of Religion, 35, no. 4 (October), 261-262.

KELSEN, H. "Foundations of Democracy; View of Reinhold Niebuhr." Ethics, 66, no. 1 (October), 54-62.

KERNON, WILLIAM C. "Our Love of Luxuries." L, 37, no. 47 (August 24), 12.
Review of The Nature and Destiny of Man.

MASSE, B. L. "Does the Bell Toll for Socialism?" America, 94 (October 29), 122-124.

MEYER, D. B. "The Protestant Social Liberals in America, 1919-1941." Ph.D. dissertation, Harvard University.

MILLER, WILLIAM L. "The Irony of Reinhold Niebuhr." The Reporter, 12, no. 1 (January 13), 11-15.

MOODY, J. N. "The Mystery of Human Personality." Commonweal, 62, no. 15 (July 15), 381-382.
Review of The Self and the Dramas of History.

SHEERIN, J. B. "Niebuhr Looks at the Church." Homiletics and Pastoral Review, 55 (September), 997-1001.

THOMPSON, K. W. "Beyond National Interest: A Critical Evaluation of Reinhold Niebuhr's Theory of International Politics." Review of Politics, 17, no. 2 (April), 167-188.

YODER, JOHN H. "Reinhold Niebuhr and Christian Pacifism." Mennonite Quarterly Review, 29, no. 2 (April), 101-117.

1956

BLOESCH, DONALD G. "Reinhold Niebuhr's Re-evaluation of the Apologetic Task." Ph.D. dissertation, University of Chicago.

1956

COTTON, J. H. "Dialogues of God." Interpretation, 10, no. 1
     (January), 100-102.
     Review of The Self and the Dramas of History.

CUNNINGHAM, G. W. Review of The Self and the Dramas of History.
     Ethics, 66, no. 2 (January), 145-146.

FACKENHEIM, EMIL L. "Judaism, Christianity and Reinhold Niebuhr--A
     Reply to Levi Olan." Judaism, 5, no. 4 (Fall), 316-324.

FRANKEL, CHARLES. The Case for Modern Man. New York: Harper and
     Brothers, pp. 85-116, 193-194, 218-225.

GOOD, ROBERT C. "The Contribution of Reinhold Niebuhr to the Theory
     of International Relations." Ph.D. dissertation, Yale University.

GREENE, THEODORE, et al. "Reinhold Niebuhr: A Symposium." Union
     Seminary Quarterly Review, 11, no. 4 (May), 3-7.

HARVEY, VAN A. "Reinhold Niebuhr and His Interpreters." Religion in
     Life, 26, no. 1 (Winter), 110-121.

HEIMANN, EDUARD. "Niebuhr's Pragmatic Conservatism." Union Seminary
     Quarterly Review, 11, no. 4 (May), 7-11.

HERBERG, WILL. "Christian Apologist to the Secular World." Union
     Seminary Quarterly Review, 11, no. 4 (May), 11-16.

HOFMANN, HANS. The Theology of Reinhold Niebuhr. New York:
     Scribner's.

KEGLEY, CHARLES, and BRETALL, ROBERT W., eds. Reinhold Niebuhr: His
     Religious, Social, and Political Thought. New York: The
     Macmillan Co.

LANGLEY, JAMES A. "A Critique of Contemporary Interpretations of the
     Sermon on the Mount, with Special Reference to Albert Schweitzer,
     Reinhold Niebuhr, and C. H. Dodd." Th.D. dissertation, South-
     western Baptist Theological Seminary.

MARGOLIS, JOSEPH. "In the Name of Human Finitude: An Examination of
     Reinhold Niebuhr's Christian Realism and Political Problems."
     The Journal of Philosophy, 53, no. 8 (April 12), 276-284.

ODEGARD, HOLTAN P. Sin and Science, Reinhold Niebuhr as Political
     Theologian. Yellow Springs, Ohio: The Antioch Press.

1958

OLAN, LEVI A. "Reinhold Niebuhr and the Hebraic Spirit: A Critical Inquiry." Judaism, 5, no. 2 (Spring), 108–122.

RAUN, GEORGE M. "Christology in the Thought of H. Ortan Wiley, Reinhold Niebuhr, and W. Norman Pittenger." Ph.D. dissertation, Boston University.

1957

ANON. "Niebuhr on Wyszynski." America, 98, no. 5 (November 2), 128.

BROWN, CARL H. "The Moral Theory of Reinhold Niebuhr." Th.D. dissertation, Northern Baptist Theological Seminary.

CARNELL, E. J. "Can Billy Graham Slay the Giant?" Christianity Today, 1, no. 16 (May 13), 3–5.

HORNIG, G. "Die Theologie Reinhold Niebuhrs im Lichte seiner Lehre von der Sünde." Erasmus, 10 (1957), 531–534.

HOROSZ, WILLIAM. "Philosophical Critique of Niebuhr's Doctrine of Man." Ph.D. dissertation, The University of New York at Buffalo.

HUDGINS, WALTER E. "The Changing Conception of Pacifism in American Protestantism of the Twentieth Century, with Special Reference to the Critique of Reinhold Niebuhr." Ph.D. dissertation, Duke University.

SCOTT, WILLIAM E. "Niebuhr's Ideal Man and Protestant Christian Education." Ph.D. dissertation, Stanford University.

SHINN, ROGER L. Review of Sin and Science: Reinhold Niebuhr As Political Theologian. The Journal of Religion, 37, no. 1 (January), 57–58.

VIGNAUX, GEORGETTE PAUL. La Théologie de l'histoire chez Reinhold Niebuhr. Paris: Delachaux and Niestlé.

WURTH, G. B. "Theological Climate in America." Christianity Today, 1, no. 4 (February 18), 10–13.

1958

ALLEN, JIMMY R. "A Comparative Study of the Concept of the Kingdom of God in the Writings of Walter Rauschenbusch and Reinhold Niebuhr." Th.D. dissertation, Southwestern Baptist Theological Seminary.

1958

ANON. Review of Pious and Secular America. Kirkus, 26, no. 2 (January 15), 72.

BENCKERT, HEINRICH. Review of Christian Realism and Political Problems. Theologische Literaturzeitung, 83, no. 2 (1958), 137-138.

BOEMESDETER, SAMUEL H. Review of Leaves From the Notebook of a Tamed Cynic. The Journal of Bible and Religion, 26, no. 2 (April), 174-175.

BUKSBAZEN, VICTOR. "Niebuhr and the Gospel for the Jew." Christianity Today, 3, no. 5 (December 8), 10-12.

COIT, JOHN K. "Reinhold Niebuhr and a Protestant Philosophy of Education." Ph.D. dissertation, New York University.

CULLY, KENDIG B. Review of Love and Justice. Anglican Theological Review, 40, no. 3 (July), 251-252.

DANFORTH, JOHN C. "Christ and Meaning: An Interpretation of Reinhold Niebuhr's Christology." M.A. thesis, Princeton University.

DAVID, WILLIAM E. "A Comparative Study of the Social Ethics of Walter Rauschenbusch and Reinhold Niebuhr." Ph.D. dissertation, Vanderbilt University.

DICKINSON, ROGER. "Rauschenbusch and Niebuhr: Brothers Under the Skin." Religion in Life, 27, no. 2 (Spring), 163-171.

FITCH, ROBERT E. "Niebuhr as Political Observer." NL, 41, no. 2 (January 13), 17-18.
    Review of Love and Justice.

_____. "Essays by Niebuhr." NL, 41, no. 25 (June 23), 25-26.
    Review of Pious and Secular America.

GILBERT, RABBI ARTHUR. "Christian Approach to the Jew." Christianity Today, 3, no. 5 (December 8), 7-9.

GLAUBER, ROBERT H. Review of Pious and Secular America. The Living Church, 136, no. 14 (April 6), 4.

HAMILTON, DAVID S. M. "Christology and Ethics: A Discussion of the Theological Foundations of Christian Ethics, with Special Reference to the Thought of Reinhold Niebuhr and Dietrich Bonhoeffer." S.T.M. thesis, Union Theological Seminary.

1958

HILTNER, SEWARD. "Rogers and Niebuhr." Pastoral Psychology, 9, no. 85 (June), 7-8.

HUNT, G. L., ed. Ten Makers of Modern Protestant Thought. New York: Association Press, pp. 78-88.

KERNON, WILLIAM C. "Personalities and Social Forces." NL, 41, no. 44 (December 1), 7-8.
    Review of The Nature and Destiny of Man.

LANGSTON, J. W. "Niebuhr Themes." The Christian Evangelist, 96, no. 26 (June 30), 17.
    Review of Pious and Secular America.

LANTERO, ERMINIE H. Review of Pious and Secular America (along with Maritain's Reflections on America). Religion in Life, 27, no. 3 (Summer), 467-468.

LOCHMAN, J. M. "Problem of Realism in Reinhold Niebuhr's Christology." Scottish Journal of Theology, 11 (September), 253-264.

LOOMER, B. M., et al. "Reinhold Niebuhr and Carl Rogers." Pastoral Psychology, 9, no. 85 (June), 17-25.

McKERNAN, L. F. "Reinhold Niebuhr: Still 'Number One Protestant?'" Catholic World, 187 (June), 173-178.

McMINN, J. B. Review of The Nature and Destiny of Man. The Journal of Bible and Religion, 26, no. 1 (January), 23-28.

MANN, GOLO. "Reinhold Niebuhr und Die Kritik des Liberalismus." Merkur (February), pp. 131-144.

MILLER, ROBERT M. American Protestantism and Social Issues, 1919-1936. Raleigh: University of North Carolina Press, pp. 106-109.

MINNEMA, THEODORE. The Social Ethic of Reinhold Niebuhr, A Structural Analysis. Amsterdam: J. H. Kok, N. V. Kampen.

MOORE, JACK W. "Love and Justice: A Study of the Christian Ethical Theory of Reinhold Niebuhr." Ph.D. dissertation, Duke University.

MOSCALL, E. L. "The Importance of Being Human." NR, 139, no. 25 (December 22), 17.
    Review of The Nature and Destiny of Man.

PHILIPSON, MORRIS. "The Misery vs. Dignity of Man." The Saturday Review of Literature, 41, no. 18 (May 3), 18-19.
    Review of Pious and Secular America.

1958

RICH, JOHN M. "Aspects of the Social Philosophies of John Dewey and Reinhold Niebuhr as They Relate to Education." Ph.D. dissertation, Ohio State University.

ROGERS, CARL. "Reinhold Niebuhr's The Self and the Dramas of History." Pastoral Psychology, 9, no. 85 (June), 15-17.

SANDERSON, J. W. "Historical Fact or Symbol? The Philosophies of History of Paul Tillich and Reinhold Niebuhr." Westminster Theological Journal, 20 (May-November), 158-169.

SCHALL, J. V. "The Political Theory of Reinhold Niebuhr." Thought, 33, no. 128 (Spring), 62-80.

SMITH, ROBERT V. Review of Love and Justice. The Journal of Bible and Religion, 26, no. 3 (July), 260-261.

WEST, CHARLES C. "An American Encounter: Reinhold Niebuhr," in Communism and the Theologians. Philadelphia: The Westminster Press, pp. 117-176.

1959

ANON. Review of The Structure of Nations and Empires. Kirkus, 27, no. 12 (June 15), 426-427.

BENEDICT, JOHN. "What Religion Does Reinhold Niebuhr Peddle?" American Mercury, 39, no. 429 (October), 18-27.

DIBBLE, ERNEST F. "Reinhold Niebuhr's Search for Social Justice." Ph.D. dissertation, American University.

FITCH, ROBERT. Review of The Structure of Nations and Empires. CCY, 76, no. 36 (September 9), 1025.

GAEDE, ERWIN A. "Reinhold Niebuhr and the Relationships of Politics and Ethics." Ph.D. dissertation, Notre Dame University.

GOTTWALD, NORMAN K. "Niebuhr on Nuclear War." CCY, 76, no. 45 (November 11), 1311-1312.
    Reader's response to Niebuhr article "The Test of Christian Faith Today." CCY (October 28).

GUTHRIE, SHIRLEY C. The Theological Character of Reinhold Niebuhr's Ethic. Winterthur: Verlag P. G. Keller.
    Inaugural dissertation, University of Basel.

1959

HARLAND, HARRY G. "Love and Justice in the Thought of Reinhold
Niebuhr." Ph.D. dissertation, Drew University.

HERBERG, WILL. "Reinhold Niebuhr and Paul Tillich." The Chaplain,
16, no. 5 (October), 3-9.

HERTZBERG, ARTHUR. "To Believe--and to Wait." CCY, 76, no. 37
(September 16), 1051-1054.
   On the issues raised by Niebuhr's article about the Christian
mission to the Jews.

HUNT, ARNOLD D. "The Nature of Human Existence: A Comparative Study
of the Doctrine of Man as Found in Reinhold Niebuhr and Sri
Aurobindo." Ph.D. dissertation, The Hartford Seminary Foundation.

KIRKLAND, WILLIAM. "Prophet From America." CCY, 76, no. 19
(May 13), 585-586.
   Review of Essays in Applied Christianity.

_____. "Something Lost." Interpretation, 13, no. 3 (July),
353-354.
   Review of Pious and Secular America.

LINDBECK, GEORGE A. "Revelation, Natural Law, and the Thought of
Reinhold Niebuhr." Natural Law Forum, 4, no. 1 (1959), 146-151.
   Reflections prompted by the publication of Love and Justice.

RIEMAN, TIMOTHY W. "A Comparative Study of the Understanding of Man
in the Writings of Reinhold Niebuhr and John Dewey and Some Implications for Education." Ph.D. dissertation, Northwestern
University.

ROBERTS, HENRY L. Review of The Structure of Nations and Empires.
Foreign Affairs, 38, no. 1 (October), 146.

SCHOTT, WEBSTER. "Dr. Niebuhr's View of National Structures."
The Louisville Courier-Journal (September 27), Sect. 4.

STRAUSZ-HUPE, ROBERT. "History's Value in a Nuclear Age." The
Saturday Review of Literature, 42, no. 35 (August 29), 12-13.
   Review of The Structure of Nations and Empires.

SWEAZEY, G. E. "Are Jews Intended to be Christians?" CCY, 76,
no. 17 (April 29), 514-516.

THOMPSON, KENNETH W. Review of The Structure of Nations and Empires.
United Church Herald, 2, no. 20 (October 29), 30.

1959

VOSS, DAVID. "The Concept of the Self in Psychology of Religion--A Comparative Study of Erich Fromm and Reinhold Niebuhr." M.A. thesis, Harvard Divinity School.

WALTZ, KENNETH N. The State and War. New York: Columbia University Press, pp. 20-41.

1960

ANON. "Reinhold Niebuhr Retires." Time, 75, no. 23 (June 6), 55.

ANON. Review of Reinhold Niebuhr on Politics. Edited by Davis and Good. Kirkus, 28, no. 5 (March 1), 216-217.

BOULDING, KENNETH E. Review of The Structure of Nations and Empires. Review of Religious Research, 1 (Winter), 122-124.

CALDWELL, G. L. "Reinhold Niebuhr and the Crisis of Our Times." Ethics, 70, no. 4 (July), 306-315.

FARLEY, EDWARD. The Transcendence of God: A Study of Contemporary Philosophical Theology. Philadelphia: The Westminster Press, pp. 42-74.

GILL, JERRY H. "Reinhold Niebuhr and Apologetics." Theology Today, 17, no. 2 (July), 200-212.

GOOD, ROBERT C. "The National Interest and Political Realism: Niebuhr's 'Debate' With Morgenthau and Kennan." Journal of Politics, 22, no. 4 (November), 597-619.

HARLAND, GORDON. The Thought of Reinhold Niebuhr. New York: Oxford University Press.

HERBERG, WILL. "Niebuhr's Three Phases." CCY, 77, no. 32 (August 10), 926-927.

HUNTINGTON, SAMUEL P. "Patterns of Political Order." NL, 43, no. 9 (February 29), 27-28.
      Review of The Structure of Nations and Empires.

KOHRS, ELDEAN V. "The Concept of Authority and the Criteria for Moral Action as Expressed by Henry Nelson Wieman and Reinhold Niebuhr With Implications for Pastoral Counseling." Ph.D. dissertation, New York University.

McBRIDE, ROBERT E. "A Study of the Philosophy of History in Selected Contemporary Theologians: With Special Reference to the Writings of Reinhold Niebuhr, Henry Nelson Wieman, and the Process Theologians." Ph.D. dissertation, University of Chicago.

MORGENTHAU, HANS. "The Intellectual and Moral Dilemma of History." CC, 20, no. 1 (February 8), 3-7.
    Review of The Structure of Nations and Empires.

PATTERSON, BOBBY E. "Sin and Grace in the Light of Reinhold Niebuhr's Writings." Th.D. dissertation, Southern Baptist Theological Seminary.

POWELL, RICHARD V. "The Concept of the End of History in the Writings of Reinhold Niebuhr." Th.D. dissertation, Union Theological Seminary in Virginia.

RAMSEY, PAUL. "A Prophet With Honor in His Own Time and Country." The New York Times Book Review (June 19), p. 6.
    Review of Harland and Gordon's The Thought of Reinhold Niebuhr and Davis and Good's Reinhold Niebuhr on Politics.

ROBERTSON, D. B. "Reinhold Niebuhr," in Weltkirchen Lexikon. Edited by F. Littell and H. Walz. Stuttgart: Freuz-Verlag, 1960, p. 1019.
    Niebuhr's contribution to the ecumenical movement.

SCHLITZ, MICHAEL F. Review of The Structure of Nations and Empires. Cross Currents, 10, no. 1 (Winter), 87-88.

STEVENS, GEORGE H. "The Gospel and the Jew." Christianity Today, 4, no. 13 (March 28), 528-529.

THOMPSON, KENNETH. Political Realism and the Crisis in World Politics. Princeton, N. J.: Princeton University Press, pp. 23-25, 148-149.

WURTH, G. B. Niebuhr. Translated by D. H. Freeman. Philadelphia: Presbyterian and Reformed Publishing Co., 41 pp.

1961

ADEN, LEROY H. "The Vicious Inevitability of Sin: A Theological and Psycholoanalytic Study of Human Bondage." Ph.D. dissertation, University of Chicago.

AL FARUQI, ISMA'IL. "On the Significance of Niebuhr's Ideas of Society." Canadian Journal of Theology, 7, no. 2 (1961), 99-107.

1961

BINGHAM, JUNE. "Theologian in the Making." Union Seminary Quarterly Review, 16, no. 2 (January), 149-162.

_____. "Reinhold Niebuhr in Detroit." CCY, 78, no. 10 (March 8), 296-298.

_____. Courage to Change. New York: Charles Scribner's Sons. Postscript added to 1972 printing.

CALLAHAN, DANIEL J. "Sin, Power & Politics: Niebuhr's Contribution." Commonweal, 73, no. 21 (February 17), 527-529.

GOSSETT, EARL F. "The Doctrine of Justification in the Theology of John Calvin, Albrecht Ritschl, and Reinhold Niebuhr." Ph.D. dissertation, Vanderbilt University.

GUTTMANN and BECKWITH. "Niebuhr's History: An Exchange." Forum (Fall).
    Responses to Niebuhr's article "Reflections on Democracy as An Alternative to Communism."

JONES, GEORGE. "A Critical Examination of the Religious and Moral Thought of Reinhold Niebuhr." Ph.D. dissertation, Brown University.

MEYER, DONALD B. "Reinhold Niebuhr: Political Morality" and "Reinhold Niebuhr: Religion and Politics," in The Protestant Search for Political Realism, 1919-1941. Berkeley: University of California Press, pp. 217-238, 238-269.

1962

BLANSHARD, BRAND. "Niebuhr's Life and Thought." NL, 45, no. 10 (May 14), 22-23.
    Review of June Bingham's The Courage to Change.

BOISON, ANTON T. "Niebuhr and Fosdick on Sin." The Chicago Theological Seminary Register, 52, no. 1 (January), 31-33.

BRUNNER, EMIL. "Reply to Interpretation and Criticism," in The Theology of Emil Brunner. Edited by Charles W. Kegley. New York: The Macmillan Co., pp. 349-351.

Writings about Reinhold Niebuhr

1963

BULKELEY, MORGAN. "Stockbridge Theologian II." The Berkshire Eagle,
71, no. 89 (August 16), 21.

CHANG, DONALD M. "Ethical and Economic Aspects of Labor-Management
Power Relationships in the Thought of Reinhold Niebuhr and
John R. Commons." Ph.D. dissertation, University of Southern
California.

COBB, JOHN B. Living Options in Protestant Theology. Philadelphia:
The Westminster Press, pp. 284-311.

DELLBRUGGE, GEORG H. "Simul Justus et Peccator: A Study in the
Theologies of Martin Luther and Reinhold Niebuhr." Ph.D. dissertation, Yale University.

DONIGER, SIMON, ed. The Nature of Man in Theological and Psychological Perspective. New York: Harper and Brothers, pp. 53, 71.

GIBSON, RAYMOND E. "Temporal and Eternal: Perspectives on Human
Destiny and Fulfillment in Recent American Religious Thought."
Ph.D. dissertation, Columbia University, pp. 188-238.

KING, RACHEL H. "The Holy Spirit's Off-Schedule Acts." CCY, 79,
no. 49 (December 5), 1478-1480.

LANDON, HAROLD R., ed. Reinhold Niebuhr: A Prophetic Voice in Our
Time, Essays in Tribute by Paul Tillich, John C. Bennett and Hans
Morgenthau. Cambridge: Seabury Press.

RHOADES, DAN. "Christian Ethics and Political Realism." Ph.D. dissertation, Yale University.

1963

ANON. Review of A Nation So Conceived. Virginia Quarterly Review,
39, no. 3 (Summer), 100-102.

AYERS, ROBERT M. "Biblical Criticism and Faith in Tillich and
Niebuhr." Journal of Bible and Religion, 31, no. 4 (October),
311-319.

_____. "To the Defense of Reinhold Niebuhr." CCY, 80, no. 5
(January 30), 143-145.
Comment on an article by Rachel King.

BROWN, ROBERT McAFEE. "To the Defense of Reinhold Niebuhr." CCY,
80, no. 5 (January 30), pp. 142-143.

187

1963

DAMHORST, DONALD E. "Social Norms and Protestant Ethics: The
    Ethical Views of Reinhold Niebuhr and H. Richard Niebuhr."
    Ph.D. dissertation, St. Louis University.

ELMORE, JOE E. "The Theme of the Suffering of God in the Thought
    of Nicholas Berdyaev, Charles Hartshorne, and Reinhold Niebuhr."
    Ph.D. dissertation, Columbia University.

LAZARETH, WILLIAM H. "Was Luther a Christian Realist?" L, NS 1,
    no. 3 (January 30), 8-9, 45-46.
    Commentary on Niebuhr.

MACQUARRIE, JOHN. "Post-Liberal Theology in the United States," in
    Twentieth-Century Religious Thought. New York: Harper and Row,
    pp. 344-347.

MAIER, VICTOR E. "Ideology and Utopia in International Politics:
    A Critique of the Ethics of International Politics of Reinhold
    Niebuhr and Edward Hallett Carr." Ph.D. dissertation, University
    of Chicago.

NEUBAUER, REINHARD. "Geschenkte und umkämpfte Gerechtigkeit: eine
    Untersuchung zur Theologie und Sozialethik Reinhold Niebuhrs im
    Blick auf Martin Luther." Heidelberg: Vandenhoeck and Ruprecht.
    Ph.D. dissertation, Heidelberg University, 1963.

SCOTT, NATHAN, JR. Reinhold Niebuhr. University of Minnesota
    Pamphlets on American Writers, No. 31. Minneapolis: University
    of Minnesota Press.

WISE, RALPH E. "Irrational Man and the Modern Dilemma: World and
    Thought of P. E. More and Reinhold Niebuhr." Ph.D. dissertation,
    Syracuse University.

1964

ANON. "Out of the World." Times Literary Supplement (May 14),
    p. 410.
    Review of A Nation So Conceived.

DICKINSON, JOHN M. "Aggression and the Status of Evil in Man: A
    Critical Analysis of Freud's Assumptions From the Theological
    Perspective of Reinhold Niebuhr." Ph.D. dissertation, Boston
    University.

HOMANS, PETER. "The Meaning of Selfhood in the Thought of Reinhold
    Niebuhr and Sigmund Freud." Ph.D. dissertation, University of
    Chicago.

1965

KING, RACHEL H. The Omission of the Holy Spirit From Reinhold
    Niebuhr's Theology. New York: Philosophical Library.

LANGE, DIETZ. Christlicher Glaube und soziale Probleme: Eine
    Darstellung der Theologie Reinhold Niebuhrs. Gutersloh:
    Verlagshaus Gerd Mohn.

LICHTHEIM, GEORGE. Review of A Nation So Conceived. The New
    Statesman, 67, no. 1717 (February 7), 214.

POTTS, HAL. "The Development of Apologetic Method: A Study of
    Reinhold Niebuhr's Experimental Years." Th.D. dissertation,
    Southwestern Baptist Theological Seminary.

RHOADES, DAN. "The Prophetic Insight and Theoretical-Analytical
    Inadequacy of 'Christian Realism.'" Ethics, 75, no. 2 (October),
    79-99.

STUMP, HARLEY H. "The Educational Philosophy of Reinhold Niebuhr."
    Ph.D. dissertation, University of Oklahoma.

1965

ANON. "Taking Inventory." Time, 87, no. 19 (November 5), 79.

BARKAT, ANWAR M. "The Fellowship of Socialist Christians and its
    Antecedents." Ph.D. dissertation, Duke University.

BARNES, E. WAYNE. "The Element of Accommodation in the Basic Social
    Ethic of Reinhold Niebuhr." Th.D. dissertation, Southwestern
    Baptist Theological Seminary.

DANIELSON, JEAN M. "The Evolution of the Political Thought of
    Reinhold Niebuhr." Ph.D. dissertation, University of Kansas.

GRAHAM, LEROY S. "An Examination and Analysis of the Relevance of
    the Christian Ethic of Sex with Respect to Premarital Sexual
    Intercourse: An Inquiry into the Thought of Reinhold Niebuhr
    and Emil Brunner in View of the Findings of Alfred Kinsey and
    Margaret Mead." Ph.D. dissertation, Drew University.

HOFMANN, HANS. "Reinhold Niebuhr," in A Handbook of Christian
    Theologians. Edited by D. G. Peerman and Martin E. Marty.
    New York: Meridian Books, pp. 355-374.

STACKHOUSE, MAX L. "Eschatology and Ethical Method: A Structural
    Analysis of Contemporary Christian Social Ethics in America With

1966

Primary Reference to Walter Rauschenbusch and Reinhold Niebuhr."
Ph.D. dissertation, Harvard University.

1966

AHN, CHESOON. "A Comparative Study of the Political Ideas of Two
Contemporary Theologians, Reinhold Niebuhr and Jacques Maritain."
Ph.D. dissertation, Florida State University.

ANDERSON, DONALD N. "The Political Ethics of Karl Barth and Reinhold
Niebuhr." Ph.D. dissertation, University of Chicago.

DANIELSON, JEAN M. "The Evolution of the Political Thought of
Reinhold Niebuhr." Ph.D. dissertation, Stanford University.

FARLEY, GARY E. "Authority in Contemporary Christian Ethics: A
Study of How one May Know the 'Will of God' as Discussed in the
Writings of Carl F. H. Henry, Jacques Maritain, Emil Brunner,
Reinhold Niebuhr, and Nels F. S. Ferre." Th.D. dissertation,
Southwestern Baptist Theological Seminary.

FITCH, ROBERT E. "Giant in the Earth." The New York Times Book
Review (January 2), pp. 10, 14.

HARLAND, GORDON. "A Realist's View." CCY, 83, no. 1 (January 5),
15-16.
    Review of Man's Nature and His Communities.

HUMPHREY, HUBERT. "The Great Work of Dr. Reinhold Niebuhr." CC, 26,
no. 9 (May 30), 120-123.
    From an address to the banquet celebrating the twenty-fifth
anniversary of Christianity and Crisis.

HYSLOP, RALPH D. "How Relevant is Reinhold Niebuhr?" Judaism, 15,
no. 4 (Fall), 419-425.

LEITH, ADDISON H. Winds of Doctrine. Westwood, N. J.: Fleming H.
Revell Co., pp. 39-42.

LEKACHMAN, ROBERT. "Progress of a Christian Realist." NL, 49,
no. 17 (August 29), 18-20.
    Review of Man's Nature and His Communities.

MERKLEY, PAUL C. "Reinhold Niebuhr: The Decisive Years (1916-1941);
A Study of the Interaction of Religious Faith and Political Commitment in an American Intellectual." Ph.D. dissertation, University of Toronto.

1966

MEYERS, LEONARD L. "Reactions to Relativism: An Investigation into the Ethical Thought of Reinhold Niebuhr and Dietrich Bonhoeffer." Ph.D. dissertation, University of Iowa.

PALMER, T. VAIL, JR. "Eschatology and Foreign Policy in the Thought of Reinhold Niebuhr, William E. Hocking, and John Courtney Murray." Ph.D. dissertation, University of Chicago.

PORTEOUS, ALVIN C. "Reinhold Niebuhr: The Implications of Christian Realism," in Prophetic Voices in Contemporary Theology. Nashville, Tenn.: Abingdon Press, pp. 130-164.

RAMSEY, PAUL. "Farewell to Christian Realism." America, 114, no. 18 (April 30), 618-622.

RANDALL, JOHN H., JR. Review of Man's Nature and His Communities. The Journal of Philosophy, 63, no. 4 (February 17), 46-53.

SAMIS, FRANCIS W. "Moral Development as an Educational Aim with Particular Reference to the Views of Reinhold Niebuhr." Ph.D. dissertation, University of Alberta.

SCHWARTZSCHILD, STEVEN S. "The Religious Demand for Peace." Judaism, 15 (Fall), 412-418.

SHEFFIELD, WESLEY. "Niebuhr and the Death of God." CC, 26, no. 12 (July 11), 163.

SHINN, ROGER L. Review of Man's Nature and His Communities. Union Seminary Quarterly Review, 21, no. 3 (March), 350-351.

SPICER, JAMES E. "A Critical and Analytical Study of the Concept of the Self as Seen from the Psychological Perspective of Gardner Murphy and Harry Stack Sullivan and from the Theological Perspective of Reinhold Niebuhr and Paul Tillich." Ph.D. dissertation, University of Chicago.

THOMPSON, WARREN K. A. "Reinhold Niebuhr on Ethics." The Hibbert Journal, 64, no. 254 (March), 99-105.

TILLEY, WILLIAM C. "The Relationship of Self-Love to Love for the Other with Special Reference to the Thought of Reinhold Niebuhr and Erich Fromm." Th.D. dissertation, Southern Baptist Theological Seminary.

TROBAUGH, ROBERT J. "The Nature of Man in the Writings of Reinhold Niebuhr and William Faulkner." Ph.D. dissertation, Vanderbilt University.

1966

WILLIAMSON, R. VISME.   Review of <u>Man's Nature and His Communities</u>.
    <u>The American Political Science Review</u>, 60, no. 3 (September),
    707-708.

WRIGHT, PALMER W.   "The New Liberalism of the Fifties: Reinhold
    Niebuhr, David Riesman, Lionel Trilling and the American Intel-
    lectual." Ph.D. dissertation, University of Michigan.

YODER, JOHN H.   <u>Reinhold Niebuhr and Christian Pacifism</u>. Washington,
    D. C.: The Church Peace Union.

<u>1967</u>

COBB, WILLIAM D.   "Moral Relativity and Christian Ethics: A Study
    in Response to the Theology of Emil Brunner and Reinhold Niebuhr."
    Ph.D. dissertation, University of Chicago.

KLEIN, ARTHUR W.   "Reinhold Niebuhr's Appraisal of Karl Barth."
    Ph.D. dissertation, Northwestern University.

SMITH, ROBERT V.   Review of <u>Man's Nature and His Communities</u>.
    <u>Journal of the American Academy of Religion</u>, 35, no. 1 (March),
    80, 82.

SPEER, JAMES P.   "Reinhold Niebuhr Plays Hamlet." CCY, 84, no. 11
    (March 15), 336-339.
        On Niebuhr's skepticism about world government.

STOWE, DAVID M.   "Mission to the Jews." CC, 27, no. 1 (February 6),
    12, 14.
        Letter to the Editor.

WILLIAMS, PRESTON N.   "Religious Responses to the New Deal: The
    Reaction of William Henry Cardinal O'Connell, Monsignor John A.
    Ryan, Clarence E. Macartney, and Reinhold Niebuhr to the Economic
    Polities of the New Deal." Ph.D. dissertation, Harvard
    University.

WOGAMAN, PHILIP.   "The Critical Realism of Reinhold Niebuhr," in
    <u>Protestant Faith and Religious Liberty</u>. Nashville, Tenn.:
    Abingdon Press, pp. 100-104.

<u>1968</u>

BENNETT, JOHN C.   "The Contribution of Reinhold Niebuhr." <u>Union
    Seminary Quarterly Review</u>, 24, no. 1 (Fall), 3-16.

1969

_____, et al. "Christian Realism: A Symposium." CC, 28, no. 14
(August 5), 175-190.
     Other writers: Roger Shinn, Harvey Cox, Richard Shaull, Alan
Geyer, Tom Driver and Robert W. Lynn.

DOYLE, MATHIAS F. "Theology and Politics in the Works of Reinhold
Niebuhr." Ph.D. dissertation, Notre Dame University.

LeFEVRE, PERRY. "Reinhold Niebuhr: Man As Sinner," in Man: Six
Modern Interpretations. Philadelphia: The Geneva Press,
pp. 95-108.

MAY, HENRY F. "A Meditation on an Unfashionable Book, The Irony of
American History." CC, 28, no. 9 (May 27), 120-122.

PARK, BONG M. "An Analysis of the Ideas of John Dewey and Reinhold
Niebuhr on Social Justice and the Implications of these Ideas
for Korean Education." Ph.D. dissertation, New York University.

STONE, RONALD H. "Reinhold Niebuhr's Perspective on United States
Foreign Policy." Ph.D. dissertation, Columbia University.

1969

ANON. "Niebuhr's Strategies of Justice." Worldview, 12, no. 5
(May), 16-20.

HARTMAN, ROBERT H. "The Use of Theology in Reinhold Niebuhr's Interpretation of History." Ph.D. dissertation, Northwestern
University.

KEGLEY, CHARLES W. Politics, Religion and Modern Man. Quezon City:
University of the Philippines Press, pp. 1-47.

LONGWOOD, WALTER M. "The Ends of Government in the Thought of
Reinhold Niebuhr and Jacques Maritain: A Study in Christian
Social Ethics." Ph.D. dissertation, Yale University.

MARGERIE, BERTRAND de. Reinhold Niebuhr. Théologien de la
Communauté Mondiale. Paris and Bruges: Desclée De Browver.

MICKEL, HOWARD A. "Reinhold Niebuhr's Thought on War and Peace, An
Analysis of the Development of His Views, 1916-1966." Ph.D.
dissertation, Claremont Graduate School.

STRICKLAND, WILLIAM R., JR. "Reinhold Niebuhr's Interpretation of
Sin as Pride." M.A. thesis, Duke University.

1970

1970

ANON. "The Resurrection of Utopia." CCY, 87, no. 12 (March 25), 347.

FACKRE, GABRIEL. "Realism and Vision." CC, 30, no. 6 (April 13), 72-72.

_____. The Promise of Reinhold Niebuhr. Philadelphia: Lippincott.

GAEDE, ERWIN A. "Reinhold Niebuhr and the Religious Dimension." Journal of the Liberal Ministry, 10, no. 2 (Spring), 40-47.

HOMANS, PETER. "Anthropological Response to Freud: Reinhold Niebuhr," in Theology After Freud, An Interpretative Inquiry. New York: The Bobbs-Merrill Co., pp. 23-65.

MARTY, MARTIN E. Righteous Empire. New York: The Dial Press, pp. 237-243.

RUETHER, ROSEMARY R. "Niebuhr and Neoorthodoxy," in The Radical Kingdom: The Western Experience of Messianic Hope. New York: Harper and Row, pp. 118-130.

SHANER, DONALD W. "The Marxian Doctrine and Practice of Race Relations in the Light of the Theology of Reinhold Niebuhr." Ph.D. dissertation, Drew University.

1971

ANON. "A Prophet Among Us...." CC, 31, no. 11 (June 2), 126-127.

BENNETT, JOHN C. "The Greatness of Reinhold Niebuhr." Union Seminary Quarterly Review, 27, no. 1 (Fall), 3-8.

BLANCHARD, MAURICE. "Right Answers, Wrong Questions." Christianity Today, 15, no. 22 (August 6), 996-998.
    Mainly makes use of a quotation from The Nature and Destiny of Man, Vol. II, p. 59, on the Greek mind and the Christian message.

COFFEY, JOHN W. "Realist Social Thought in America, Reinhold Niebuhr and George F. Kennan." Ph.D. dissertation, Stanford University.

DAUGHERTY, JAMES D. "The Concept of Community in the Thought of Reinhold Niebuhr: An Analysis of Niebuhr's Political Realism and its Relationship to the Achievement of Community with a

1972

Special Emphasis on the American National Community." Ph.D. dissertation, Graduate Theological Union.

ECKHARDT, A. ROY. "A Tribute to Reinhold Niebuhr, 1892-1971." Midstream, 17, no. 6 (June/July), 11-18.

EDWARDS, HERBERT O. "Racism and Christian Ethics in America." Katallagete (Winter), pp. 15-24.

FACKRE, GABRIEL J., and BRAUN, THEODORE C. "Appraisal and Comment: The Life and Work of Reinhold Niebuhr." United Church Herald, 14, no. 8 (August), 42-43.

FINN, JAMES. "Reinhold Niebuhr." Commonweal, 94, no. 14 (June 25), 324.

GREENLAW, WILLIAM A. "Reinhold Niebuhr as Theologian: A New Interpretation." Ph.D. dissertation, Duke University.

KUHN, HAROLD B. "The Legacy of Niebuhr." Christianity Today, 15, no. 19 (June 18), 891.

RIZZO, ROBERT F. "Christian Vision and Pacifism: A Study of Charles Earle Raven with a Comparison to Reinhold Niebuhr." Ph.D. dissertation, Catholic University of America.

SHAW, LONEL E., JR. "The Political Theory of Reinhold Niebuhr." Ph.D. dissertation, University of North Carolina, Chapel Hill.

SUZUKI, YUGO. "An Examination of the Doctrine of Man of Erich Fromm and Reinhold Niebuhr." Th.D. dissertation, Union Theological Seminary in Virginia.

WINGEIER, DOUGLAS. "Doing Ministry in a 'Future-Shock' Age." The Christian Advocate (February 15), p. 7.

1972

BENNETT, JOHN C. "Realism and Hope After Niebuhr." Worldview, 15, no. 5 (May), 4-14.

_____. "Response." CC, 32, no. 7 (May 1), 106-108. Response to Williamson's "The Pentagon Papers and the Desecration of Pragmatica."

BOULTON, WAYNE G. "Ethics and Vision: The Role of Myth in the Thought of Reinhold Niebuhr." Ph.D. dissertation, Duke University.

1972

EARLY, TRACY. "Reinhold Niebuhr for the 70's." CCY, 89, no. 24
(June 14), 688-690.

HARRISON, BEVERLY. "Response." CC, 32, no. 7 (May 1), 104-106.
Response to Williamson's "The Pentagon Papers and the Desecration of Pragmatica."

KOOPS, HUGH A. "The Knowledge of Good and Evil: A Study of the
Criteria of the Good as Reflected in the Theological Ethics of
H. Richard Niebuhr, Reinhold Niebuhr, and Dietrich Bonhoeffer."
Ph.D. dissertation, University of Chicago.

McFAUL, THOMAS R. "A Comparison of the Ethics of H. Richard Niebuhr
and Reinhold Niebuhr." Ph.D. dissertation, Boston University.

MARTIN, THOMAS M. "Reinhold Niebuhr and Charles Chaplin: A Comparative Study Through the Ironic Ingredients of Niebuhr's
Thought." Ph.D. dissertation, Syracuse University.

MAYERS, RONALD B. "The Problem of Meaning and Function of 'Transcendence' in the Social Ethic with Particular Reference to the
Social Ethics of John Dewey and Reinhold Niebuhr." Ph.D. dissertation, Syracuse University.

NELSON, GORDON L. "A Consideration of Reinhold Niebuhr's Concept
of Government as an 'Organizing Center': The Case of
Minneapolis." Ph.D. dissertation, University of Chicago.

NOVAK, MICHAEL. "Politics as Drama." The Center Magazine
(May/June), pp. 4-24.

_____. "Needing Niebuhr Again." Commentary, 54, no. 3 (September),
52-62.

RICHARDSON, ARTHUR W. "Mishpat as the Basis for Human Community:
A Study of Justice in Jeremiah and Reinhold Niebuhr." Ph.D.
dissertation, School of Theology at Claremont.

ROTHSTEIN, ROBERT L. "On the Costs of Realism." Political Science
Quarterly, 87, no. 3 (September), 347-362.
Not specifically on Niebuhr but especially pertinent to
Niebuhr's relationship to "realism" in foreign policy.

SCHLESINGER, ARTHUR, JR. "Prophet for a Secular Age." NL, 55,
no. 2 (January 24), 11-14.

SHAULL, RICHARD. "Response." CC, 32, no. 1 (May 1), 108-109.
Response to Williamson's "The Pentagon Papers and the Desecration of Pragmatica."

SIEGEL, SEYMOUR. "Reinhold Niebuhr: In Memoriam," in American Jewish Year Book: 1972. New York: The American Jewish Committee, pp. 605-610.

STONE, RONALD H. Reinhold Niebuhr: Prophet to Politicians. Nashville, Tenn.: Abingdon Press.

TAYLOR, LARRY M. "The Role of General Revelation in American Neo-orthodoxy: Reinhold Niebuhr, Paul Tillich, and H. Richard Niebuhr." Th.D. dissertation, Southwestern Baptist Theological Seminary.

WILLIAMSON, GEORGE, JR. "The Pentagon Papers and the Desecration of Pragmatica." CC, 32, no. 7 (May 1), 99-104.

1973

ALVES, RUBEM A. "Christian Realism: Ideology of the Establishment." CC, 33, no. 15 (September 17), 173-176.

ANON. "Reinhold Niebuhr Speaks to a Future-Shocked Age." Christian Advocate (June 7), 7-8.

ANON. "The Realists and Their Critics." Worldview, 16, no. 6 (June), 19-28.

BENNETT, JOHN C. "Continuing the Discussion: Liberation Theology and Christian Realism." CC, 33, no. 17 (October 15), 197-198.

BROWN, ROBERT McAFEE. "Continuing the Discussion: Liberation Theology and Christian Realism." CC, 33, no. 17 (October 15), 199-200.

FISHMAN, HERTZEL. American Protestantism and A Jewish State. Detroit: Wayne State University Press, pp. 69-80, 121-122, 168-171.

GRIFFIN, DAVID. "Whitehead and Niebuhr on God, Man and the World." The Journal of Religion, 53, no. 2 (April), 149-175.

HAUERWAS, STANLEY. "Messianic Pacifism." Worldview, 16, no. 6 (June), 29-33.

HILTNER, SEWARD. "Kinsey and the Church--Then and Now." CCY, 90, no. 22 (May 30), 624-629.

1973

HILTNER, SEWARD. "What Was Reinhold Niebuhr?" CCY, 90, no. 39 (October 31), 1086.

JUERGENSMEYER, MARK. "The Unfinished Tasks of Reinhold Niebuhr." CCY, 90, no. 32 (September 12), 884–887.

KOZUB, JACQUES. "Continuing the Discussion: Liberation Theology and Christian Realism." CC, 33, no. 17 (October 15), 202–204.

McCOLLOUGH, CHARLES. "Up to Our Steeples in Realism: Ethics After Vietnam." Worldview, 16, no. 6 (June), 24–28.

McFAUL, THOMAS R. "Reinhold Niebuhr: An Alleged 'Individualist.'" Religion in Life, 42, no. 2 (Summer), 194–205.

MIDDLETON, ROBERT G. "Hubris in Camelot." CCY, 90, no. 32 (September 12), 887–888.

PLANK, JOHN. "Continuing the Discussion: Liberation Theology and Christian Realism." CC, 33, no. 17 (October 15), 198–199.

QUIGLEY, THOMAS. "Continuing the Discussion: Liberation Theology and Christian Realism." CC, 33, no. 17 (October 15), 200–202.

RAINES, JOHN C. "Theodicy and Politics." Worldview, 16, no. 4 (April), 44–48.

SANDERS, THOMAS G. "The Theology of Liberation: Christian Utopianism." CC, 33, no. 15 (September 17), 167–173.

SMYLIE, JAMES H. "Reinhold Niebuhr: Quadragesimo Anno." Religion in Life, 42, no. 1 (Spring), 25–36.

STONE, RONALD. "The Realists and Their Critics." Worldview, 16, no. 6 (June), 19–24.

_____. "The Responsibility of the Saints." CCY, 90, no. 32 (September 12), 881–883.

THORN, EDWARD W. "Implications for Rhetoric in the Works of Reinhold Niebuhr." Ph.D. dissertation, Indiana University.

VANDERPOOL, HAROLD Y. "Reinhold Niebuhr: Religion Fosters Social Criticism and Promotes Social Justice," in Critical Issues in Modern Religion. By Roger Johnson, et al. Englewood Cliffs, N. J.: Prentice-Hall, Inc., pp. 175–208.

1974

WILDE, ALEXANDER. "Continuing the Discussion: Liberation Theology and Christian Realism." CC, 33, no. 17 (October 15), 204-206.

1974

AIGNER, GEORGE F. "Emergent Relations of Freedom: An Analysis of the Thought of Erik Erikson and Reinhold Niebuhr Toward a More Comprehensive Theory of Moral Development." Ph.D. dissertation, Graduate Theological Union.

ANON. Review of Justice and Mercy. CCY, 91, no. 26 (July 17), 728.

BROWN, ROBERT McAFEE. "Reinhold Niebuhr: A Study in Humanity and Humility." The Journal of Religion, 54, no. 4 (October), 325-331.

BURNS, EMMETT C. "Love, Power, and Justice as Central Elements in a View of Social Change: A Comparison and Evaluation of the Thought of Reinhold Niebuhr and Martin Luther King, Jr." Ph.D. dissertation, University of Pittsburgh.

COATS, WILLIAM. God in Public: Political Theology Beyond Niebuhr. Grand Rapids, Mich.: Eerdman's.
Scattered references; see index.

COLES, ROBERT. "The Nature and Destiny of Man by Reinhold Niebuhr (Twentieth-Century Classics Revisited)." Daedalus, 103, no. 1 (Winter), 103; no. 1 (Winter), 96-97.

CONLEY, JOHN J. Review of Justice and Mercy. America, 131, no. 5 (September 7), 96-97.

FAHEY, JOSEPH J. "The Relationship Between Theological Anthropology and International Peace in the Thought of Reinhold Niebuhr: With Certain Implications for Contemporary Higher Education." Ph.D. dissertation, New York University.

GAMWELL, FRANKLIN I. "Reinhold Niebuhr's Theistic Ethic." The Journal of Religion, 54, no. 4 (October), 387-408.

GILKEY, LANGDON. "Reinhold Niebuhr's Theology of History." The Journal of Religion, 54, no. 4 (October), 360-386.

HOOK, SIDNEY. "The Moral Vision of Reinhold Niebuhr," in Pragmatism and the Tragic Sense of Life. New York: Basic Books, Inc., pp. 184-189.

1974

MARTY, MARTIN E. "Reinhold Niebuhr: Public Theology and the American Experience." The Journal of Religion, 54, no. 4 (October), 332–359.

NOVAK, MICHAEL. "Beyond Niebuhr: Symbolic Realism," in Choosing Our King. New York: Macmillan, pp. 95–102.

REYNOLDS, JAMES G. "Justification by Faith in Reinhold Niebuhr's Thought." Ph.D. dissertation, Graduate Theological Union.

SHINN, ROGER L. "Realism, Radicalism, and Eschatology in Reinhold Niebuhr: A Reassessment." The Journal of Religion, 54, no. 4 (October), 409–423.

STROUT, CUSHING. "Crisis Theology from the Crash to the Bomb," in New Heavens and New Earth. New York: Harper and Row, pp. 268–284.

THOMPSON, KENNETH W. "Niebuhr as Thinker and Doer." The Journal of Religion, 54, no. 4 (October), 424–434.

1975

HARRISVILLE, ROY A. "Porter of Yale––Teacher of the Niebuhrs: A Tiny Page in the History of American Biblical Scholarship." Dialog, 14, no. 4 (Fall), 283–288.

LINK, MICHAEL. The Social Philosophy of Reinhold Niebuhr: An Historical Introduction. Chicago: Adams Press.

LONGWOOD, MERLE. "Niebuhr and a Theory of Justice." Dialog, 14, no. 4 (Fall), 253–262.

MERKLEY, PAUL. Reinhold Niebuhr: A Political Account. Montreal: McGill-Queen's University Press.

MILNE, BRUCE A. "The Idea of Sin in Twentieth-Century Theology." Tyndale Bulletin, 26: 3–33.

RAH, HALK JIN. "The Political Relevance of Jen in Early China and Agape in the Theology of Reinhold Niebuhr." Ph.D. dissertation, Princeton University.

SCOTT, NATHAN, JR., ed. The Legacy of Reinhold Niebuhr. Chicago: The University of Chicago Press.
    Also appears without Scott's introduction, in The Journal of Religion, 54, no. 4 (December).

1976

VELDHUIS, RUURD. <u>Realism versus Utopianism? Reinhold Niebuhr's</u>
<u>Christian Realism and the Relevance of Utopian Thought for Social</u>
<u>Ethics</u>. Assen, The Netherlands: van Gorcum.

1976

BURNHAM, J. "Politics and Review." <u>National Review</u>, 28, no. 43
(November 12), 1226.

CHO, SEOP WHAT. "The Theological Critique of the Marxist Idea of
Man and the State in the Thought of Reinhold Niebuhr and Paul
Tillich." Ph.D. dissertation, Emory University.

GREENLAW, WILLIAM A. "Revelation and the Problem of Apologetics:
An Exploration in the Theology of Reinhold Niebuhr." <u>Dialog</u>,
15, no. 4 (Autumn), 253-262.

HOLIFIELD, E. BROOKS. "The Three Strands of Jimmy Carter's Religion."
NR, 174, no. 23 (June 5), 15-17.

IRWIN, JOHN E. G. "Psychoanalysis and Christian Thought: In Search
of Man Through the <u>Gestaltkreis</u>." <u>The Drew Gateway</u>, 46,
nos. 1-3 (1975-76), 107-108.

McCANN, DENNIS P. "Religious Symbols and Social Criticism in the
Thought of Reinhold Niebuhr." Ph.D. dissertation, University
of Chicago.

MARTY, MARTIN E. "The Lost Worlds of Reinhold Niebuhr." <u>The</u>
<u>American Scholar</u>, 45, no. 4 (Autumn), 566-572.

NELSON, JANE V. "Navigating the Straits of Messina: Science and
Art in Reinhold Niebuhr's Philosophy of History." Ph.D. dissertation, University of Utah.

PARK, SEONG MO. "Reinhold Niebuhr's Perspective on Marxism." Ph.D.
dissertation, Drew University.

PLASKOW, JUDITH E. "Sex, Sin, and Grace: Women's Experience and
the Theologies of Reinhold Niebuhr and Paul Tillich." Ph.D.
dissertation, Yale University.

REID, JAMES F. "A Critique of the Political Philosophy of the
Berrigans From the Perspectives of Augustine and Niebuhr." Ph.D.
dissertation, University of Missouri.

1976

SCHLESINGER, ARTHUR, JR. "God and the 1976 Election." The Wall
Street Journal, 187, no. 83 (April 28), 18.

SCOTT, GEOFFREY D. "Reinhold Niebuhr and the Concept of Virtue."
Ph.D. dissertation, Southern Methodist University.

THOMPSON, DEAN K. "Moral Duty and Divine Grace: A Union Seminary
Case Study." Religion in Life, 45, no. 1 (Spring), 82–88.
"The Van Dusen–Niebuhr argument over moral will served as a
classic illustration of the greater liberal–neo–orthodox clash."

VILLA-VICENCIO, CHARLES M. L. "History in the Thought of Reinhold
Niebuhr and Wolfhart Pannenberg." The Drew Gateway, 46,
nos. 1–3 (1975–76), 119–120.

1977

BINGHAM, JUNE. "Carter, Castro and Reinhold Niebuhr." CCY, 94,
no. 28 (September 14), 775–776.

BOWDEN, HENRY W. "Reinhold Niebuhr." Dictionary of American Biography. Westport, Conn.: Greenwood Press, pp. 332–334.

CHRYSTAL, WILLIAM G. "Reinhold Niebuhr and the First World War."
Journal of Presbyterian History, 55 (Fall), 285–298.

JONES, ALAN H. "A Psychological and Theological Response to a Case
of Demon Possession, With Particular Reference to the Theology
of Reinhold Niebuhr." D.Min. dissertation, School of Theology
at Claremont.

PATTERSON, BOB E. Reinhold Niebuhr. Waco, Tex.: Word Books,
Publishers.
In the series Makers of the Modern Theological Mind.

1978

CUDDIHY, JOHN M. "Protestant: The Reinhold Niebuhr––Will Herberg
'Treaty,'" in No Offense: Civil Religion and Protestant Taste.
New York: Seabury Press, pp. 31–47.

1978

DIBBLE, ERNEST F. Young Prophet Niebuhr: Reinhold Niebuhr's Early
    Search for Social Justice. Washington, D. C.: University Press
    of America.

LOVIN, ROBIN W. "The Constitution as Covenant: The Moral Foundation
    of Democracy and the Practice of Desegregation." Ph.D. disserta-
    tion, Harvard University.

McCANN, DENNIS. "Reinhold Niebuhr and Jacques Maritain on Marxism:
    A Comparison of Two Traditional Models of Practical Theology."
    The Journal of Religion, 58, no. 2 (April), 140-168.

MARTY, MARTIN E. "Fit for a Giant." CCY, 95, no. 11 (March 29),
    343.

_____. "We Get Letters." CCY, 95, no. 16 (May 3), 487.
    Responses to March 29 article.

Index to Reinhold Niebuhr's
Shorter Writings and Writings about Him

Index